711.

131014

W9-CHR-844

Teacher's Edition

Summer Success®

Math

Patsy F. Kanter • Karen M. Hardin • Alanna Arenivas

Grade 5

GReaT S✦uRCe®
EDUCATION GROUP
A Division of Houghton Mifflin Company

ELEMENTARY GRADES REVIEWERS

Charles Keith Case
Math Teacher
Aldine ISD
Houston, TX

Judy Chambers
Math Consultant
Fayette County Schools
Fayetteville, GA

Cynthia Fontenot
Retired 2nd Grade Teacher
Lafayette Parish School District
Lafayette, LA

Sharon Greenwald
Elementary Mathematics District
  Facilitator
Broward County Public Schools
Ft. Lauderdale, FL

Shelly Gufert
Special Education Teacher
Boston Public Schools
Boston, MA

Elma G. Jones
5th Grade Teacher
Wallingford-Swarthmore School
  District
Wallingford, PA

Jerrilynn Lawless
Math Professional Developer
New York City, NY

Stephen Paterwic
Math Department Chair
Springfield High School of
  Science and Technology
Springfield, MA

Karen Reid
Teacher
Rosemead School District
Rosemead, CA

Jeannine M. Shirley
2nd Grade Teacher
Taylor Elementary School
White Hall, AR

Sharon Fields Simpson
Educational Consultant
Denver, CO

Kathryn Tobon
Curriculum Support
Broward County Public Schools
Ft. Lauderdale, FL

CREDITS

Writing: Barbara Irvin

Design/Production: Taurins Design

Illustration: Debra Spina Dixon

Cover and Package Design: Kristen Davis/Great Source

Copyright © 2008 by Great Source Education Group, a division of Houghton Mifflin Company. All rights reserved.

Permission is hereby granted to the teacher who has purchased the Grade 5 *Summer Success: Math* kit (ISBN 978-0-669-53468-9) to reprint or photocopy in quantities for classroom use and with accompanying Great Source material the Planner on page 152 that carries a copyright notice, provided each copy made shows the copyright notice. Such copies may not be sold and further distribution is expressly prohibited. Except as authorized above, prior written permission must be obtained from Great Source Education Group to reproduce or transmit this work or portions thereof in any other form, or by any other electronic or mechanical means, including any information storage or retrieval system, unless expressly permitted by federal copyright law. Address inquiries to Permissions, Great Source Education Group, 181 Ballardvale Street, Wilmington, MA 01887.

Printed in the United States of America.

Great Source® and *Summer Success*® are registered trademarks of Houghton Mifflin Company.

International Standard Book Number–13: 978–0-669–53716–1

International Standard Book Number–10: 0–669–53716–0

 2 3 4 5 6 7 8 9 10 MZ 11 10

Visit our web site: http://www.greatsource.com/

TABLE OF CONTENTS

Summer Success: Math

MATHEMATICAL UNDERSTANDING AND PROFICIENCY FOR ALL STUDENTS

The Summer Success: Math program is designed to:

- focus on grade level standards while reviewing required prior skills and concepts
- introduce concepts incrementally and keep them in front of students for the entire session
- include and connect all strands every day
- include a variety of instructional formats, including direct instruction, group work, partner activities, and independent practice
- connect ordinary language with the language of mathematics, including notation
- include two forms of practice: independent paper-and-pencil work and games
- include algebraic thinking in all grade levels
- focus on math as reasoning and thinking; develop quantitative reasoning and number sense
- provide daily assessment opportunities

INSTRUCTIONAL COMPONENTS

Summer Success: Math consists of four basic instructional components that blend a variety of teaching formats. The combination of approaches provides multiple points of entry to engage all students. This helps students build a solid understanding of key math concepts at the same time as they develop mathematical proficiency.

1. The **Number Names** lessons are the cornerstone of *Summer Success: Math.* With a bulletin board display as the focus of whole-group instruction, students review the major strands of mathematics—**Number, Operations, Patterns and Algebra, Geometry,** and **Measurement**—with **Problem Solving** woven into each lesson. In addition, one key math **Vocabulary** term is discussed in depth each day.

   The Number Names discussions relate concepts in the different math strands to each other by focusing on a specific number of the day. Lessons are designed for incremental learning to allow students multiple opportunities to grasp key concepts, to learn by listening to each other's explanations of solutions, and to see patterns develop through visual models.

2. The daily instruction is reinforced with daily **Practice.** These pages allow students to work independently to apply the various concepts and skills they have discussed.

3. Daily **Game** experiences encourage students to question and further explore key grade-level math topics. The Games are simple to teach and learn, yet powerful in both the rich quality and the quantity of practice they provide.

4. The fourth element, **Focus,** provides yet another format for presenting a key concept or skill. Each week in grades K–5, Focus includes a two-day **Data Study,** a two-day **Concept Builder,** and, a special Friday problem-solving opportunity called **Read and Reason.**

© Great Source. Copying is prohibited.

Kit Contents

Each grade-level specific **Summer Success: Math** kit provides ready-to-use materials for an entire summer school course including:

- Teacher's Edition packed with Weekly Planners, detailed lessons, Pretest and Post test, math vocabulary guides, and daily assessment guides
- Student Edition (copy masters also available as consumable student books)
- Recording Pads for Number, Operations, Patterns and Algebra, Geometry, Measurement, Vocabulary
- Great Source Math Handbook (*Math to Learn, Math to Know, Math at Hand,* or *Math on Call*) (Grades 1–8 only)
- Great Source Math Handbook Teacher Resource Book (Grades 1–8 only)
- Cardstock for Games
- Clear plastic counters in packs of 100
- Blank number cubes
- Cardstock solids (6 sheets)
- Cardstock rulers (2 sheets)
- Hundred Chart/Blank Hundred Chart
- Visuals on Overhead Transparencies (6–8 only)
- Visuals on CD-ROM (6–8 only)
- Cardstock clocks, pack of 10 (1–2 only)
- Cardstock Demo Clock (K only)
- 1 roll paper tape (adding machine tape)
- 1 pack 6 Recording Pad labels (English and Spanish)
- 1 pack plastic hooks for Recording Pads
- Fine-tip marker for cubes, transparencies, hundred chart, recording pads
- Zip-close sandwich bags for Games pieces (72)
- 1 pack 10 brads for clocks (K–2 only)
- 1 pack self-stick notes, 100 sheets (K–1 only)

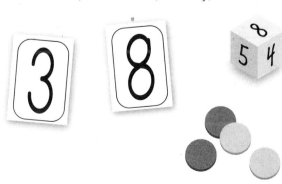

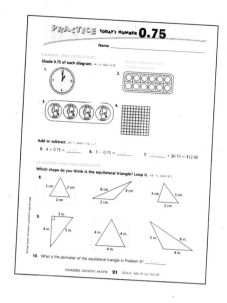

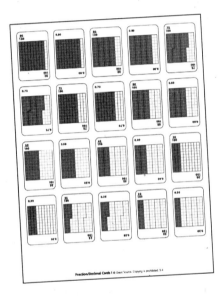

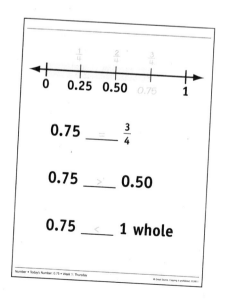

© Great Source. Copying is prohibited.

USING SUMMER SUCCESS: MATH

Summer Success: Math provides for as much as six weeks of instruction with up to two hours of class time each day of the week. The complete program offers a powerful review of the grade level concepts and skills identified by NCTM and state standards. Abbreviated versions of the program can provide a briefer, more focused review.

PLAN YOUR SUMMER SESSION

If possible, begin with Week 1, Monday, and continue page by page through each week of the program. Otherwise, use the Scope and Sequence on pages xviii and xiv along with the adaptation suggestions on pages xv to plan where to begin and what to cover each week.

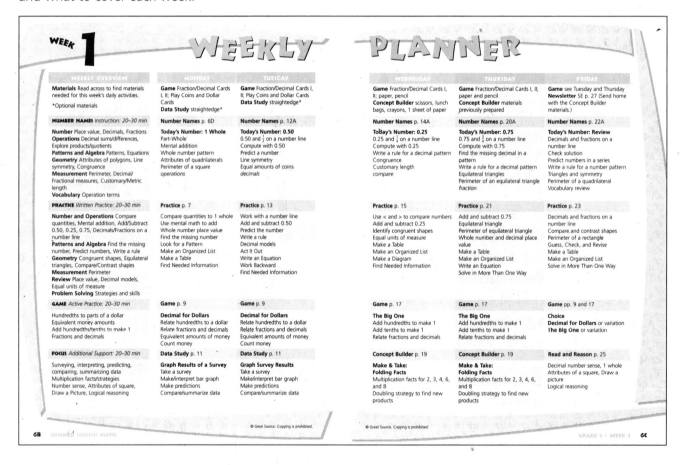

PLAN THE WEEK

- *Summer Success: Math* has been designed to provide multiple exposures to each key grade level topic over the course of each week, so if possible, follow the program as outlined by the Weekly Planners, beginning on page 6B.

- If time is limited, study the Weekly Planner's detailed Overview of concepts and skills addressed that week as well as the pacing suggestions, then choose those elements that best address your students' needs and schedule.

© Great Source. Copying is prohibited.

- Variety is built into *Summer Success: Math* to offer students multiple representations and different points of entry. Be sure that as you plan your week you maintain this variety.
- Also notice that each Game, Data Study, and Concept Builder activity takes place over the course of two days.

BEGIN THE DAY

- Begin each day with classroom discourse in a Number Names discussion. This direct instruction is your opportunity to focus students' attention on the math they will be encountering that day, to encourage students to share ideas and mathematical reasoning, and to address students' misconceptions.
- Follow the Number Names discussion with at least part of the corresponding Practice pages.
- Follow Practice with either a Game or Focus activity. For the richest possible *Summer Success: Math* experience, do both.

AT THE END OF EACH WEEK

- Send home the weekly Newsletter found in the Student Book with the Concept Builder materials used during the week.
- Newsletter activities are an opportunity for students to extend practice beyond school using their own materials, and for family members to become active participants in the child's learning.

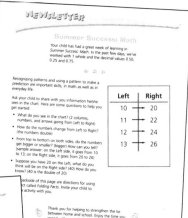

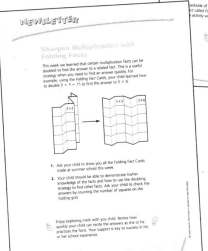

Daily Routine

© Great Source. Copying is prohibited.

PART 1: NUMBER NAMES

Daily Group instruction and discourse
- Connect six strands plus vocabulary; use Recording Pads to reflect collective thinking.

PART 2: PRACTICE

Daily Independent work and problem solving
- Reinforce day's instruction and review.

PART 3: GAMES

Daily Active paired practice
- Day 1: Introduce game, math concepts, vocabulary; play a model game.
- Day 2: Play in pairs; verbalize strategy and mental math; record.

PART 4: FOCUS

Two days—Data Study: Group instruction and paired work
- Discuss, collect, organize data; then graph and analyze data.

Two days—Concept Builder: Whole group and pairs
- Build manipulative materials and introduce math concept; then use materials to explore concept in depth.

One day—Read and Reason: Guided problem solving
- Develop problem-solving skills, logical reasoning, and reading for meaning.

Number Names Instruction

Number Names provides daily instruction covering five different math strands plus **Vocabulary. Problem Solving** is integrated throughout. Today's Number, unique to each day, is the connecting thread that ties the discussion together. For example, if Today's Number is 0.50, students may look at the number in terms of:

Number: If there were 100 marks on the number line, which one would be halfway between 0 and 100?

Operations: If you add 1 whole and 0.50 will the sum be more or less than 2?

Patterns and Algebra: : How do the numbers in the left column and right column compare?

Measurement: What part of a dollar is fifty cents?

GET STARTED

- Choose a Number Names display area that allows students to sit as close as possible. Some teachers prefer to have the students sit on the floor or in chairs in front of the Number Names wall to focus their attention.

- Post the six Recording Pads and their labels, leaving a space for Today's Number.

DISCUSSION

- During each day's discussion, detailed in the Teacher's Edition, students consider questions displayed on the day's Recording Pads. Answers are collectively agreed upon and then written on the pads, providing a lasting representation of the concepts covered.

- Encourage students to interact with each other by listening to one another, sharing their reasoning, and respectfully questioning each other. To raise their level of thinking, follow up student responses with questions such as: *How do you know? How can we figure out if you're right? Does anyone else have another answer?*

- Reaching All Learners hints can help struggling students, including English Language Learners, who may benefit from another approach. References to the Great Source Math Handbook, *Math at Hand*, follow each discussion strand and provide a resource for re-teaching.

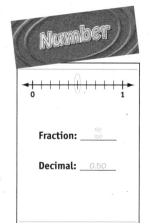

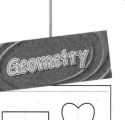

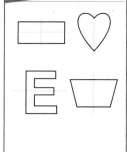

© Great Source. Copying is prohibited.

If possible, collect and display all the Recording Pad pages throughout the entire week so past discussions can be easily referred to. Use the paper adding machine tape in your kit to organize the sheets by Today's Number. Hang the tape at least 66 inches above the floor, and hang the Recording Pads pages in the same order each day. Friday's Number Names summarizes the week's work; having the pages displayed will enhance student's recall capacity.

Written Practice and Problem Solving

Practice pages in the student book reinforce the key math topics discussed in Number Names.

- Students work independently on the first sections; references to *Math at Hand* follow each direction line for any who may need another explanation.

- Each Practice includes a Problem Solving section with a multi-step or otherwise challenging problem for small-group cooperative work. Guide students as necessary in approaching the problem, sorting out the information, and selecting a strategy.

- Optional additional features in the Teacher's Edition include Glossary to Go, which suggests that students complete a personal glossary entry (on pages 139 to 144 of the student book) for the vocabulary term of the day, and a Math Journal writing prompt to give students practice expressing mathematical thinking in writing.

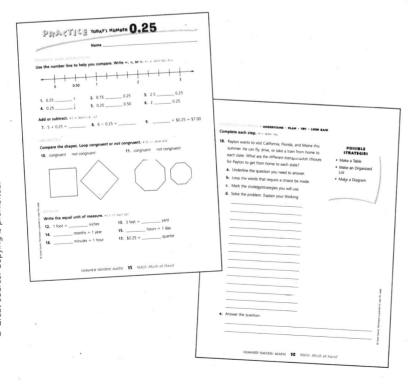

© Great Source. Copying is prohibited.

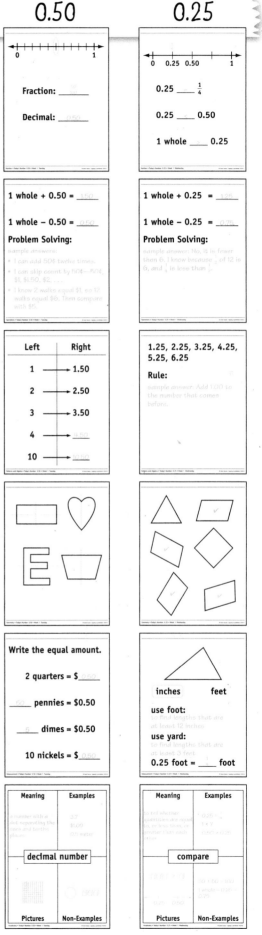

Active Practice with Games

Games in *Summer Success: Math* provide hands-on, verbal, and auditory experiences with number facts, computation, mental-math strategies, and problem-solving strategies to complement the Number Names instruction.

GET STARTED

- Introduce the idea of playing the Games as a form of practice from the outset. Let students know that the games are work to help them achieve the goals of summer school math.

- Each day students should be either learning a Game or playing a Game, so setting ground rules is very important. Keep the rules short and simple. You might make a poster for the room like the one shown of the "Partner Pledge."

- Have the students say the partner pledge before beginning game play, to ensure their understanding of the expectations. Students who cannot participate constructively should be removed from the group quickly and allowed to return when ready.

USING THE GAMES

- Each week of *Summer Success: Math* includes two Games, each of which is a two-day activity.

- **Day 1** is instruction day. Review background vocabulary and concepts, and model one or two full sample games. Modeling the games provides an opportunity to teach the language of mathematics and to have students share their strategies for playing the game.

- On **Day 2** students play the game in pairs while the teacher observes. Assessment guidelines are provided along with suggestions for re-teaching as needed. *Math at Hand* references are listed for both student and teacher, and a simpler version of each game is provided for any students who may need it.

Spinner for Build a Net

© Great Source. Copying is prohibited.

- On Fridays students replay any prior game or one of the suggested variations in order to reinforce or expand upon concepts and skills they previously encountered.

- Discussion is a key ingredient of the games, especially for those students for whom learning is largely auditory. Be sure that students follow the examples in the game instructions to explain their thinking on each move.

- Prompt students to be aware of their thinking using the Reflect on the Math questions in the Teacher's Edition. If class size dictates that students play in groups of three, have students take turns playing the "judge" responsible for fact-checking all statements and moves made by the other two.

- Materials for 18 students (9 pairs) to play each game (cardstock cards, plastic counters, and blank wooden cubes) are included in your *Summer Success: Math* kit. Use the fine-tip marker in the kit to label the faces of the cubes as shown in the table below.

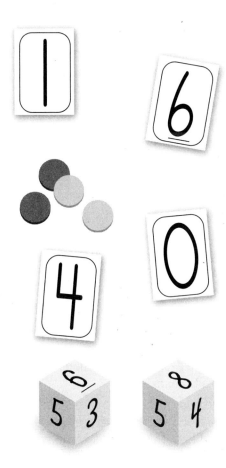

Cube Faces	How Many	Where Used
1, 2, 3, 4, 5, 6	9	Weeks 2, 3
4, 5, 6, 7, 8, 9	18	Weeks 2, 3

Focus with Data Study

Data Study in *Summer Success: Math* is a weekly two-day focus on various facets of data, including collecting, organizing, graphing, interpreting, and analyzing.

USING DATA STUDY

- On **Day 1,** students may collect data through a probability experiment or a class survey. Alternatively, data are provided to students in a list or table format. Have students work in pairs or small groups to create a graph or other meaningful visual representation of the data.

- On **Day 2,** after a brief review, guide students to analyze their data or graphs from the previous day. Conclude each Data Study with a What if? question such as the one suggested in the Teacher's Edition to encourage students to consider the possible outcomes of changing one aspect of the data.

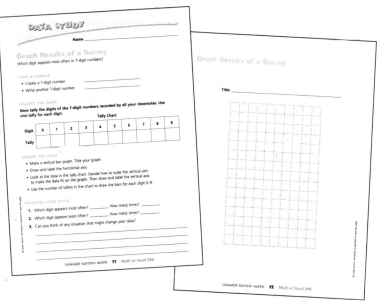

How would the data change if we collected 7-digit numbers from 100 more people?

© Great Source. Copying is prohibited.

Focus with Concept Builder

A Concept Builder is a two-day make-and-take project in which students focus on the most fundamental math concepts for their grade level. Using pages from the student book and basic classroom supplies, students build manipulative materials that they will work with to solidify conceptual understandings. With one unique Concept Builder each week, students explore concepts of number, operations, fractions, facts, and more as they create their own models, games, and flash cards for school and home use.

USING CONCEPT BUILDER

- On **Day 1,** show students a completed sample of what they will be making and explain how it will be used. Then walk students through the step-by-step instructions in the Teacher's Edition for making the materials.

- Provide lunch bags or sandwich bags for students to use to store their materials until the next day, and later to carry materials home.

- On **Day 2,** demonstrate the activity using the materials. Again, step-by-step instructions are provided in your Teacher's Edition.

- At the end of the week have students take these materials home along with the Newsletter containing activity instructions. This essential home-school link reinforces the students' sense of ownership while providing opportunities for further practice at home.

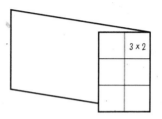

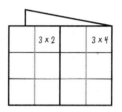

Can you use your Folding Facts cards to show that 3 × 4 is twice 3 × 2?

Focus with Read and Reason

Each Friday of *Summer Success: Math* includes a Read and Reason special focus on using mathematical reasoning with analytical reading skills in a grade-level context. Each exercise consists of a short paragraph depicting some mathematical scenario with four words or numbers omitted and replaced with blank write-on-lines. Only when those blanks are filled in with correct numbers, measurements, or mathematical terms, does the paragraph make sense.

USING READ AND REASON

- Begin by reading the paragraph aloud, then have a volunteer re-read the paragraph. Allow students to work independently, in pairs, or in small groups to complete the activity. Remind students to use a combination of number sense, estimation, measurement and geometry knowledge, and/or the process of elimination to "solve the puzzle."

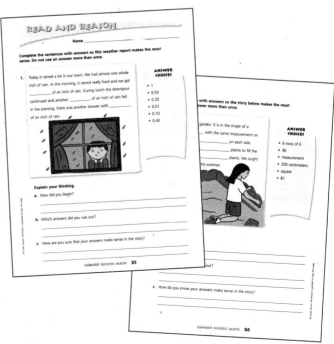

© Great Source. Copying is prohibited.

ASSESSMENT

Assessment

Assessment in *Summer Success: Math* is both summative and formative. Opportunities are provided for assessing students' strengths and weaknesses at the beginning and the end of the summer session, as well as daily opportunities for continuous monitoring of student progress.

PRETEST AND POST TEST

The Pretest and Post Test are provided to assess the needs and achievements of both individual students and of the class as a whole. Use the tests as a pair to measure each student's overall growth.

- A 6-page Pretest provides a full page of multiple choice or short answer questions for each math content strand including Number, Operations, Patterns and Algebra, Geometry, Measurement, and Data as well as a page of open-response Problem-Solving questions similar to those found on many high-stakes tests.

- A Pretest Correlation Chart identifies the Week or Weeks in which the concept or skill represented is taught. Use this chart to help choose activities that will address the students' specific needs.

- A 6-page Post Test mirrors the Pretest to facilitate evaluating and reporting of progress.

ONGOING ASSESSMENT

Summer Success: Math includes daily informal assessment opportunities for teachers to consider each day during each activity.

- Discussion questions provided in Number Names help you to monitor student understanding and to correct possible misconceptions on an on-going basis.

- Practice pages are designed to help identify and remediate areas that are troublesome for students.

- Assessment of problem solving is supported by a scoring suggestion in the Teacher's Edition for the Problem Solving portion of each day's Practice.

- Glossary to Go entries are the student's own representation of the meaning of the day's Vocabulary term. Whether words or drawings, these will reveal how well students have absorbed the meaning of the math term and related concepts.

- Math Journal prompts with Practice in the Teacher's Edition can be used to gain insight into students' thinking and to address misconceptions as they arise.

- Ongoing Assessment with Games and Concept Builders in the Teacher's Edition help you use the activities to identify students' strengths and weaknesses and to monitor their progress daily.

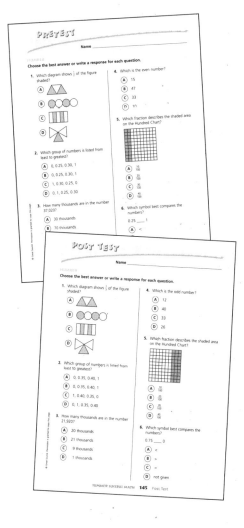

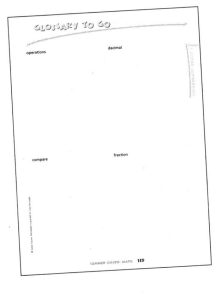

© Great Source. Copying is prohibited.

Summer Success: Math

SPECIAL FEATURES

Summer Success: Math includes special features that address the needs of the English language learner.

- Each day's Number Names discussion includes a focus on one key Vocabulary term and closely associated words or phrases.

- Math Talk in the Teacher's Edition provides clear and meaningful definitions for key math terms essential to each activity.

- Reaching All Learners throughout the Teacher's Edition provides additional hints for concrete, visual, tactile, and language scaffolding for English learners and other students needing additional support. Suggested manipulative materials for Reaching All Learners demonstrations include items such as clocks, number lines, counters, and hundreds chart. For a complete list of materials, see page xvii.

GENERAL TEACHING STRATEGIES FOR ENGLISH LANGUAGE LEARNERS

When working with English language learners in mathematics, be careful not to "water down" the lesson content in an attempt to explain it. Use appropriate mathematics vocabulary and stress understanding rather than rote computational procedures.

- Use a variety of teaching strategies to express yourself and make your meaning more widely understandable.

- Use pictures and diagrams, real objects, gestures and body language to provide additional clues to your meaning, engage students, help them make connections, and help them remember and understand language that they are hearing and learning.

- Key vocabulary must be represented in every lesson. This is critical to an ELL student. You must not only have a content area objective but must also include a language objective to ensure language development.

- Adjust your speaking for English learners. Speak slowly and clearly and avoid idioms and slang; but do not water down the lesson by simplifying vocabulary.

- Use cooperative learning activities that allow English learners to interact with peers and be actively involved with group activities.

- Provide interactive learning opportunities which support "hands-on" learning experiences. In particular, allow students time to manipulate new materials and practice language as they work with Games and Concept Builders.

- Model everything when explaining classroom or homework activities. Show the students a finished product or physically demonstrate, step by step, what is expected.

- List and review instructions step by step and have students work on each step individually before moving on to the next. This process works well when teaching students to solve word problems or when preparing Concept Builders.

- Ask inferential and higher-order thinking questions that will develop metacognitive skills. For example, "Can you explain this in another way? Does this rule always work?" Allow for alternate solutions and keep expectations high!

- Increase your wait time, allowing time after each question for students to think and raise their hands to respond. Do not interject additional thoughts or prompts at this time.

© Great Source. Copying is prohibited.

CUSTOMIZING

Summer Success: Math is planned for maximum flexibility. Although developed for a six-week program that meets five days per week, it can be adapted to meet a variety of different schedules. Use the blank planner provided in the Teacher's Edition to make your own plans for Summer Success. Here are just a few ideas.

FOUR DAYS A WEEK FOR 5 OR 6 WEEKS

Friday lessons provide a valuable opportunity for students to consolidate the week's concepts, but no new material is introduced. Fridays may be omitted from the program if necessary to accommodate a four-day schedule. Practice pages from Friday might be assigned as homework.

FOUR WEEKS OR LESS

Prioritize based on test results. Select the three most critical strands of Number Names, and do two days' worth in each class. Assign only related problems from corresponding Practice pages. Use the Scope and Sequence to select a variety of activities from Game, Data Study, Concept Builder, Read and Reason that best address identified needs.

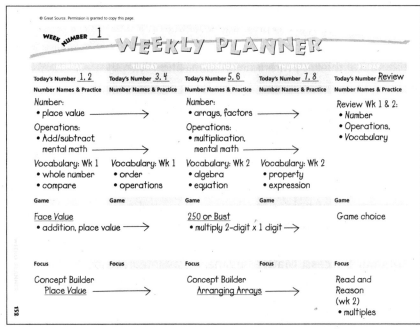

Grade 4 Sample Planner for condensed schedule

USING SUMMER SUCCESS: MATH DURING THE SCHOOL YEAR

- **As a full-year program** Use *Summer Success: Math* as a supplement to any math program, spreading one day's material from *Summer Success* over the course of a full week. A single week becomes a 5-week unit; the 30 days of the program cover 30 weeks of school.

- **As remediation** Place students in a remediation class according to their level of performance. Use the corresponding level of *Summer Success: Math* for a 30-day remediation program. At the end of 30 days, have successful students move up to the next level; have others repeat the program.

- **In a bilingual program** Implement *Summer Success: Math* in Spanish at a level a year or two below the student's actual grade. After the full 30 days, repeat the same program in English. Then repeat the process at the next higher level.

© Great Source. Copying is prohibited.

RESEARCH BASE & PROGRAM EFFECTIVENESS

Summer Success: Math has a proven track record of success that is supported by a sound research base as well as effectiveness studies. The program applies the findings of current research in math education. Below are sample excerpts; for complete research and effectiveness information please visit www.greatsource.com/grants.

Research Base

RESEARCH SAYS

When children talk about mathematical concepts they are actually increasing their understanding of that concept. Language allows them to reflect on and revise thoughts.[1]

In Summer Success: Math the daily whole-class Number Names discussion helps to promote a deeper understanding of key concepts. Students organize and consolidate their mathematical thinking through communication with the teacher and with classmates. A daily focus on Vocabulary helps students develop appropriate terminology for discussing their mathematical thinking.

RESEARCH SAYS

Assessment . . . should be an integral part of instruction that informs and guides teachers as they make instructional decisions.[2]

In Summer Success: Math assessment is an integral aspect of the program. A pre-test and a post-test provide points of reference and measures of student progress. Daily informal assessment questions allow the teacher to monitor student progress and provide individualized assistance. Students reap the benefits of immediate assessment by correcting any flawed reasoning and applying this corrected thinking to subsequent problems.

1. Andrews, A. G. (1997, January). Doing what comes naturally: Talking about mathematics. Teaching children mathematics, 236–239.

2. National Council of Teachers of Mathematics. (2000). *Principles and standards for school mathematics.* Reston, VA: National Council of Teachers of Mathematics.

Effectiveness

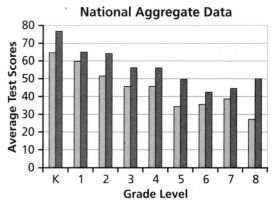

National Aggregate Data

Key: ▢ Pretest ■ Post Test

Pre-test scores at the beginning of the Summer Success: Math *program and post-test scores at the end of the course reflect significant improvement in students' math proficiency nationwide.*

Data collected in summer of 2001 from 4747 students in grades K–8.

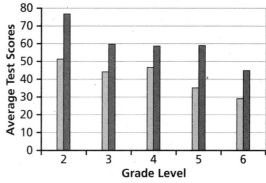

Brockton School District, Brockton, MA

Key: ▢ Pretest ■ Post Test

The Brockton School District is an urban district in Massachusetts.

Summer Success: Math *helped student test scores rise by at least 15.68% across participating grade levels with some grades improving as much as 23.97%.*

© Great Source. Copying is prohibited.

Required

	Weeks					
	1	2	3	4	5	6
Play Dollars ($1)*	✔	✔		✔		
Play Coins*	✔	✔		✔		✔
Fraction/Decimal Cards I*	✔			✔		
Fraction/Decimal Cards II*	✔			✔		
Play Money I ($100)*		✔				
Play Money II ($1,000)*		✔				
0-9 Digit Cards*			✔		✔	✔
Spinner*				✔		
Square and Triangle Cards*				✔		
Rectangle Cards*				✔		
Cardstock Solids*			✔	✔		
Number Cubes*		✔	✔			
Rulers*					✔	
counters*	✔		✔	✔	✔	✔
Hundred Chart*	✔	✔		✔	✔	✔
adding machine tape*			✔	✔		
paper clips, large				✔		
yarn or string	✔			✔		
paper	✔	✔	✔	✔	✔	✔
pencils	✔	✔	✔		✔	✔
scissors	✔	✔	✔	✔	✔	✔
crayons or markers	✔		✔	✔	✔	
storage bags	✔	✔		✔	✔	✔
glue or tape			✔	✔		

Optional

	Weeks					
	1	2	3	4	5	6
12-in ruler or straightedge	✔	✔	✔	✔	✔	
yardstick				✔		
calculator	✔	✔		✔		
grid paper	✔					✔
tape measure				✔		
tracing paper	✔			✔		✔
cereal box		✔	✔			
soup cans			✔			
tissue box			✔			
colored paper						✔
calendar						✔

*Materials included in *Summer Success: Math* kit.

© Great Source. Copying is prohibited.

SCOPE AND SEQUENCE

WEEK 1	WEEK 2	WEEK 3

Number Names: 1 whole, 0.50, 0.25, 0.75 | **Number Names: 0.20, 0.30, 0.40, 0.60** | **Number Names:** $\frac{1}{2}$, $\frac{1}{4}$, $\frac{3}{4}$, $\frac{1}{3}$

Number Place Value, decimals, fractions
Operations Decimal sums and differences, explore products and quotients
Patterns and Algebra Patterns, equations
Geometry Attributes of polygons, line symmetry, congruence
Measurement Perimeter, decimal and fractional measures, customary and metric length
Vocabulary Operation terms

Number Compare, order and round decimals, relate fractions and decimals
Operations Decimals, mental math
Patterns and Algebra Number pattern, write a rule, function table, equations
Geometry Lines, interior angles, coordinate grid, ordered pairs
Measurement Customary weight, metric mass, time
Vocabulary Algebra terms

Number Equivalent fractions and decimals, order fractions
Operations Compute with fractions
Patterns and Algebra Number patterns, prediction, write a rule, order of operations
Geometry Solids, nets
Measurement Area, time, customary capacity and length, circumference
Vocabulary Geometry terms

Practice

Number and Operations Compare quantities, mental addition, add and subtract decimals, decimals and fractions on a number line
Patterns and Algebra Find the missing number, predict numbers, write a rule
Geometry Congruent shapes, equilateral triangles
Measurement Perimeter
Problem Solving Strategies and skills

Number and Operations Compare and order decimals and fractions
Patterns and Algebra Patterns, function table
Geometry Map geometry, coordinate grid, ordered pairs
Measurement Customary weight
Problem Solving Strategies and skills

Number and Operations Fraction concepts, compute with fractions, use symbols, fractions on number lines
Patterns and Algebra Number patterns and rules
Geometry Solids, nets
Measurement Area of rectangle, triangle, fractions and time
Problem Solving Strategies and skills

Game

Decimal for Dollars Relate hundredths to cents, relate fractions and decimals, equivalent amounts of money, count money
The Big One Add hundredths to make 1, add tenths to make 1, relate fractions and decimals

A Whole in One Review decimal place value, add and subtract decimals
Collect $10,000 Review place value, add large numbers, read and write large numbers

Division Estimation Estimate quotients, whole number division, remainders, compare mixed numbers
Factor Frenzy Factors and products, multiplication and division facts

Focus

Data Study Surveying, interpreting, predicting, comparing, summarizing data
Concept Builder Multiplication facts and strategies
Read and Reason Decimal number sense, attributes of square, logical reasoning

Data Study Read a table, bar graph; range, mean, and median
Concept Builder Add decimals, decimal place value, decimal amounts, estimate sums, mental math
Read and Reason Factor numbers, make inferences, prisms, cubes

Data Study Use a table, make a line graph, data, metric units in decimal or fraction form
Read and Reason Multiplication, volume concept, elapsed time, compute with units of time

© Great Source. Copying is prohibited.

Number Names: $\frac{1}{5}$, $\frac{1}{6}$, $\frac{1}{8}$, $\frac{1}{100}$

Number Fractions, decimals, percents
Operations Compute with fractions
Patterns and Algebra Fraction pattern, expressions and equations
Geometry Transformations, ordered pairs, coordinate grid
Measurement Volume, area, customary weight, metric length
Vocabulary Measurement terms

Practice

Number and Operations Equivalent fractions, decimals, and percents; model, compare and compute with fractions
Patterns and Algebra Table of values, rules
Geometry Rotation, cubes
Measurement Volume, area
Problem Solving Strategies and skills

Game

Build a Net Geometric solid faces, nets
Ordering Fractions and Decimals Equivalent fractions and decimals, order fractions and decimals, models for decimals and fractions

Focus

Data Study Gather data; line plot; compare and summarize data; find range, mode, median
Concept Builder Fractions and adding fractions
Read and Reason Multiplication and division, logical reasoning, data, mean, range

---

Number Names: 10; 1000; 100,000; 1,000,000

Number Place value, large numbers
Operations Exponents, compute with large numbers
Patterns and Algebra Tables of values, write equations and rules, predictions
Geometry Polygons, prisms, interior angles
Measurement Area, volume, kilometers
Vocabulary Data and Problem Solving terms

Practice

Number and Operations Groups of 10; standard, expanded, exponential forms; place value; add, subtract, multiply powers of 10
Patterns and Algebra Write an equation, predictions
Geometry Interior angles
Measurement Area, volume
Problem Solving Strategies and skills

Game

Ten Times Ten Read and write large numbers, understand powers of 10, apply exponents
Eagle-Eye Estimation Estimate product, calculate exact product compare numbers

Focus

Data Study Data, tables, bar graphs, range, mean, median, rounding
Concept Builder Fractions and equivalent fractions
Read and Reason Decimals, triangles, customary weight, logical reasoning

---

Number Names: 0, 2, 3, 5

Number Place value, even and odd, prime and composite
Operations Compute with 0, divisibility by 2, 3, 5, sum of primes
Patterns and Algebra Commutative and Associative Properties, square and triangular number pattern
Geometry Transformations, tessellations, polygons
Measurement Area, perimeter
Vocabulary Data terms

Practice

Number and Operations Place value and the digit 0, even and odd, compute with zero, divisibility, prime and composite
Patterns and Algebra Commutative and Associative Properties, number sequences
Geometry Transformations
Measurement Perimeter, area
Problem Solving Strategies and skills

Game

Prime Time Prime and composite numbers, add and subtract whole numbers
Inverse Estimations Estimate sums and differences, calculate exact sums and differences

Focus

Data Study Events, outcomes, combinations, tree diagram, probability
Concept Builder Spatial relationships, recognize congruence, similarity, and symmetry
Read and Reason Fraction concepts, number types

© Great Source. Copying is prohibited.

PRETEST

The Pretest for *Summer Success: Math* is intended to provide baseline data for each student beginning the program. At the end of your summer session, if you are administering the Post Test you will have data to analyze and measure the student's growth. Whether you use this Pretest or student data from the school district, test data can be used to choose areas to emphasize with students attending summer school.

NUMBER

Choose the best answer or write a response for each question.

1. Which diagram shows $\frac{1}{2}$ of the figure shaded?

   (A)

   (B)

   (C)

   (D)

2. Which group of numbers is listed from least to greatest?

   (A) 0, 0.25, 0.30, 1

   (B) 0, 0.25, 0.30, 1

   (C) 1, 0.30, 0.25, 0

   (D) 0, 1, 0.25, 0.30

3. How many thousands are in the number 37,020?

   (A) 30 thousands

   (B) 70 thousands

   (C) 37 thousands

   (D) 7 thousands

4. Which is the even number?

   (A) 15

   (B) 47

   (C) 33

   (D) 10

5. Which fraction describes the shaded area on the Hundred Chart?

   (A) $\frac{10}{100}$

   (B) $\frac{20}{100}$

   (C) $\frac{30}{100}$

   (D) $\frac{40}{100}$

6. Which symbol best compares the numbers?

   0.25 _____ 1

   (A) <

   (B) >

   (C) =

   (D) not given

© Great Source. Permission is granted to copy this page.

ABOUT NUMBER

A student's number sense and ability to apply it is key to success in mathematics. The comprehension and application of number sense are the underpinnings of computation, operations, and place value understanding.

© Great Source. Copying is prohibited.

Pretest Correlation

Test Question	Frequency Missed	Math Concept Assessed	Week: Day
1		Relate parts to a whole	1: Monday 3: Thursday 6: Friday
1		Use fraction concepts and models	3: Monday–Friday 4: Monday–Friday
2		Compare and order decimals between 0 and 1	1: Monday–Friday 2: Monday–Friday 4: Wednesday–Friday
3		Understand place value	1: Monday, Thursday–Friday 2: Wednesday, Thursday 5: Monday–Friday
3		Understand powers of 10	5: Monday–Friday
4		Understand odd and even numbers, factors	1: Wednesday, Thursday 3: Wednesday, Thursday 6: Tuesday–Wednesday, Friday
5		Relate fractions and decimals with models	1–4: Monday–Friday
6		Use < and > to compare decimals	1: Wednesday–Friday 3: Monday–Friday 4: Wednesday–Friday

MAKING THE MOST OF THE PRETEST RESULTS FOR NUMBER

Use the results of the Pretest as a guide to what number concepts to emphasize over the course of the summer. For each concept tested, does one student, one fourth of the class, one half of the class, or the whole class need review? Note which concepts need the greatest emphasis.

© Great Source. Copying is prohibited.

PRETEST

OPERATIONS

7. Which model shows $\frac{1}{6}$?

Ⓐ

Ⓑ

Ⓒ

Ⓓ

8. Which is the factored form for the number 100,000?

Ⓐ $10 \times 10 \times 10 \times 10 \times 10$

Ⓑ $10 \times 1,000$

Ⓒ 10×10

Ⓓ $10 \times 10 \times 10$

9. What is the sum?

$\$6.25 + \$0.75 = $ ____

Ⓐ $6.00

Ⓑ $7.00

Ⓒ $6.25

Ⓓ $1.75

10. What is the product?

$10 \times 0.30 = $ ____

Ⓐ 0.30

Ⓑ 3.0

Ⓒ 30

Ⓓ 300

11. What is the difference?

$1 - \frac{2}{3} = $ ____

Ⓐ $\frac{2}{3}$

Ⓑ $1\frac{2}{3}$

Ⓒ $\frac{1}{3}$

Ⓓ 1

12. Which operation best completes the equation?

$597 \underline{\quad} 0 = 0$

Ⓐ $\times$

Ⓑ $+$

Ⓒ $-$

Ⓓ $\div$

© Great Source. Permission is granted to copy this page.

ABOUT OPERATIONS

A student's success with applying operations is dependent on two factors. The student must understand the language of the operation, for example, what it means to add, subtract, or multiply, and the student must know how to do the computation involved.

© Great Source. Copying is prohibited.

Pretest Correlation

Test Question	Frequency Missed	Math Concept Assessed	Week: Day
7		Use fraction models	3: Monday, Thursday 4: Monday–Friday
8		Understand powers of ten	5: Monday–Friday
9		Relate hundredths to a dollar	1: Monday–Tuesday, Friday
9		Add decimals	2: Monday–Friday
10		Multiply decimals	2: Monday–Friday
10		Understand powers of 10	5: Monday–Friday
11		Compute with fractions	3: Monday–Friday
12		Use algebraic properties	6: Monday–Friday

MAKING THE MOST OF THE PRETEST RESULTS FOR OPERATIONS

Use the results of the Pretest as a guide to what operations concepts and skills to emphasize over the course of the summer. For each concept or skill tested, does one student, one fourth of the class, one half of the class, or the whole class need review? Note which concepts and skills need the greatest emphasis.

© Great Source. Copying is prohibited.

PATTERNS AND ALGEBRA

Use the fractions to answer problems 13–14.

$$\frac{1}{10}, \frac{2}{10}, \frac{3}{10}, \frac{4}{10}, \underline{\quad}$$

13. What is the missing fraction?

(A) 5

(B) $\frac{5}{10}$

(C) $\frac{5}{5}$

(D) $\frac{5}{20}$

14. Which rule best describes the pattern?

(A) count backwards by $\frac{1}{10}$

(B) subtract by $\frac{1}{10}$

(C) count on by $\frac{1}{10}$

(D) multiply by $\frac{1}{10}$

15. Look at the equations.

$\frac{1}{2} \times 1 = \frac{1}{2}$

$100 \times 1 = 100$

$0.75 \times 1 = 0.75$

$648 \times 1 = 648$

Now, complete the sentence.
Any number times 1...

_____ is that number.

16. Which number pattern follows the rule shown?

Add 0.5 to the term before.

(A) 1.0, 1.5, 2.0, 2.5

(B) 0.5, 0.55, 0.6, 0.65

(C) 2.0, 1.5, 1.0, 0.5

(D) 0.5, 0.5, 0.5, 0.5

Use the table to answer problems 17–18.

In	Out
3	3.5
10	10.5
7	7.5
4	4.5
___	6.5

17. What is the missing term?

(A) 4

(B) 5

(C) 6

(D) 7

18. Which equation best describes the terms in the table?

(A) In − 0.5 = Out

(B) In × 0.5 = Out

(C) In ÷ 0.5 = Out

(D) In + 0.5 = Out

© Great Source. Permission is granted to copy this page.

SUMMER SUCCESS: MATH **3** Pretest

ABOUT PATTERNS AND ALGEBRA

Seeing patterns is the basis of mathematics. Help students use what they recognize in patterns to make predictions that will lead to algebraic thinking. Translating a pattern into a T-chart, into an expression, or into a graph are important building blocks of Algebra.

© Great Source. Copying is prohibited.

Pretest Correlation

Test Question	Frequency Missed	Math Concept Assessed	Week: Day
13		Complete or extend a number pattern	1–6: Monday–Friday
14		Describe rule for a number pattern	1–6: Monday–Friday
15		Generalize from patterns	1–6: Monday–Friday
16		Match a rule to an number pattern	1–6: Monday–Friday
17		Understand function tables	1: Monday–Tuesday 2: Monday, Wednesday–Friday 3: Monday, Wednesday 4: Tuesday–Friday 5: Monday–Friday
17		Complete or extend a number pattern	1–6: Monday–Friday
18		Understand function tables	1: Monday–Tuesday 2: Monday, Wednesday–Friday 3: Monday, Wednesday 4: Tuesday–Friday 5: Monday–Friday
18		Describe rule for a number pattern	1–6: Monday–Friday

MAKING THE MOST OF THE PRETEST RESULTS FOR PATTERNS AND ALGEBRA

Use the results of the Pretest as a guide to what patterns and algebra concepts and skills to emphasize over the course of the summer. For each concept or skill tested, does one student, one fourth of the class, one half of the class, or the whole class need review? Note which concepts and skills need the greatest emphasis.

© Great Source. Copying is prohibited.

Name _____

GEOMETRY AND MEASUREMENT

19. Which ordered pair names the location of Point *K*?

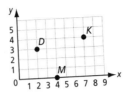

A (4, 7)

B (7, 4)

C (2, 3)

D (0, 4)

Use the diagram to answer problems 20–21.

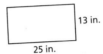

13 in.

25 in.

20. What is the perimeter of the rectangle?

A 325 inches

B 76 inches

C 38 inches

D 12 inches

21. What is the area of the rectangle?

A 325 square inches

B 100 square inches

C 76 square inches

D 38 square inches

Use the diagram to answer problems 22–23.

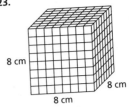

8 cm

8 cm

8 cm

22. What is the total area of the 6 faces of the cube?

A 16 square centimeters

B 24 square centimeters

C 64 square centimeters

D 384 square centimeters

23. What is the volume of the cube?

A 24 cubic centimeters

B 72 cubic centimeters

C 512 cubic centimeters

D 4,832 cubic centimeters

24. Which diagram shows a reflection?

A

B

C

D

© Great Source. Permission is granted to copy this page.

ABOUT GEOMETRY AND MEASUREMENT

Students need to visualize and see real examples of geometry in the world around them.

Geometry is built on attributes and the language of points, lines, angles, and two- and three- dimensional shapes. Graphic organizers can be useful to differentiate the extensive academic language that accompanies geometry.

In measurement, students need to understand the type of measurement (such as length, capacity, weight); recognize the units (such as inches, liters, pounds); and understand the tools used (such as ruler, measuring cup, or scale or a yardstick). Look closely at the items students missed to see if you can discern which aspect(s) of measurement students do not understand.

© Great Source. Copying is prohibited.

Pretest Correlation

© Great Source. Copying is prohibited.

	Frequency Missed		
19		Understand coordinate grids	2: Wednesday, Friday 4: Monday, Thursday, Friday
20		Find perimeter	1: Thursday 2: Thursday, Friday 3: Thursday 5: Tuesday 6: Friday
21		Find area	1: Friday 3: Monday, Wednesday 5: Monday, Thursday 6: Wednesday, Friday
22		Find area	1: Friday 3: Monday, Wednesday 5: Monday, Thursday 6: Wednesday, Friday
22		Identify nets of cubes and rectangular prisms	4: Monday–Tuesday, Friday
23		Find volume of a prism	3: Friday 4: Monday, Friday 5: Wednesday
24		Understand transformations	6: Monday–Tuesday, Friday

MAKING THE MOST OF THE PRETEST RESULTS FOR GEOMETRY AND MEASUREMENT

Use the results of the Pretest as a guide to what geometry and measurement concepts and skills to emphasize over the course of the summer. For each concept or skill tested, does one student, one fourth of the class, one half of the class, or the whole class need review? Note which concepts and skills need the greatest emphasis.

Name _____

DATA

Use the table to answer problems 25–26.

School Planner

Store 1	Store 2	Store 3	Store 4
$4.89	$4.59	$5.00	$3.99

25. Which equation would you use to find the range of prices for the planner?

- (A) $5.00 + $3.99 = $8.99
- (B) $5.00 × $3.99 = $19.95
- (C) $5.00 − $3.99 = $1.01
- (D) $5.00 ÷ $3.99 = $1.25

26. Which two operations would you use to find the average price?

- (A) addition and division
- (B) subtraction and division
- (C) multiplication and division
- (D) subtraction and multiplication

27. Which number is the median for the data?

11, 28, 31, 31, 55, 55, 67

- (A) 28
- (B) 31
- (C) 55
- (D) 67

Use the diagram to answer problems 28–30.

28. What type of diagram is this?

- (A) line plot
- (B) line graph
- (C) tree diagram
- (D) stem-and-leaf plot

29. What does the diagram tell you?

- (A) survey results
- (B) possible outcomes
- (C) mean, median, mode
- (D) probability

30. How many possible outcomes are there?

- (A) 2
- (B) 3
- (C) 6
- (D) 12

© Great Source. Permission is granted to copy this page.

SUMMER SUCCESS: MATH **5** Pretest

ABOUT DATA

Data is an easy topic to connect to the real world. When looking at data, students must be able to understand what the content the data refers to, decode the representation of the data, know the language of data (most, least, in the middle, mean, median, mode, range, etc.) and be able to use a key. If a student has missed a question about data, try to determine the cause of the difficulty.

© Great Source. Copying is prohibited.

Pretest Correlation

| --- | --- | --- | --- |
25		Find range	2–5: Monday–Tuesday
26		Find mean	2: Monday–Tuesday 3: Monday–Wednesday 5: Monday–Tuesday
27		Find median	2: Monday–Tuesday 4–5: Monday–Tuesday
28		Recognize a data displays such as tree diagram, line plot	1: Monday–Wednesday 2: Monday–Tuesday 3: Monday–Tuesday 5: Monday–Tuesday 6: Monday–Tuesday
29		Interpret a tree diagram	1: Wednesday 6: Monday–Tuesday, Friday
30		Use a tree diagram	1: Wednesday 6: Monday–Tuesday, Friday
30		Identify possible outcomes	1: Wednesday, Friday 5: Monday 6: Monday–Tuesday, Friday

MAKING THE MOST OF THE PRETEST RESULTS FOR DATA

Use the results of the Pretest as a guide to what data concepts and skills to emphasize over the course of the summer. For each concept or skill tested, does one student, one fourth of the class, one half of the class, or the whole class need review? Note which concepts and skills need the greatest emphasis.

© Great Source. Copying is prohibited.

PRETEST

PROBLEM SOLVING

Solve each problem. Show your work.

31. Andy needs to set up 25 chairs in the gym. He has to put them in equal rows. How many different arrangements are possible?

Answer: _____ There are 2 arrangements. _____

Sample work:

□□□□□□□□□□□□□□□□□□□□□□□□□

25 chairs, 1 row

□□□□□
□□□□□
□□□□□
□□□□□
□□□□□

5 chairs, 5 rows

32. I am a hundredth decimal with one digit that is not zero. I am less than $\frac{7}{10}$, but greater than 0.40. I am between 0.50 and 1 on the number line. What decimal number am I?

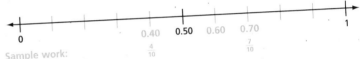

0   0.40   0.50   0.60   0.70   1
           $\frac{4}{10}$ $\frac{7}{10}$

Sample work:

Answer: _____ 0.60 _____

© Great Source. Permission is granted to copy this page.

ABOUT PROBLEM SOLVING

Students who answer problem solving questions incorrectly are not always getting the computation wrong. Sometimes students have difficulty with reading the problem; other times students do not know what extra information is included; and other students do not know which mathematical process to choose to solve the problem. *Summer Success: Math* offers daily opportunities for the teacher to help the student overcome all of those barriers. If a student has scored low on the pretest for problem solving, be sure to allow adequate time for problem solving every day.

© Great Source. Copying is prohibited.

Pretest Correlation

Test Question	Frequency Missed	Math Concept Assessed	Week: Day
31		Solve problems that involve multiplication facts and arrays	1: Wednesday-Friday 3: Wednesday–Friday 4: Thursday, Friday 5: Wednesday, Friday
31		Use appropriate strategies to solve problems	1–6: Monday–Friday
32		Use a number line to compare and order decimals and fractions	1: Monday–Friday 2: Tuesday–Friday 3: Tuesday–Friday 4: Monday–Friday
32		Use appropriate strategies to solve problems	1–6: Monday–Friday

MAKING THE MOST OF THE PRETEST RESULTS FOR PROBLEM SOLVING

Use the results of the Pretest as a guide to what problem-solving concepts and skills to emphasize over the course of the summer. For each of the two problems given, do students seem to have a strategy? Are they able to identify the question that needs to be answered? Are they able to explain their thinking? Note which aspects of problem solving need the greatest emphasis.

© Great Source. Copying is prohibited.

WEEKLY OVERVIEW	MONDAY	TUESDAY
Materials Read across to find materials needed for this week's daily activities. *Optional materials	**Game** Fraction/Decimal Cards I, II; Play Coins and Dollar Cards **Data Study** straightedge*	**Game** Fraction/Decimal Cards I, II; Play Coins and Dollar Cards **Data Study** straightedge*
NUMBER NAMES *Instruction: 20–30 min*	**Number Names** p. 6D	**Number Names** p. 12A
Number Place value, Decimals, Fractions **Operations** Decimal sums/differences, Explore products/quotients **Patterns and Algebra** Patterns, Equations **Geometry** Attributes of polygons, Line symmetry, Congruence **Measurement** Perimeter, Decimal/Fractional measures, Customary/Metric length **Vocabulary** Operation terms	**Today's Number: 1 Whole** Part-Whole Mental addition Whole number pattern Attributes of quadrilaterals Perimeter of a square *operations*	**Today's Number: 0.50** 0.50 and $\frac{1}{2}$ on a number line Compute with 0.50 Predict a number Line symmetry Equal amounts of coins *decimals*
PRACTICE *Written Practice: 20–30 min*	**Practice** p. 7	**Practice** p. 13
Number and Operations Compare quantities, Mental addition, Add/Subtract 0.50, 0.25, 0.75, Decimals/Fractions on a number line **Patterns and Algebra** Find the missing number, Predict numbers, Write a rule **Geometry** Congruent shapes, Equilateral triangles, Compare/Contrast shapes **Measurement** Perimeter **Review** Place value, Decimal models, Equal units of measure **Problem Solving** Strategies and skills	Compare quantities to 1 whole Use mental math to add Whole number place value Find the missing number Look for a Pattern Make an Organized List Make a Table Find Needed Information	Work with a number line Add and subtract 0.50 Predict the number Write a rule Decimal models Act It Out Write an Equation Work Backward Find Needed Information
GAME *Active Practice: 20–30 min*	**Game** p. 9	**Game** p. 9
Hundredths to parts of a dollar Equivalent money amounts Add hundredths/tenths to make 1 Fractions and decimals	**Decimal for Dollars** Relate hundredths to a dollar Relate fractions and decimals Equivalent amounts of money Count money	**Decimal for Dollars** Relate hundredths to a dollar Relate fractions and decimals Equivalent amounts of money Count money
FOCUS *Additional Support: 20–30 min*	**Data Study** p. 11	**Data Study** p. 11
Surveying, interpreting, predicting, comparing, summarizing data Multiplication facts/strategies Number sense, Attributes of square, Draw a Picture, Logical reasoning	**Graph Results of a Survey** Take a survey Make/interpret bar graph Make predictions Compare/summarize data	**Graph Survey Results** Take a survey Make/interpret bar graph Make predictions Compare/summarize data

© Great Source. Copying is prohibited.

PLANNER

Game Fraction/Decimal Cards I, II; paper, pencil
Concept Builder scissors, lunch bags, crayons, 1 sheet of paper

Number Names p. 14A

Today's Number: 0.25
0.25 and $\frac{1}{4}$ on a number line
Compute with 0.25
Write a rule for a decimal pattern
Congruence
Customary length
compare

Practice p. 15

Use < and > to compare numbers
Add and subtract 0.25
Identify congruent shapes
Equal units of measure
Make a Table
Make an Organized List
Make a Diagram
Find Needed Information

Game p. 17

The Big One
Add hundredths to make 1
Add tenths to make 1
Relate fractions and decimals

Concept Builder p. 19

Make & Take:
Folding Facts
Multiplication facts for 2, 3, 4, 6, and 8
Doubling strategy to find new products

Game Fraction/Decimal Cards I, II; paper and pencil
Concept Builder materials previously prepared

Number Names p. 20A

Today's Number: 0.75
0.75 and $\frac{3}{4}$ on a number line
Compute with 0.75
Find the missing decimal in a pattern
Write a rule for a decimal pattern
Equilateral triangles
Perimeter of an equilateral triangle
fraction

Practice p. 21

Add and subtract 0.75
Equilateral triangle
Perimeter of equilateral triangle
Whole number and decimal place value
Make a Table
Make an Organized List
Write an Equation
Solve in More Than One Way

Game p. 17

The Big One
Add hundredths to make 1
Add tenths to make 1
Relate fractions and decimals

Concept Builder p. 19

Make & Take:
Folding Facts
Multiplication facts for 2, 3, 4, 6, and 8
Doubling strategy to find new products

Game see Tuesday and Thursday
Newsletter SE p. 27 (Send home with the Concept Builder materials.)

Number Names p. 22A

Today's Number: Review
Decimals and fractions on a number line
Check solution
Predict numbers in a series
Write a rule for a number pattern
Triangles and symmetry
Perimeter of a quadrilateral
Vocabulary review

Practice p. 23

Decimals and fractions on a number line
Compare and contrast shapes
Perimeter of a rectangle
Guess, Check, and Revise
Make a Table
Make an Organized List
Solve in More Than One Way

Game pp. 9 and 17

Choice
Decimal for Dollars or variation
The Big One or variation

Read and Reason p. 25

Decimal number sense, 1 whole
Attributes of a square, Draw a picture
Logical reasoning

© Great Source. Copying is prohibited.

6C

NUMBER NAMES TODAY'S NUMBER **1 Whole**

1 whole pizza
1 whole hour
1 whole set of cards
1 whole carton of eggs
1 whole class of students
1 whole mile

- *What does 1 whole mean?* (sample answer: all of something)
- ✎ *Let's name some examples.* (sample answers: 1 whole apple, 1 whole brick, 1 whole pencil, and so on)
- ✎ *Sometimes we can group things together to make 1 whole. What are some examples?* (sample answers: 100 pennies in 1 dollar, 100 yards in a football field, 7 days in a week, 15 kids on a team, and so on)

Math at Hand 002

---

mental math

$60 + 30 =$ ___90___

$75 + 25 =$ ___100___

Answers will vary.

___ + ___ = 100
red   blue

OPERATIONS Mental math

- *What does mental math mean?* (sample answers: figure the answer in my head; don't use paper and pencil)
- ✎ *Can you tell how you used mental math to add the problems?* (sample answers: $60 + 30$, I used counting-on by 10s starting with 60 → 60, 70, 80, 90; or, 6 tens plus 3 tens = 9 tens; $75 + 25$, I used money → 75 cents plus 25 cents = 1 dollar; I know 1 dollar equals 100 cents, so the answer is 100)
- ✎ **Problem Solving** *Suppose you have 100 marbles. Some are red and some are blue. How many of each color can you have?* (use the Blank Hundred Chart to model sums of 100)

Math at Hand 073–076

Left	Right
1 →	2
2 →	4
3 →	6
4 →	8

PATTERNS AND ALGEBRA Patterns

- *What do you see?* (sample answer: two columns of numbers and arrows going from Left to Right)
- *Describe how the pattern changes from Left to Right.* (sample answers: 2 of the Left side equals 4 of the Right side; the Left side is half of the Right side)
- ✎ *What do you think is the missing number?* (8)

REACHING ALL LEARNERS Help students recognize the movement from Left to Right. Point to a number in the Left column and move across to the number in the Right column.

Math at Hand 401

6D   SUMMER SUCCESS: MATH

KEY ✎ = record on pad

© Great Source. Copying is prohibited.

GEOMETRY Quadrilaterals

- *What do you see?* (shapes, closed figures, or polygons)
- *Which shape is different from the others?* (The one with 5 sides.) *How are the others alike?* (They have 4 sides.)
- ✎ *Polygons with 4 sides are called* quadrilaterals. *Can you draw another quadrilateral?* (any 4-sided closed figure)
- ✎ *Can you draw one more polygon that is not a quadrilateral?* (any 3-sided closed figure; any closed figure with 5 or more sides)

Math at Hand 364–366

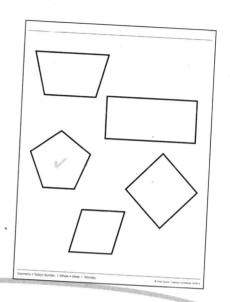

MEASUREMENT Perimeter

- *Here is a special quadrilateral. What is its name?* (square) *What is special about a square?* (It has 4 sides with the same length, and 4 right angles.)
- *How do you find the distance around the big square?* (count the number of units on each side) *What is the name for the distance around the outside of a shape?* (perimeter)
- ✎ *Show how you would find the perimeter of a square. Can you come up with a shortcut?* (count the little squares to get 40; count-on by 10s; use 4 times 10)

Math at Hand 295

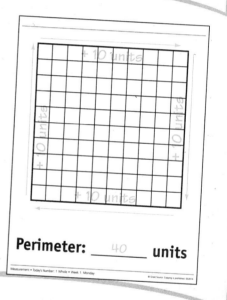

Perimeter: ___40___ units

VOCABULARY *operations*

- *Can you name the 4 operations?* (addition, subtraction, multiplication, division)
- *What are the symbols?* (+, −, ×, ÷ or ⟌ or fraction bar)
- *Is a square an operation?* (no) *Why?* (because there is no adding, subtracting, multiplying, or dividing)
- *How would you define* operations? (work with numbers using addition, subtraction, multiplication, and/or division)

Math at Hand 529

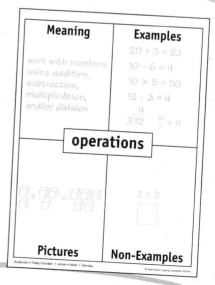

© Great Source. Copying is prohibited.

PRACTICE

Written Practice

CONCEPTS AND SKILLS

- Compare quantities to 1 whole
- Use mental math to add
- Review whole number place value
- Problem Solving Strategies and Skills: *Look for a Pattern, Make an Organized List, Make a Table; Find Needed Information*

PREVIEW THE PRACTICE

- To help students prepare, brainstorm some equivalent amounts. *How many pennies are in 1 dime?* (10)

SUPPORT THE PRACTICE

- Problems 1–4 ask students to compare different quantities. If necessary, discuss the answer choice for Problem 1.

- Problems 5–9 should be done using mental math. Review mental grouping strategies. *How many tens are in 150?* (15)

- Problem 10 asks students to articulate their mental math strategy. Encourage students to share their thinking.

- Problems 11–12 present patterns for students to analyze and complete. Encourage students to look back at the Patterns and Algebra recording pad, if needed.

- Problems 13–14 review writing large numbers in standard form. Use a place value chart, if necessary.

Name _____

NUMBER AND OPERATIONS

Compare the amount to 1 whole. Loop *less than, greater than,* or *equal to.* ◄1–4. MAH 002

1. $1.14	less than	(greater than)	equal to	$1
2. 12 months	less than	greater than	(equal to)	1 year
3. 90 minutes	less than	(greater than)	equal to	1 hour
4. 12 inches	less than	greater than	(equal to)	1 foot

Loop the problems with answers *equal to* or *greater than* 100. You don't need to write the answer. ◄5–10. MAH 073–076

5. (87 + 23)   6. (150 + 10)   7. (55 + 65)   8. 20 + 60   9. (75 + 55)

10. How did you know which problem(s) to loop?

Sample answers: I worked with numbers in my head; I looked to see how many 10s are in the numbers.

PATTERNS AND ALGEBRA

What is the missing number? ◄11–12. MAH 401

11.
Left		Right
2	→	4
4	→	8
5	→	10
8	→	16

12.
Left		Right
10	→	20
20	→	40
30	→	60
40	→	80

REVIEW

Write in standard form. ◄13–14. MAH 005–006

13. eighty-two thousand, forty-two   82,042

14. one million, sixteen thousand, eight   1,016,008

SUMMER SUCCESS: MATH   **7**   MAH: *Math at Hand*

© Great Source. Permission is granted to copy this page.

REACHING ALL LEARNERS

Some students may need help rewriting numbers from word form to standard form. Remind students that the comma is used to separate the different place value periods.

Math at Hand

If students need help, encourage them to refer to the MAH items shown on the student page.

© Great Source. Copying is prohibited.

Complete each step. ◄15. MAH 396

15. Tammy is playing a board game. On her first turn she wins (15 points.) On her second turn, she wins (30 points.) On her third and fourth turns she wins (45 and 60 points.) Tammy continues to win points at the same rate. How many points will she win on her sixth turn?

a. Underline the question you need to answer.

b. Loop the points Tammy wins.

c. Mark the strategy/strategies you will use.

d. Solve the problem. Explain your thinking.

first turn	15 points
second turn	30 points
third turn	45 points
fourth turn	60 points
fifth turn	?
sixth turn	?

e. Answer the question.

She will win 90 points on the sixth turn.

POSSIBLE STRATEGIES

- Look for a Pattern
- Make an Organized List
- Make a Table

sample strategies:
Look for a Pattern
Make an Organized List

© Great Source. Permission is granted to copy this page.

SUMMER SUCCESS: MATH **8** MAH: *Math at Hand*

REACHING ALL LEARNERS

If students have difficulty with the problem, draw a table and label the columns "Turn" and "Points." Fill in the first row of the table with the correct values. Then invite students to complete the remainder of the table.

© Great Source. Copying is prohibited.

PROBLEM SOLVING

Work in small groups of 3 or 4 students.

- Encourage students to find ways to identify needed information to solve the problem.
- *What do you need to answer the question?* (the record of Tammy's points per turn)
- *How can you use the information?* (to predict, to generalize, to see a pattern)

SCORING

a. Last sentence underlined: 1 pt

b. Circled points won: 1 pt

c. Choose and apply an appropriate strategy: 1 pt

d. Explanation of solution: 1 pt

e. Correct answer: 1 pt

GLOSSARY TO GO

Today's Vocabulary *operation*

Have students complete an entry for today's vocabulary term in their Glossaries. Encourage students to use both words and drawings.

MATH JOURNAL

- *Describe your strategy for finding patterns.* (Help students articulate methods that focus on pattern recognition or grouping to identify patterns.)

GAME

Active Practice

CONCEPTS AND SKILLS

- Relate hundredths to parts of a dollar
- Relate fractions and decimals
- Compare equivalent money amounts
- Count money

MATH TALK

Model the correct use of these words and encourage students to use them as they work.

- **decimal number** a number containing a decimal point
- **denominator** the number of equal parts into which a whole is divided
- **one-hundredth** one part of 100 equal parts of the whole

MATERIALS

For each pair: 1 set of Fraction/Decimal Cards I; 1 set of Fraction/Decimal Cards II (use only 0.10 and $\frac{10}{100}$); Play Coins and Dollar Cards (6 nickels, 40 dimes, 10 one-dollar bills)

GAME

Decimals for Dollars

Object: Be the first to exchange decimal/fraction cards for matching money amounts, enough to collect at least $3.00.

MATERIALS

1 set of Fraction/Decimal Cards I; 1 set of Fraction/Decimal Cards II (use only 0.10 and $\frac{10}{100}$); Play Coins and Dollar Cards (6 nickels, 40 dimes, 10 one-dollar bills)

DIRECTIONS

1. Spread out the play money pieces, face up.
2. Collect the Fraction/Decimal cards, mix the cards, and put them in a stack face down.
3. Players take turns drawing one card from the stack of Fraction/Decimal cards. When you draw a card, you collect coins to match the amount shown on the card. For example, if you draw the 0.25 card or the $\frac{25}{100}$ card, you collect 2 dimes and 1 nickel. After collecting your money, tell how much more money you need to have $3.00. Then place the card you drew face down on the bottom of the draw pile. **(I got the 0.40 card. So, I can collect 40 cents in coins. Now, I only need two more dollars and 60 cents to make three dollars!)**
4. As soon as you have 2 nickels, trade them in for a dime; as soon as you have 10 dimes, trade them in for a dollar bill. Before you trade, you have to explain what you are doing. **(I've got 2 nickels. I can trade them for 1 dime.)**
5. The first player to collect $3.00 or more wins.

© Great Source. Permission is granted to copy this page.

REACHING ALL LEARNERS

Simplify Make the game a little easier by using only decimal cards. When students are more familiar with how to play the game, then merge in the fraction cards.

Variation Instead of addition, use subtraction to play the game. Players start with $3.00 credit. Each time a card is drawn, players subtract that amount from $3.00. If subtraction is not possible because the player doesn't have enough money, the player must pass. The first player to reach $0 is the winner.

Math at Hand

- Decimals: Place Value, 012
- Relating Decimals to Fractions, 019
- Counting Money, 025

© Great Source. Copying is prohibited.

Day 1

- Review the relationships among decimals, fractions, and money amounts. *What part of a dollar is one cent?* (1 one-hundredth) *What part of a dollar is a nickel?* (5 one-hundredths) *What part of dollar is a dime?* (10 one-hundredths or 1 tenth)
- *How do you write a value that equals a dime as a decimal?* (0.10 or 0.1) *As a fraction?* ($\frac{10}{100}$ or $\frac{1}{10}$)
- *Why is the denominator of the fractional amounts of money always 100?* (There are 100 cents in a dollar, so hundredths is used to represent 100 cents.)

Demonstrate with a volunteer how to exchange coins for a matching fraction or decimal card.

- Have volunteers play a demonstration game.

Day 2

- Review the directions for playing the game.
- Assign no more than 3 players in each group.
- Assign pairs of students to play together.

Encourage students to ask themselves:

- *How much more money do I need to equal a dollar?*
- *What card draw will help me win the game?*
- *Who is ahead and by how much?*
- *What amount do I need to get ahead?*

Teacher: I have $\frac{30}{100}$. How much money in coins is that?

Student: 30 cents.

T: Which coins do I collect?

S: 3 dimes.

T: What if on my next turn, I draw the 0.75 card? Which coins do I add to what I already have?

S: 7 dimes and 1 nickel.

T: Do I have enough coins to trade for a dollar bill?

S: Yes. Trade in your 10 dimes for a dollar bill.

T: Now I have a total of $1.05. What do I need to make 3 dollars?

S: Let's see. You still need $1.95.

T: How did you figure that out?

S: I know one nickel plus 95 cents equals $1.00. Then you would have $2.00, and you would need only another $1.00 to make $3.00.

T: Is there another way to find the answer?

If students need more help, use the hints below, or refer to the *Math at Hand* items shown to the left.

- **Are students having trouble converting to money amounts?** Encourage students to read the decimals or fractions aloud. Remind students that 0.9 and 0.90 are equal.

© Great Source. Copying is prohibited.

Additional Support

CONCEPTS AND SKILLS

- Take a survey
- Make and interpret a bar graph
- Make predictions using samples
- Compare and summarize data

MATH TALK

Model the correct use of these words and encourage students to use them as they work.

- **axis** the horizontal or vertical number line that supports the labeled data; the plural of axis is axes
- **data** information, especially numerical information
- **sample** a small representative number of the entire group
- **scale** a system of marks

MATERIALS

For each pair of students:
straightedge or ruler*

*Optional materials

GET STARTED

- Read and discuss the directions on student page 11.
- Assign partner pairs of mixed abilities to work together.

DATA STUDY

Name _____

Graph Results of a Survey

Which digit appears most often in 7-digit numbers?

TAKE A SAMPLE

- Create a 7-digit number.   _____
- Write another 7-digit number. _____

COLLECT THE DATA

Now tally the digits of the 7-digit numbers recorded by all your classmates. Use one tally for each digit.

Tally Chart

Digit	0	1	2	3	4	5	6	7	8	9
Tally										

GRAPH THE DATA

- Make a vertical bar graph. Title your graph.
- Draw and label the horizontal axis.
- Look at the data in the tally chart. Decide how to scale the vertical axis to make the data fit on the graph. Then draw and label the vertical axis.
- Use the number of tallies in the chart to draw the bars for each digit 0–9.

ANALYZE YOUR DATA

1. Which digit appears most often? _____ How many times? _____   Answers will vary.
2. Which digit appears least often? _____ How many times? _____
3. Can you think of any situation that might change your data?
   Sample answers: I entered the same numbers more than once; by setting rules about repeating numbers.
   _____
   _____

© Great Source. Permission is granted to copy this page.

REACHING ALL LEARNERS

- Review how to record and read tally marks.
- Review the names for the different parts of a bar graph, including axis (axes), labels, bars, and title.

Math at Hand

- Taking Samples, 249–251
- Recording Data, 253–254
- Labeling the Axes, 270
- Choosing the Scales, 271
- Single-Bar Graphs, 273

© Great Source. Copying is prohibited.

Day 1

After students have completed the Take a Sample section, talk about the word *sample* and the digits in their samples. Invite them to predict the results and to explain their reasoning.

Have students take turns reading aloud the digits of their numbers to complete the class tallies. Make sure they do not re-tally the digits of their own number.

Day 2

Review with students how they collected data and about the predictions they made on Day 1. You might ask students how they can check if all the digits have been recorded for all the numbers. (The total should equal 7 times all the numbers collected.)

- Work with students to help them create an accurate graph of the data. Be sure they think about what information they want someone else to see when the graph is completed.

- Discuss as a group how to choose an appropriate scale for the vertical axis.

Before discussing the answers to the questions, invite students to show each other their graphs. Then have students consider the following questions:

- **What if?** *Suppose we collected 7-digit numbers from 100 more people. How do you think the graph might change?* (Each bar would be longer if we use the same scale. We would probably have to change the scale to fit all the data on the graph.)

- *Based on our data, do you think every digit, 0–9, might appear an equal number of times if all the people in the city named a 7-digit number? In the state?* (Answers will vary.)

Teacher: Look at the squares along the left side of the grid. How many squares are there?

Student: I count 15 squares.

T: Now look at the data in the tally chart for the digit that appears the most. To fit the data on the graph, would it be better to use a scale that increases by 1 or by a greater number?

S: Since there are more than 15 tallies for the digit 6, we could use a scale that increases by 2, 3, or 10 to fit the data on the graph.

T: Can we use more than one square on the grid to mark the scale?

S: Sure, as long as the number of squares is the same between each number on the scale.

T: Can we also use one square for each tally mark?

S: We could if the grid was bigger, but we have 27 sixes and only 15 squares. It won't fit.

Sample graph: Answers will vary. Bars in graph should correspond to data in the tally chart.

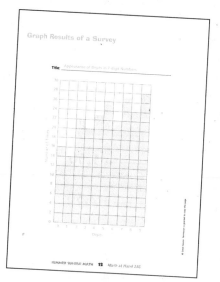

© Great Source. Copying is prohibited.

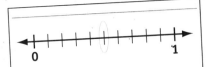

Fraction: _____ $\frac{50}{100}$

Decimal: _____ 0.50

NUMBER Number line

- *What do you see on the number line?* (equally spaced marks, 0, and 1)

✎ *Show the mark that is halfway between 0 and 1. How do you know?* (sample answers: if folded on that mark, 0 and 1 meet; the same number of marks are on each side.)

✎ *If there were 100 marks, which one would be halfway between 0 and 100?* (50th) *How would you write 50 out of 100 as a fraction?* ($\frac{50}{100}$) *Decimal?* (0.50) *So, what can you tell about $\frac{50}{100}$, 0.50, and $\frac{1}{2}$?* (They are all equal.)

REACHING ALL LEARNERS Shade 50 squares on the Blank Hundred Chart to show $\frac{1}{2} = \frac{50}{100}$.

Math at Hand 031, 035

---

1 whole + 0.50 = _____ 1.50

1 whole − 0.50 = _____ 0.50

Problem Solving:

sample answers:

- I can add 50¢ twelve times.
- I can skip count by 50¢—50¢, $1, $1.50, $2, . . .
- I know 2 walks equal $1, so 12 walks equal $6. Then compare with $5.

OPERATIONS Compute with 0.50

✎ *If you add 1 whole and 0.50, will the sum be greater than or less than 2?* (less than) *What is the sum?* (1.50)

✎ *If you have 1 whole and you subtract 0.50, will the difference be greater than or less than 1?* (less than) *What is the difference?* (0.50)

✎ **Problem Solving** *Sam gets 50¢ each time he walks the dog. So far, he's walked the dog 12 times. What would you do to see if Sam has earned more than $5?*

Math at Hand 118, 127

Left	Right
1	→ 1.50
2	→ 2.50
3	→ 3.50
4	→ 4.50
10	→ 10.50

PATTERNS AND ALGEBRA Predict a number

- *Can you describe what you see on the pad?* (two columns of numbers going from Left to Right)

- *Tell how the pattern changes from Left to Right.* (sample answers: the Right side has a decimal part; the Right side has 0.50 in the number)

✎ *What is the missing number for the Right side of 4?* (4.50)

✎ *Can you predict the number for the Right side of 10?* (10.50)

Math at Hand 401

© Great Source. Copying is prohibited.

KEY ✎ = record on pad

GEOMETRY Symmetry

- *What does* symmetry *mean?* (when something can be divided into two halves that are exactly the same size and shape)

- ✎ *Look at the shapes. How would you draw the line symmetry for each one?* (see recording pad)

- *What is one quick way to see if a shape has line symmetry?* (fold the shape to see if the two parts fit exactly over one another)

Math at Hand 380

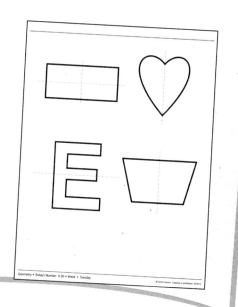

MEASUREMENT Equal amounts

- *Another way to write 50 cents is $0.50 or 50¢. What part of a dollar is 50¢?* (one-half)

- ✎ *Tell how many pennies are in $0.50?* (50) *How many nickels?* (10) *How many dimes?* (5) *How many quarters?* (2)

- *What do 0.50, $\frac{1}{2}$, and one-half have in common?* (all 3 name the same amount)

Math at Hand 024

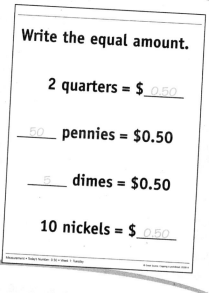

Write the equal amount.

2 quarters = $ _0.50_

_50_ pennies = $0.50

_5_ dimes = $0.50

10 nickels = $ _0.50_

VOCABULARY *decimal number*

- *Tell where you see decimal numbers used in everyday life.* (sample answers: money amounts, batting averages, radio station names)

- ✎ *What are examples of decimal numbers you know?* (sample answers: 3.7, $1.00, 0.5 meter)

- ✎ *How would you define* decimal number*?* (A number with a decimal point.)

Math at Hand 011

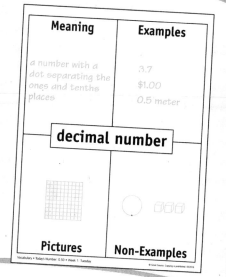

© Great Source. Copying is prohibited.

PRACTICE

Written Practice

CONCEPTS AND SKILLS

- Work with a number line
- Add and subtract 0.50
- Write a rule
- Review decimal models
- Problem Solving Strategies and Skills: *Act It Out, Write an Equation, Work Backward; Find Needed Information*

PREVIEW THE PRACTICE

- Remind students about their work with the number line in today's Number Names. ***What are the labels on the number line?*** (0, 0.50, 1, and the Points *A, B, C*) ***What do Point B and 0.50 have in common?*** (They both name the halfway mark between 0 and 1.)

SUPPORT THE PRACTICE

- Problems 1–4 ask students to read and interpret a number line. Be sure they recognize the position of Point *C* as somewhere between 0.50 and 1.
- Problems 5–7 involve simple addition and subtraction with 0.50. Remind students of their work on the Operations recording pad today.
- Problems 8–9 require students to examine a number pattern, then write a rule that describes the pattern. Remind students of their work on the Patterns and Algebra recording pad today.
- Problems 10–12 review pictorial representation for decimals.

© Great Source. Permission is granted to copy this page.

Name _____

NUMBER AND OPERATIONS

Look at the number line to answer Problems 1–4. ◄1–4. MAH 031, 035

A number line with 0 at left, 0.50 at middle, 1 at right. Point A between 0 and 0.50, Point B at 0.50, Point C between 0.50 and 1.

1. Is Point *A* greater than or less than 0.50? _____ less than _____
2. How would you use a fraction to name Point *B*? _____ $\frac{1}{2}$ or $\frac{50}{100}$ _____
3. Which point is greater than 0 *and* closest to 1? _____ Point C _____
4. Use a decimal to name Point *B*. _____ 0.5 or 0.50 _____

Add or subtract. ◄5–7. MAH 118, 127

5. 2 + 0.50 = _____2.50_____   6. 8 − 0.50 = _____7.50_____   7. _____$2.50_____ + $0.50 = $3.00

PATTERNS AND ALGEBRA

Fill in the blank, then write a rule for the pattern. ◄8–9. MAH 401

8.
Left		Right
1.50	→	1
2.50	→	2
3.50	→	3
4.50	→	4
10.50	→	10

Rule: Sample answer: Subtract 0.50 from the Left number.

9.
Left		Right
10	→	20
20	→	40
30	→	60
40	→	80
100	→	200

Rule: Sample answer: The Left number is half the Right number.

SUMMER SUCCESS: MATH **13** MAH: *Math at Hand*

REACHING ALL LEARNERS

Use strings or strips of paper to help students visualize $0.50 = \frac{1}{2}$.

Math at Hand

If students need help, encourage them to refer to the MAH items shown on the student page.

© Great Source. Copying is prohibited.

Write the decimal modeled by the shaded area. ◄ 10–12. MAH 012

10.

0.5 or 0.50

11.

0.32

12.

0.05

PROBLEM SOLVING • **UNDERSTAND** • **PLAN** • **TRY** • **LOOK BACK**

Complete each step. ◄ 13. MAH 396

13. Sera spent $3.65 on a magazine and $4.29 on a hairbrush. When she got home, she still had $5.81 in her wallet. How much money did Sera have before she bought the magazine and hairbrush?

   a. Underline the question you need to answer.

   b. Loop the amounts Sera spent and what she had left.

   c. Mark the strategy/strategies you will use.

   d. Solve the problem. Explain your thinking.

   _____

   _____

   _____

   _____

   _____

   e. Answer the question.

   Sera had $13.75 before she bought the magazine and hairbrush.

   _____

POSSIBLE STRATEGIES

• Act It Out

• Write an Equation

• Work Backward

sample strategy:
Write an Equation

$3.65 + $4.29 + $5.81 = $13.75

© Great Source. Permission is granted to copy this page.

SUMMER SUCCESS: MATH **14** MAH: *Math at Hand*

REACHING ALL LEARNERS

If students have difficulty with the problem, present a similar one using whole dollar amounts. Once they understand the concept, then use the decimal amounts.

© Great Source. Copying is prohibited.

PROBLEM SOLVING

Work in small groups of 3 or 4 students.

• Encourage students to find ways to identify needed information to solve the problem.

• *What are some things to consider when you go shopping?* List considerations on the chalkboard. Focus on the necessity to have enough money.

• *What do you need to answer the question?* (the amount of money spent and what is left over)

• *How can you use the information?* (to find how much money Sera had before buying the two items)

SCORING

   a. Last sentence underlined: 1 pt

   b. Money amounts circled: 1 pt

   c. Choose and apply an appropriate strategy: 1 pt

   d. Explanation of solution: 1 pt

   e. Correct answer: 1 pt

GLOSSARY TO GO

Today's Vocabulary *decimal number*

Have students complete an entry for today's vocabulary term in their Glossaries. Encourage students to use both words and drawings.

MATH JOURNAL

• *Write a story problem about shopping. Ask a classmate to solve it.* (Problems will vary. Check student's work and answer.)

NUMBER NAMES TODAY'S NUMBER **0.25**

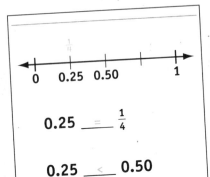

0.25 __=__ $\frac{1}{4}$

0.25 __<__ 0.50

1 whole __>__ 0.25

NUMBER Decimals and fractions

- *Who knows what is one-half of 50?* (25)
- *Look at the number line. What is halfway between 0 and 50 hundredths?* (twenty-five hundredths) *How do you write that?* (0.25)
- ✎ *Look at the 4 equal sections on the number line. What is the simplest fraction you can use to label the mark between 0 and 0.50?* ($\frac{1}{4}$) Invite a volunteer to plot $\frac{1}{4}$ on the number line.
- ✎ *What can you tell about 25 hundreths and $\frac{1}{4}$?* (They are equal.) Invite a volunteer to complete the comparisons.

Math at Hand 008, 016, 019, 031

---

1 whole + 0.25 = __1.25__

1 whole − 0.25 = __0.75__

Problem Solving:

sample answer: No, it is fewer than 6. I know because $\frac{1}{2}$ of 12 is 6, and $\frac{1}{4}$ is less than $\frac{1}{2}$.

OPERATIONS Compute with 0.25

- ✎ *If you add 1 whole and 0.25, will the sum be greater than or less than 2?* (less than) *What is the sum?* (1.25)
- ✎ *If you have 1 whole and you subtract 0.25, will the difference be greater than or less than 1?* (less than) *What is the difference?* (0.75)
- ✎ **Problem Solving** *There are 12 students in your summer school class. Suppose $\frac{1}{4}$ of the students walk to school. Is that more than 6 students? How do you know?*

Math at Hand 118, 127

1.25, 2.25, 3.25, 4.25, 5.25, 6.25

Rule:

sample answer: Add 1.00 to the number that comes before.

PATTERNS AND ALGEBRA Write a rule

- *Can you describe what you see on the pad?* (decimal numbers)
- *Starting with 1.25, would you say the numbers are getting bigger or smaller?* (bigger) *How can you tell?* (The whole number parts go from 1 to 6.)
- ✎ *What is a rule that describes the pattern?* (sample answer: add 1.00 to the number that comes before)

REACHING ALL LEARNERS Help students see the number pattern by listing the numbers vertically. Be sure to line up the decimal points.

Math at Hand 401

© Great Source. Copying is prohibited.

KEY ✎ = record on pad

GEOMETRY Congruence

- *How can you tell if two shapes are exactly the same size and shape?* (put one shape on top of the other to see if they fit exactly)
- ✎ *When shapes fit exactly, they are congruent. Which shapes are congruent?* (all but the triangle and diamond)
- ✎ *Draw a shape that is not congruent.* (any closed polygon)

REACHING ALL LEARNERS Students may need to trace the shapes to make cutouts. Then, place one on top of the other to find the congruent ones.

Math at Hand 372

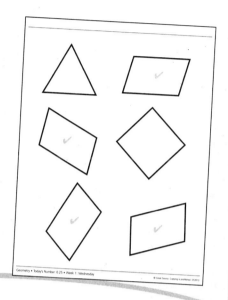

MEASUREMENT Customary length

- *Suppose you want to measure the side of the triangle on the Geometry recording pad. Would you use inches or feet?* (inches) *Tell why.* (because the triangle is small)
- *When do you use a foot to measure?* (to find lengths that are at least 12 inches)
- *When do you use a yard to measure?* (to find longer lengths that are at least 3 feet)
- *What is a fraction name for 0.25 foot?* ($\frac{1}{4}$ foot)

Math at Hand 294

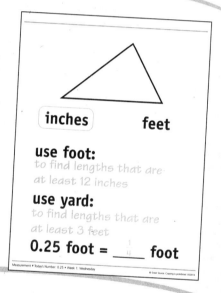

VOCABULARY *compare*

- *What are some words you use to compare?* (sample answers: bigger, smaller, greater than, less than, equal to)
- *What are some symbols you use to compare numbers?* (sample answers: $>$, $<$, $=$, $\neq$, $\geq$, $<$)
- *Is 25 + 75 = 100 a comparison?* (no) *Tell why.* (It shows an operation.)
- ✎ *How would you define* compare? (tell how things are the alike or different)

Math at Hand 008, 016

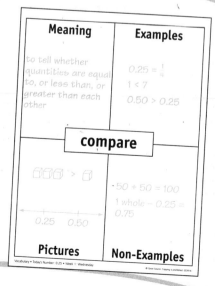

© Great Source. Copying is prohibited.

PRACTICE

Written Practice

CONCEPTS AND SKILLS

- Use =, <, or >
- Add and subtract with 0.25
- Identify congruent shapes
- Review equal units of measure
- Problem Solving Strategies and Skills: *Make a Table, Make an Organized List, Make a Diagram; Find Needed Information*

PREVIEW THE PRACTICE

- Write the greater than (>) and less than (<) symbols on the board. ***Does anyone have a way for telling the difference between these two symbols?*** (sample answer: the bigger end has the greater number; the pointy end has the lesser number)

SUPPORT THE PRACTICE

- Problems 1–6 ask students to compare numbers. Point out that the number line goes from 0 to 3, and the shorter marks show 0.25 intervals between whole numbers.
- Problems 7–9 involve simple addition and subtraction with 0.25. If necessary, work on Problem 9 together. Remind students that it can be read *what plus 25 cents equals 7 dollars.*
- Problems 10–11 work with congruence. Revisit the Geometry recording pad, if needed.
- Problems 12–17 review familiar equal measures. Remind students that $0.25 can be read *25 cents.*

PRACTICE TODAY'S NUMBER **0.25**

Name _____

NUMBER AND OPERATIONS

Use the number line to help you compare. Write =, <, or >. ◀1–6. MAH 008, 016

1. 0.25 __<__ 1
2. 0.75 __>__ 0.25
3. 2.5 __>__ 0.25
4. 0.25 __=__ $\frac{1}{4}$
5. 0.25 __<__ 0.50
6. 2 __>__ 0.25

Add or subtract. ◀7–9. MAH 118, 127

7. 5 + 0.25 = __5.25__
8. 6 − 0.25 = __5.75__
9. __$6.75__ + $0.25 = $7.00

GEOMETRY

Compare the shapes. Loop *congruent* or *not congruent*. ◀10–11. MAH 372

10. (congruent)   not congruent
11. congruent   (not congruent)

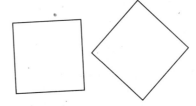
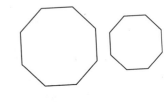

REVIEW

Write the equal unit of measure. ◀12–17. MAH 327

12. 1 foot = __12__ inches
13. 3 feet = __1__ yard
14. __12__ months = 1 year
15. __24__ hours = 1 day
16. __60__ minutes = 1 hour
17. $0.25 = __1__ quarter

© Great Source. Permission is granted to copy this page.

SUMMER SUCCESS: MATH   **15**   MAH: *Math at Hand*

REACHING ALL LEARNERS

You may wish to allow students to work in pairs for Problems 10–11. Some students might need to trace a copy of the square in Problem 10 to make a cutout. Then, position it on top of the second shape to recognize that it is identical in shape and size.

Math at Hand

If students need help, encourage them to refer to the MAH items shown on the student page.

© Great Source. Copying is prohibited.

Complete each step. ◄18. MAH 396

18. Payton wants to visit California, Florida, and Maine this summer. He can fly, drive, or take a train from home to each state. What are the different transportation choices for Payton to get from home to each state?

a. Underline the question you need to answer.

b. Loop the words that require a choice be made.

c. Mark the strategy/strategies you will use.

d. Solve the problem. Explain your thinking.

_____

_____

_____

_____

_____

_____

_____

_____

_____

_____

e. Answer the question.

Payton's choices are: California-fly/drive/train, Florida-fly/drive/train, Maine-fly/drive/train.

POSSIBLE STRATEGIES

• Make a Table

• Make an Organized List

• Make a Diagram

sample strategy:
Make a Diagram

fly

State — drive

train

© Great Source. Permission is granted to copy this page.

PROBLEM SOLVING

Work in small groups of 3 or 4 students.

• Encourage students to find ways to identify needed information to solve the problem.

• *What kinds of situations come up that may require you to make a choice?* (sample answer: when ordering a sandwich, sometimes I need to pick the types of toppings)

• *What do you need to answer the question?* (the states Payton wants to visit and the ways to get there)

• *How can you use the information?* (to see what are the possible combination of choices)

SCORING

a. Last sentence underlined: 1 pt

b. Choice words circled: 1 pt

c. Choose and apply an appropriate strategy: 1 pt

d. Explanation of solution: 1 pt

e. Correct answer: 1 pt

GLOSSARY TO GO

Today's Vocabulary *compare*

Have students complete an entry for today's vocabulary term in their Glossaries. Encourage students to use both words and drawings.

MATH JOURNAL

• *Make an organized list of three places in your neighborhood that you can reach by bike, on foot, or by car.* (Check student's work.)

REACHING ALL LEARNERS

Explain to students that the answer to a question that asks "how many . . ." is often a number. And, the answer to a question that asks "what are . . ." is often a list.

© Great Source. Copying is prohibited.

GAME

Active Practice

CONCEPTS AND SKILLS

- Add hundredths to make 1
- Add tenths to make 1
- Relate fractions and decimals

MATH TALK

Model the correct use of these words and encourage students to use them as they work.

- **denominator** a number that tells the number of equal parts into which a whole is divided
- **numerator** a number that tells how many equal parts are described by the fraction
- **one-hundredth** one of 100 equal parts of the whole
- **one-tenth** one of 10 equal parts of the whole

MATERIALS

For each pair: 1 sheet each of Fraction/Decimal Cards I and II; paper and pencil

GAME

The Big One

Object: Be the first to collect 8 pairs of decimal cards, each pair with the sum of 1.

Al	|||
Elka	₩₩	
Frank	|||
Tory	₩₩

MATERIALS

1 set each of Fraction/Decimal Cards I and II; paper and pencil

DIRECTIONS

1. Shuffle and deal 1 card to each player. The player with the greatest value starts the game. You will need a scorekeeper and a dealer.

2. Collect and shuffle all the cards again. Deal 7 cards to each player. Place left-over cards facedown in a draw pile.

   If any player is dealt pairs of cards that make 1, that player can choose to show the cards right away and score 1 point for each pair. Or, the player can keep the cards and play the game.

3. The game begins with Player 1 and moves to the left. When it is your turn, draw a card either from the pile or from the player on your left and place it faceup. If you can, pair the new card with one you already have to make a sum of 1, now place the two cards together faceup. These cards form a "Big One." You explain the sum, and you score 1 point. If you can't pair the card to make a sum of 1, you keep the card. **(Big One! $\frac{25}{100}$ is the same as 0.25. Add that to 0.75 and it equals 1. I get the point.)**

> Big One! $\frac{25}{100}$ is the same as 0.25. Add that to 0.75 and it equals 1. I get the point.

4. If the player on your left has only one card when it is your turn, draw your next card from the pile. If you have no cards in your hand when it is your turn, draw one card from the pile to play your round. Then, continue to play as directed in step 3.

5. When there are no more cards in the pile, collect all the paired cards, shuffle very well, and make a new draw pile. Continue playing.

6. The first player to score 8 points wins.

© Great Source. Permission is granted to copy this page.

REACHING ALL LEARNERS

Simplify Make the game a little easier by using only decimal cards or only fraction cards. When students are more familiar with how to play the game, then merge in the second set of cards.

Variation Use 3 cards to make a "Big One": two cards from the dealt hand paired with the one card drawn. The winner is the first player to score 5 points.

Math at Hand

- Equivalent Decimals, 015
- Adding with Decimals, 125–126
- Relating Decimals to Fractions, 019

© Great Source. Copying is prohibited.

Day 1

- Have students make a table of sums that equal 1 using two decimal addends. The decimal addends are limited to benchmark decimals, 0.25, 0.50, and 0.75, and multiples of 0.1 and 0.10.
- Talk about ways to combine tenths and hundredths to create 1. *Do 0.1 and 0.90 equal 1?* (Yes) *How do you know?* (sample answers: 0.1 is the same as 0.10, and 0.90 plus 0.10 equals 1. Or, 0.90 is the same as 0.9, and 0.9 plus 0.1 equals 1.) *Are there other examples of tenths and hundredths that can be added to make a "Big One"?* (Record students' suggestions. Provide assistance when a student suggests a combination that does not equal 1.)

- Demonstrate with a volunteer how to analyze a hand of 7 cards to find a sum that equals 1 when paired with a card drawn.
- Model writing decimal sentences with sums that equal 1.
- Have volunteers play a demonstration game under the Play the Game.

Day 2

- Review the directions for playing the game.
- Assign pairs of students to play together.

Encourage students to ask themselves:

- *What card do I need to make a sum of 1?*
- *What is another name for this decimal?*
- *Is it better to draw a card from the pile, or to take one from the player on my left? Which strategy will help me win?*
- *How can I be sure the other players are making correct pairs?*

Teacher: Look. I have $\frac{25}{100}$, 0.1, 0.50, $\frac{6}{10}$, 0.8, 0.10, and 0.60. I just picked up $\frac{7}{10}$ from the pile. Can I make a sum of 1 with $\frac{7}{10}$?

Student: No. You put the $\frac{7}{10}$ card in your hand, and the next player takes a turn.

T: So, when it is my turn, what are my two choices?

S: You take from the pile or pick a card from the player on your left.

S: Yes. but only if that player has more than one card.

T: Okay, what if I get 0.75? Can I make a Big One?

S: Yes. $\frac{25}{100}$ is the same as 0.25. And, 0.25 plus 0.75 makes 1.

T: Terrific. I put these 2 cards face up, and score 1 point.

S: What happens when no cards are left in the pile?

S: We remix the paired Big One cards to make a new pile.

S: Mix them real well! Or else the cards will be paired already.

If students need more help, use the hints below, or refer to the *Math at Hand* items shown to the left.

- **Are students having a hard time?** Ask students to read aloud the decimals and fractions.
- **How are students finding pairs of cards?** Have students talk to you about their strategies and ideas.
- **Do students use the correct vocabulary?** Model how to use the targeted vocabulary.

© Great Source. Copying is prohibited.

CONCEPT BUILDER
MAKE & TAKE

Additional Support

CONCEPTS AND SKILLS

- Visualize multiplication facts for 2, 3, 4, 6, and 8
- Use the doubling strategy to find new products

MATH TALK

Model the correct use of these terms and encourage students to use them as they work.

- **array** an arrangement of objects in equal rows
- **factors** numbers that divide evenly into a common number
- **products** the result of multiplication

MATERIALS FOR DAY 1

Folding Fact Cards for 2, 3, 4, 6, and 8 (SE pp. 19, 19A), scissors, lunch bags, crayons, 1 sheet of paper

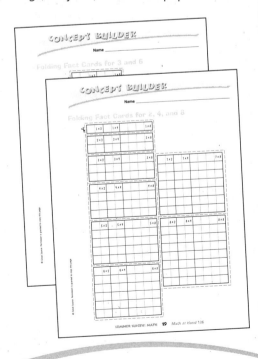

Folding Fact Cards **Day 1**

GET READY

Follow the instruction below to prepare a sample set of Folding Fact Cards to use for demonstration.

BUILD THE FOLDING FACT CARDS

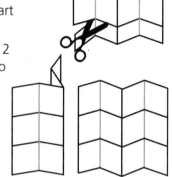

1. To demonstrate, fold a sheet of paper so that you end up with a 3 × 4 grid of squares, as shown. Cut off what is not part of the grid.

2. Then, fold so that only a 3 × 2 grid shows. Ask a volunteer to count the number of squares.

3. Next, unfold the entire grid. Help students see that now there are twice as many squares as the 3 × 2 grid. Count the squares to verify.

4. Before students cut the folding fact cards on pp. 19 and 19A of their books, have them darken the fold lines for each card.

| | 1 × 2 | | 1 × 4 | | | 1 × 8 |

5. As students cut out the cards, remind them to cut carefully along the dashed lines, or as close to the edge to each card as possible.

6. Have students write their initials on the back of each piece and store them in the bag for tomorrow.

FOCUS ON THE MATH

- *Can this 3 × 4 folded grid be used for other multiplication facts?* (yes) *Can you name some of those facts?* (1 × 3, 3 × 3, 1 × 4, 2 × 4)

- *What did you notice when the 3 × 2 grid unfolded into the 3 × 4 grid?* (the number of squares doubled from 6 to 12) *Using the same idea, how many squares do you think are on a 3 × 8 grid?* (24) *How about a 3 × 16 grid?* (48)

- *Do you think the folded grid is a good model for finding perimeter?* (no) *Why do you think so?* (It doesn't tell you the distance around the outside edge. It tells you the number of squares inside. So, this would be a great model to find area.)

© Great Source. Copying is prohibited.

Folding Fact Cards **Day 2**

1. Have students practice folding the cards and reciting the multiplication facts for each one.

2. Have students open their cards and press them flat on their desks. Focus their attention on the top row and ask them to read the facts aloud from left to right and name the products. Some students may find it helpful to use an index card to cover the other rows of the cards.

3. Here is a model of how the facts might be read aloud.

   - **For the 1 × 8 card:** 1 row of 2 equals 2 or 1 × 2 = 2; 1 row of 4 equals 4, or 1 × 4 = 4; 1 row of 8 equals 8, or 1 × 8 = 8.

   - **For the 2 × 8 card:** 2 rows of 2 equals 4, or 2 × 2 = 4; 2 rows of 4 equals 8, or 2 × 4 = 8; 2 rows of 8 equals 16, or 2 × 8 = 16.

   - **Continue through the 8 × 8 card:** 8 rows of 2 equals 16, or 8 × 2 = 16; 8 rows of 4 equals 32, or 8 × 4 = 32; 8 rows of 8 equals 64, or 8 × 8 = 64.

MODEL THE ACTIVITY

To prepare students to work on their own, draw a 5 × 5 array embedded in a 5 × 10 array on the chalkboard. Ask volunteers to recite the facts that correspond to the specific arrays.

Guide and prompt students through the explanation of the array. 1 row of 5 equals 5, or 1 × 5 = 5; 1 row of 10 equals 10, or 1 × 10 = 10. Continue this process as each subsequent row of the array is added.

REFLECT ON THE MATH

Encourage students to ask themselves:

- *Do I know the meaning of* array, factor, *and* product?
- *Is the grid unfolded so that it matches the multiplication?*
- *Can I skip count to double check the product?*

REACHING ALL LEARNERS

Have one student use a calculator to verify the facts being recited.

Math at Hand

Multiplication, 136

© Great Source. Copying is prohibited.

Folding Facts Cards for 2, 4, and 8, and for 3 and 6 assembled previously, index cards (optional).

Note: Send these materials home with the Newsletter at the end of the week.

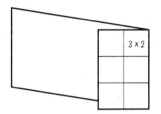

We know that 3 times 2 equals 6.

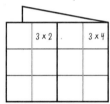

Twice 3 times 2 is the same as 3 times 4. Twice 6 is 12. So, 3 times 4 equals 12.

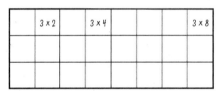

Twice 3 times 4 equals 3 times 8. Twice 12 is 24. So, 3 times 8 equals 24.

ONGOING ASSESSMENT

If students need more help, use the hints below, or refer to the *Math at Hand* items shown to the left.

- **Are students able to manipulate the cards, correctly?** Review the concept of doubling numbers in isolation beginning with different digits.

- **Are students able to recite the facts that correspond to the arrays displayed?** Assign students to work in pairs. Have students count the squares of the arrays displayed. Be sure students use the colors to guide them through the facts.

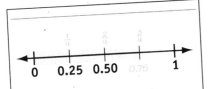

0.75 ___ $= \frac{3}{4}$

0.75 ___ $>$ 0.50

0.75 ___ $<$ 1 whole

NUMBER Decimals and fractions

✎ *Halfway between 0 and 50 hundredths is 25 hundredths. So, what is halfway between 50 hundredths and 1 whole?* (seventy-five hundredths)

✎ *Look at the 4 equal sections on the number line. What is the simplest fraction to name 75 hundredths?* ($\frac{3}{4}$) Invite a volunteer to plot $\frac{3}{4}$ on the number line. *What is one way to shade 0.75 of the number line?* (shade 3 out of the 4 sections)

✎ *What can you tell about 0.75 and $\frac{3}{4}$?* (They are equal.) Invite a volunteer to complete the comparisons.

Math at Hand 008, 016, 019, 031

---

1 whole + 0.75 = ___ 1.75

1 whole − 0.75 = ___ 0.25

Problem Solving:

sample answer: Yes, it is more than 4 seats. I know because $\frac{1}{2}$ of 8 is 4, and $\frac{3}{4}$ is greater than $\frac{1}{2}$.

OPERATIONS Compute with 0.75

✎ *If you add 1 whole and 0.75, will the sum be greater than or less than 2?* (less than) *What is the sum?* (1.75)

✎ *If you have 1 whole and you subtract 0.75, will the difference be greater than or less than 1?* (less than) *What is the difference?* (0.25)

✎ **Problem Solving** *There are 8 seats on the minibus. Suppose $\frac{3}{4}$ of them are taken. Is that more than 4 seats? How do you know?*

Math at Hand 118, 127

10.75, 9.75, ___ 8.75 **,**
7.75, ___ 6.75 **, 5.75,** ___ 4.75

Rule:

sample answer:
Subtract 1 whole from the number that comes before.

PATTERNS AND ALGEBRA Write a rule

• *What do you see on the pad?* (decimal numbers)

• *Starting with 10.75, would you say the numbers are getting bigger or smaller?* (smaller) *How can you tell?* (the whole number parts go down from 10 to 5)

✎ *What are the missing numbers?* (8.75, 6.75, 4.75)

✎ *What is a rule that describes the pattern?* (sample answer: subtract 1 whole from the number that comes before)

REACHING ALL LEARNERS Help students see the number pattern by listing the numbers vertically. Be sure to line up the decimal points.

Math at Hand 401

KEY ✎ = record on pad

© Great Source. Copying is prohibited.

GEOMETRY Equilateral triangles

- *What can you tell about the triangle?* (the sides have the same length, the sides are all equal)

- ✎ *The word* equilateral *means the same length on all sides. How can you use the word to describe this triangle?* (equilateral triangle)

- ✎ *Do the sides of all triangles have the same length?* (no) *Draw a triangle whose sides are not equilateral.*

Math at Hand 358, 362

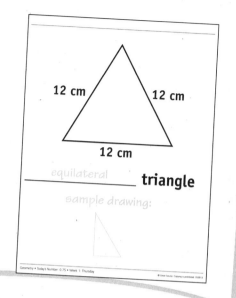

MEASUREMENT Perimeter

- *What can you tell about this triangle?* (Its sides have the same length.) *How would you name this triangle?* (equilateral triangle)

- ✎ *Show how you would find the perimeter, or distance around this triangle.* (add up the sides)

- *Can you think of a shortcut?* (sample answers: skip-count by 5s; multiply 5 by 3)

Math at Hand 295

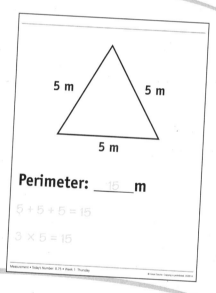

VOCABULARY *fraction*

- *Tell where you see fractions used in everyday life.* (sample answers: half an apple, $\frac{3}{4}$ of the class, quarter hour)

- ✎ *Name some fractions you have learned this week.* ($\frac{1}{2}$, $\frac{1}{4}$, $\frac{3}{4}$)

- ✎ *How would you define* fraction? (a number that tells how many equal parts a whole has been divided into, and how many you are looking at)

Math at Hand 028

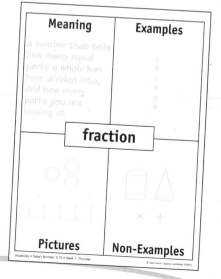

© Great Source. Copying is prohibited.

PRACTICE

Written Practice

CONCEPTS AND SKILLS

- Models of 0.75 and $\frac{3}{4}$
- Add and subtract with 0.75
- Equilateral triangle and perimeter
- Review whole number and decimal place value
- Problem Solving Strategies and Skills: *Make a Table, Make an Organized List, Write an Equation; Solve in More Than One Way*

PREVIEW THE PRACTICE

- Draw a long narrow rectangle divided into 8 equal sections. *How can you show 0.75 of this rectangle?* (shade 6 out of 8 section)

SUPPORT THE PRACTICE

- Problems 1–4 model 0.75 or $\frac{3}{4}$ in different applications. Remind students that $0.75 = \frac{75}{100} = \frac{3}{4}$.
- Problems 5–7 involve simple addition and subtraction with 0.75. Remind students that Problem 7 can be read *what plus 75 cents equals 12 dollars.*
- Problems 8–9 require students to circle equilateral triangles. Remind students of their work on today's Geometry Recording pad.
- Problem 10 asks students to find the perimeter of the equilateral triangle in Problem 8. Help students recall the definition of perimeter.
- Problems 11–13 review whole number and decimal place value.

Name _____

NUMBER AND OPERATIONS

Check student's work.
Sample answers.

Shade 0.75 of each diagram. ◄1–4. MAH 030

1.

2.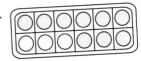

3.

4.

Add or subtract. ◄5–7. MAH 118, 127

5. $4 + 0.75 =$ ___4.75___

6. $3 - 0.75 =$ ___2.25___

7. ___$11.25___ $+ \$0.75 = \$12.00$

GEOMETRY AND MEASUREMENT

Which shape do you think is the equilateral triangle? Loop it. ◄8–10. MAH 362

8.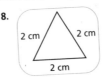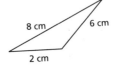

9.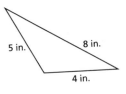

10. What is the perimeter of the equilateral triangle in Problem 8? ___6 cm___

© Great Source. Permission is granted to copy this page.

SUMMER SUCCESS: MATH **21** MAH: *Math at Hand*

REACHING ALL LEARNERS

Allow students to work in pairs to answer Problems 11–12. Some students might need to use a place value chart to help them position the digits.

Math at Hand

If students need help, encourage them to refer to the MAH items shown on the student page.

© Great Source. Copying is prohibited.

Use the digits below to make numbers that fit the description. ◀11–13. MAH 005

| 0 | 1 | 3 | 5 | 8 | 9 |

11. A number with a 5 in the hundreds place and a 8 in the hundredths place.

____ , ____ ____ ____ . ____ ____   sample answer: 1,503.98

12. Write the greatest whole number you can make with all the digits.

____ ____ ____ , ____ ____ ____   answer: 985,310

13. Explain how you decided where to place the digits to answer Problem 12.

Sample answer: I put all the digits in order from greatest to least and then lined them up from left to right.

PROBLEM SOLVING • **UNDERSTAND** • **PLAN** • **TRY** • **LOOK BACK**

Complete each step. ◀14. MAH 396

14. Abbey has a $20 gift certificate to the Music Depot, where all CDs are $8 each. During the Crazy Super Sale, Abbey can buy one CD at the regular price and the rest at half-price. What is the greatest number of CDs she can buy with the gift certificate?

POSSIBLE STRATEGIES

• Make a Table

• Make an Organized List

• Write an Equation

Sample strategy: Write an Equation

a. Underline the question you need to answer.

b. Loop the information that explains the cost of the CDs.

c. Mark the strategy/strategies you will use.

d. Solve the problem. Explain your thinking.

$20 – $8 = $12

half of $8 is $4

$12 – $4 = $8, $8 – $4 = $4

e. Answer the question.

Abbey can buy 4 CDs.

SUMMER SUCCESS: MATH **22** MAH: *Math at Hand*

© Great Source. Permission is granted to copy this page.

© Great Source. Copying is prohibited.

REACHING ALL LEARNERS

If students have difficulty with the problem, brainstorm ways to start the solution. Help students recognize the different pricing for the first CD, and the cost for each additional CD.

PROBLEM SOLVING

Work in small groups of 3 or 4 students.

• Encourage students to find ways to identify needed information to solve the problem.

• *What does it means when an item is "on sale"?* (It sells for less than the original price.)

• *What does it mean when the price is "half-off"?* (It is one-half of the original price.) *Is there a fraction or decimal that describes "half-off"?* ($\frac{5}{10}$, $\frac{1}{2}$, 0.50, or 0.5)

SCORING

a. Last sentence underlined: 1 pt

b. Pricing information circled: 1 pt

c. Choose and apply an appropriate strategy: 1 pt

d. Explanation of solution: 1 pt

e. Correct answer: 1 pt

GLOSSARY TO GO

Today's Vocabulary *fraction*

Have students complete an entry for today's vocabulary term in their Glossaries. Encourage students to use both words and drawings.

MATH JOURNAL

• *The Sneaker Barn is having a year-end sale. Describe how you will figure out the cost of an item marked $\frac{1}{2}$ off; $\frac{1}{4}$ off; $\frac{3}{4}$ off.* (Answers will vary. Check to be sure students know the difference between the discount amount and the final cost of the item.)

NUMBER NAMES TODAY'S NUMBER Review

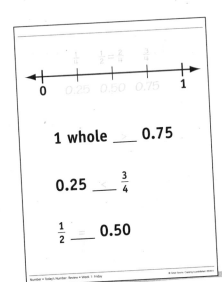

1 whole ___ 0.75

0.25 _<_ $\frac{3}{4}$

$\frac{1}{2}$ ___ 0.50

NUMBER Decimals and fractions

✎ *Let's review some of the numbers we've learned this week. How would you use decimals to label the marks on the number line?* Invite volunteers to plot 0.25, 0.50, and 0.75.

✎ *Using decimals is one way to label the marks. How would you use fractions?* Invite volunteers to plot $\frac{1}{4}$, $\frac{1}{2}$, and $\frac{3}{4}$.

✎ *Would it be okay to use the fraction $\frac{2}{4}$ instead of $\frac{1}{2}$?* (yes) *Why do you think so?* (sample answer: $\frac{2}{4}$ is another name for $\frac{1}{2}$) Invite volunteers to complete the comparisons.

Math at Hand 019

$5.00 ___ $3.50 = $ _1.50_

Check:

sample answers

• Add $1.50 to $3.50.

• Use another way to solve: $3.50 plus 50¢ is $4.00; add another dollar and that'll be $5; so the answer is $1.50.

OPERATIONS Check solution

• **Problem Solving** *Listen to this. Sam gets 10¢ for every bottle he recycles. He has earned $3.50 so far. How much more does he need to earn to have $5?*

✎ *Which operation would you use to find the answer?* (subtraction or addition) *What is the answer?* ($1.50)

✎ *Is there a way to check the answer?* (see recording pad)

REACHING ALL LEARNERS Some students might benefit from using play money or counters to help them find the answer.

Math at Hand 123

1, $1\frac{1}{2}$, 2, $2\frac{1}{2}$, 3, $3\frac{1}{2}$, 4, $4\frac{1}{2}$, . . .

Next 3 numbers:

_5_, _$5\frac{1}{2}$_, _6_

Rule:

Add $\frac{1}{2}$ to the number that comes before.

PATTERNS AND ALGEBRA Write a rule

• *Can you describe what you see on the pad?* (fractions and whole numbers)

• *Starting from the left, would you say the numbers are getting bigger or smaller?* (bigger) *How can you tell?* (the whole numbers go up from 1 to 4) *What do the three dots mean?* (sample answers: and so on; more to come)

✎ *What are the next three numbers?* (5, $5\frac{1}{2}$, 6)

✎ *How would you write a rule to describe the pattern?* (sample answer: add $\frac{1}{2}$ to the number that comes before)

Math at Hand 401

© Great Source. Copying is prohibited.

KEY ✎ = record on pad

GEOMETRY Triangles and symmetry

- *What do you see?* (triangles)

- ✎ *How are they alike?* (Each is a closed figure, has 3 sides, has 3 corners, or angles.) *Different?* (sample answers: different lengths for the sides of each triangle; different angles, some big, some small)

- ✎ *Do all three triangles have line symmetry?* (no) *Which triangle seems to have line symmetry?* Invite a volunteer to mark the line of symmetry.

Math at Hand 358, 380

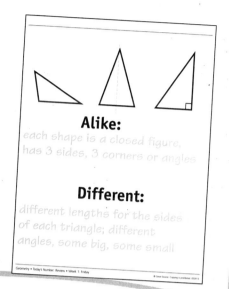

Alike:
each shape is a closed figure, has 3 sides, 3 corners or angles

Different:
different lengths for the sides of each triangle; different angles, some big, some small

Geometry • Today's Number: Review • Week 1: Friday   © Great Source. Copying is prohibited. 052913

MEASUREMENT Perimeter

- *Here is a 4-sided shape, or quadrilateral. What can you tell about this shape?* (It has 2 long sides, 2 short sides, and 4 right angles.)

- ✎ *How would you find the perimeter, or distance around the shape?* (count the number of units on each side) *Show your work.* (see recording pad)

- *Can you come up with a shortcut?* (sample answer: add one long side and one short side, then double it)

Math at Hand 295

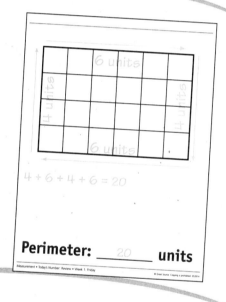

6 units

4 units

4 units

6 units

$4 + 6 + 4 + 6 = 20$

Perimeter: ___20___ **units**

Measurement • Today's Number: Review • Week 1: Friday   © Great Source. Copying is prohibited. 052913

VOCABULARY Review

- *Let's work together to do today's matching exercise. Draw a line to match each word with an example that describes it.*

- *What are you doing when you compare numbers?* (sample answer: see which one is bigger or smaller)

- *What do the different parts of a fraction tell you?* (sample answer: the numerator tells how many parts, the denominator tells how many part in all)

- *How are operation symbols useful?* (sample answer: they tell how the value of a number is changed)

Math at Hand 008, 011, 028, 529

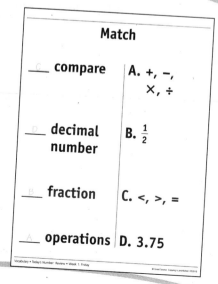

Match

__C__ compare | A. +, −, ×, ÷

__D__ decimal number | B. $\frac{1}{2}$

__B__ fraction | C. <, >, =

__A__ operations | D. 3.75

Vocabulary • Today's Number: Review • Week 1: Friday   © Great Source. Copying is prohibited. 052913

© Great Source. Copying is prohibited.

PRACTICE

Written Practice

CONCEPTS AND SKILLS

- Decimals and fractions on a number line
- Compare and contrast shapes
- Find perimeter of a rectangle
- Problem Solving Strategies and Skills: *Guess, Check, and Revise, Make a Table, Make an Organized List; Solve in More Than One Way*

PREVIEW THE PRACTICE

- Copy the number line from the Practice page. *The first point is on the number line already. Why is it a good idea to find the middle first?* (sample answer: then you can figure out how to place the points that are greater than or less than one-half)

SUPPORT THE PRACTICE

- Problems 1–6 revisit decimals and fractions on a number line. Work on Problem 1 together.
- Problems 7–11 give students a chance to be the teacher. Help students articulate a comment to answer Problem 11.
- Problems 12–13 compare and contrast a square, rectangle, and triangle. Review previous Geometry recording pads, if needed.
- Problems 14–15 ask students to find the missing length of a rectangle. Then, find the perimeter. Review previous Measurement Recording Pads, if needed.
- Problems 16–17 review place value. Provide a place value chart for students having difficulties.

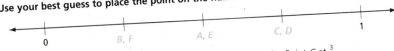

Name _____

© Great Source. Permission is granted to copy this page.

NUMBER AND OPERATIONS

Use your best guess to place the point on the number line. ◀1–6. MAH 019

```
←————|————————|————————|————————|————————|————→
     0        B, F      A, E      C, D              1
```

1. Point A at 0.50
2. Point B at 0.25
3. Point C at $\frac{3}{4}$
4. Point D at 0.75
5. Point E at $\frac{1}{2}$
6. Point F at $\frac{1}{4}$

Help the teacher correct this paper. Write a note to the student.

> **Add or subtract** ◀7–11. MAH 123
>
> 7. $5.00 + $1.75 = $ __6.75__ ✓   8. 3 − 0.50 = __2.50__ ✓
> 9. 3.25 + 0.50 = __3.75__ ✓   10. 0.25 + 0.25 + 0.25 = __3.25__ ✗
> 11. Comment: __In #10, use 3 groups of 25¢ to check your answer. You can__
> __see the answer should be 0.75.__

GEOMETRY AND MEASUREMENT

Look at the shapes. ◀12–13. MAH 357, 358, 364

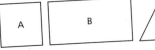

12. How are the three shapes alike?
Sample answers: They are polygons; you can find their perimeter by adding the sides; they have corners, or angles.

13. How are the three shapes different?
Sample answers: Shape A looks like a square with 4 sides that are the same length; B is rectangle, with 2 long sides, 2 short sides; and C is a triangle, it has only 3 sides

Use the diagram to answer. ◀14–15. MAH 295

The short sides of a rectangle measures 0.25 m. Each of the longer sides is double the length of the shorter side.

14. What is the length of the longer side? __0.50 m__

15. What is the perimeter of the rectangle? __1.50 m__

0.25 m   0.25 m

REACHING ALL LEARNERS

Help students visualize the dimensions of the rectangles in Problems 14–15. Draw a larger similar rectangle. Use strips of paper to show the proportions of the shorter side as compared with the longer side.

Math at Hand

If students need help, encourage them to refer to the MAH items shown on the student page.

© Great Source. Copying is prohibited.

Use the digits below to make numbers that fit the description. ◄16–17. MAH 005

| 1 | 2 | 5 | 6 | 7 | 8 |

16. Write a number with a 2 in the tens place and a 7 in the tenths place.

_____ , _____ _____ _____ . _____ _____   sample answer: 1,526.78

17. Write the greatest whole number you can make with all the digits.

_____ _____ _____ , _____ _____ _____   answer: 876,521

PROBLEM SOLVING · **UNDERSTAND** · **PLAN** · **TRY** · **LOOK BACK**

Complete each step. ◄18. MAH 396

18. How many different 2-digit numbers can be made using the digits 1, 5, 7, and 9? No digit can be repeated in the same number.

a. Underline the question you need to answer.

b. Loop the details that describe the type of numbers to be made.

c. Mark the strategy/strategies you will use.

d. Solve the problem. Explain your thinking.

_____

_____

_____

_____

_____

e. Answer the question.

A total of 12 different numbers can be made.

POSSIBLE STRATEGIES

- Guess, Check, and Revise
- Make a Table
- Make an Organized List

sample strategy:
Make an Organized List

1	15, 17, 19
5	51, 57, 59
7	71, 75, 79
9	91, 95, 97

© Great Source. Permission is granted to copy this page.

REACHING ALL LEARNERS

If students have difficulty with the problem, begin an organized list or table using the first two digits, 1 and 5, to make the numbers 15 and 51. Explain why 11 and 55 are not part of the list.

© Great Source. Copying is prohibited.

PROBLEM SOLVING

Work in small groups of 3 or 4 students.

- Encourage students to find ways to identify needed information to solve the problem.
- *What does 2-digit mean?* (having only 2 numerals) *Which 2-digit numbers can be made using 6 and 8?* (68, 86, 66, and 88)
- *This problem has as special rule. What is it?* (no repeating digits in the number)

SCORING

a. Last sentence underlined: 1 pt

b. Detail descriptors circled: 1 pt

c. Choose and apply an appropriate strategy: 1 pt

d. Explanation of solution: 1 pt

e. Correct answer: 1 pt

GLOSSARY TO GO

Today's Vocabulary Review

Have students review and share the entries they made for this week's vocabulary words, *operations*, *decimals*, *compare*, and *fraction*. Ask students to add more words and/or drawings to the maps if they can.

MATH JOURNAL

- *Think back over the past week. What is one new math skill you learned that you want to make sure to remember next week?* (Answers will vary. Check to be sure student is able to articulate clearly using appropriate math terms.)

READ AND REASON

Additional Support

CONCEPTS AND SKILLS

- Decimal number sense
- Concept of 1 whole

MATH TALK

Model the correct use of these terms and encourage students to use them as they work.

- **hundredths** decimal place value two places to the right of the decimal point
- **inch** unit of length in Customary measure, 12 inches equal 1 foot

SUPPORT PROBLEM 1

Read the story aloud, then have a volunteer read the problem again.

- *What is the story about?* (inches of rainfall)
- *What is the math about?* (decimal sum that is close to 1 whole)
- *Where do you think we should start?* (Answers will vary.)
- *Are there any answers you can rule out?* (1 and 0.01) *Why?* (1 because it is too much, and 0.01 because it was too small of a number)

Name _____

Complete the sentences with answers so this weather report makes the *most* sense. Do not use an answer more than once.

1. Today it rained a lot in our town. We had almost one whole inch of rain. In the morning, it rained really hard and we got ___0.50___ of an inch of rain. During lunch the downpour continued and another ___0.20___ of an inch of rain fell. In the evening, there was another shower with ___0.10___ of an inch of rain.

ANSWER CHOICES

- 1
- 0.50
- 0.20
- 0.01
- 0.10
- 0.40

Explain your thinking.

a. How did you begin?
Example: I decided which numbers could work and which could not work.

b. Which answers did you rule out?
I ruled out 1 because it was too much and 0.01 because it was too small.

c. How are you sure that your answers make sense in the story?
I read the story again and it sounded okay. I also added the decimals and I got 0.80, which is almost 1 whole.

© Great Source. Permission is granted to copy this page.

REACHING ALL LEARNERS

- Some students might relate better if the decimals are expressed as fractions. Use the Blank Hundred Chart to model that $0.50 = \frac{1}{2}$, $0.40 = \frac{2}{5}$, and so on.
- Help students recognize that the number we are looking for should be close to 1 whole.

Math at Hand

- Decimals: Place Value, 012
- Reading and Writing Decimals, 013
- Comparing Decimals, 018
- Adding with Decimals, 118

© Great Source. Copying is prohibited.

Complete the sentences with answers so the story below makes the *most* sense. Do not use an answer more than once.

2.

> I am building a flower garden. It is in the shape of a ___square___ with the same measurement on each side. It is ___200 centimeters___ on each side. I hope to make ___6 rows of 6___ plants to fill the garden. I need ___36___ plants. We ought to have a lot of flowers this summer.

- 6 rows of 6
- 36
- measurement
- 200 centimeters
- square
- 81

Explain your thinking.

a. How did you begin?

Example: I drew a picture and chose which blanks should have numbers and which should have words.

b. What answers did you rule out?

Example: I ruled out the word *measurement* because it didn't make any sense. I also ruled out 81 because I needed the answer to 6 × 6, not 9 × 9.

c. How do you know your answers make sense in the story?

Example: I added detail to my picture and read the story again to make sure it made sense.

© Great Source. Permission is granted to copy this page

- Attributes of a square
- Draw a picture

Model the correct use of these terms and encourage students to use them as they work.

- **centimeters** Metric unit of length, 100 centimeters equal 1 meter
- **square** a 4-sided shape with the same length for each side and 4 right-angle corners

Read the story aloud, then have a volunteer read the problem again.

- *What is the story about?* (building a flower garden)
- *What is the math about?* (finding the answer to 6 × 6)
- *Where do you think we should start?* (Answers will vary.)
- *Are there any answers you can rule out?* (measurement and 81) *Why?* (because *measurement* doesn't make sense, and 81 is not the answer to 6 × 6)

- You might wish to use grid paper to make a drawing of the square and label the sides.
- There are many ways to find the total number of plants. Students can skip-count by 3s six times, then double that number to find 6 × 6; some might recognize that 6 × 5 = 30, so 6 × 6 is 6 more, or 36.

Math at Hand

- Quadrilaterals, 364
- Make a Diagram, 398

© Great Source. Copying is prohibited.

NEWSLETTER

This Newsletter is designed to be sent home with students at the end of the week along with the completed *Folding Facts Kit* Concept Builder materials.

The first page suggests a simple way for students to share with their parent or guardian basic math skills they have been practicing in class.

NEWSLETTER

Summer Success: Math

Your child has had a great week of learning in *Summer Success: Math*. In the past few days, we've worked with 1 whole and the decimal values 0.50, 0.25 and 0.75.

Recognizing patterns and using a pattern to make a prediction are important skills, in math as well as in everyday life.

Ask your child to share with you information he/she sees in the chart. Here are some questions to help you get started:

- What do you see in the chart? (2 columns, numbers, and arrows going from Left to Right)
- How do the numbers change from Left to Right? (the numbers double)
- From top to bottom on both sides, do the numbers get bigger or smaller? (bigger) How can you tell? (sample answer: on the Left side, it goes from 10 to 13; on the Right side, it goes from 20 to 26)
- Suppose you have 20 on the Left, what do you think will be on the Right side? (40) How do you know? (40 is the double of 20)

Left	Right
10 →	20
11 →	22
12 →	24
13 →	26

On the backside of this page are directions for using the project called *Folding Facts*. Invite your child to share this activity with you.

 Thank you for helping to strengthen the tie between home and school. Enjoy the time you spend with your child!

© Great Source. Permission is granted to copy this page.

© Great Source. Copying is prohibited.

Sharpen Multiplication with Folding Facts

This week we learned that certain multiplication facts can be doubled to find the answer to a related fact. This is a useful strategy when you need to find an answer quickly. For example, using the *Folding Fact Cards*, your child learned how to double 5 × 3 = 15 to find the answer to 5 × 6.

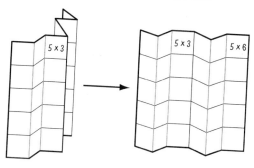

1. Ask your child to show you all the Folding Fact Cards made at summer school this week.

2. Your child should be able to demonstrate his/her knowledge of the facts and how to use the doubling strategy to find other facts. Ask your child to check the answers by counting the number of squares on the folding grid.

 Enjoy exploring math with you child. Notice how quickly your child can recite the answers as she or he practices the facts. Your support is key to success in his or her school experience.

The back side of this week's Newsletter includes instructions for the parent or guardian to help their student demonstrate the *Folding Facts Kit* Concept Builder activity at home.

© Great Source. Permission is granted to copy this page.

28

© Great Source. Copying is prohibited.

WEEKLY OVERVIEW	MONDAY	TUESDAY
Materials Read across to find materials needed for this week's daily activities. *Optional materials	**Game** 1–6 and 4–9 Number cubes **Data Study** straightedge*, calculator*	**Game** 1–6 and 4–9 Number cubes **Data Study** straightedge*, calculator*

NUMBER NAMES *Instruction: 20–30 min*

Number Compare, order and round decimals, Fractions **Operations** Decimals, Mental math **Patterns and Algebra** Number pattern, Write a rule, Function table, Equations **Geometry** Lines, Interior angles, Coordinate grid, Ordered pairs **Measurement** Customary weight, Metric mass, Time **Vocabulary** Algebra terms	**Number Names** p. 28C **Today's Number: 0.20** Compare decimals Multiply by decimals Number pattern Lines Metric length *algebra*	**Number Names** p. 34A **Today's Number: 0.30** Order decimals Compute with decimals Write a rule Interior angles of triangles Time *equation*

PRACTICE *Written Practice: 20–30 min*

Number and Operations Compare/Order, Decimals, Decimals and fractions **Patterns and Algebra** Patterns, Function table **Geometry** Map geometry, Coordinate grid, Ordered pairs **Measurement** Customary weight **Review** Decimals, Coins, Symbols to compare, Lines **Problem Solving** Strategies and skills	**Practice** p. 29 Use <, >, or = to compare Multiply by decimals Map geometry Decimal standard form Act It Out Make a Diagram Make an Organized List Solve in More Than One Way	**Practice** p. 35 Order decimals Add, subtract, multiply decimals Patterns in equations Coin values Make a Diagram Make a Table Write an Equation Find Needed Information

GAME *Active Practice: 20–30 min*

Review decimal place value Add and subtract decimals Read, write, add large numbers	**Game** p. 31 **A Whole in One** Review decimal place value Add and subtract decimals	**Game** p. 31 **A Whole in One** Review decimal place value Add and subtract decimals

FOCUS *Additional Support: 20–30 min*

Read a table, Bar graph, Range, mean, and median, Data Add decimals, Decimal place value, Decimal amounts, Estimate sums, Mental math Factor numbers, Inferred information, Prisms, Cubes	**Data Study** p. 33 **Making a Bar Graph** Making a Bar Graph Read a table Make and interpret a bar graph Range, mean, and median Compare and summarize data	**Data Study** p. 33 **Making a Bar Graph** Making a Bar Graph Read a table Make and interpret a bar graph Range, mean, and median Compare and summarize data

© Great Source. Copying is prohibited.

PLANNER

Game Play Money Cards I, II; 4–9 Number cubes; pencils
Concept Builder scissors, paper, pencils, bags

Number Names p. 36A

Today's Number: 0.40
Round decimals
Compute with decimals
Function table
Coordinate grid
Customary weight
expression

Practice p. 37

Round decimals
Add, subtract, multiply decimals
Customary weight
Ordering decimals
Act It Out
Make a Model
Make a Diagram
Find Needed Information

Game p. 39

Collect $10,000
Review place value
Add large numbers
Read and write large numbers

Concept Builder p. 41

Make & Take:
Decimal Kit
Practice adding decimals
Review place value of decimals
Decimal amounts
Estimate sums, Mental math

Game Play Money Cards I, II; 4–9 Number cubes; pencils
Concept Builder materials prepared previously

Number Names p. 42A

Today's Number: 0.60
Comparing decimals
Compute with decimals
Function table
Angles
Metric mass
variable

Practice p. 43

Decimal place value
Add, subtract, multiply decimals
Function table and equations
Using symbols to compare numbers
Make a Model
Make a Diagram
Write an Equation
Ignore Unneeded Information

Game p. 39

Collect $10,000
Review place value
Add large numbers
Read and write large numbers

Concept Builder p. 41

Make & Take:
Decimal Kit
Practice adding decimals
Review place value of decimals
Decimal amounts
Estimate sums, Mental math

Game see Tuesday and Thursday
Newsletter SE p. 49 (Send home with the Concept Builder materials.)

Number Names p. 44A

Today's Number: Review
Decimals and fractions
Mental math
Equations
Coordinate grid
Time
Vocabulary review

Practice p. 45

Write decimal and fraction names for points on a number line
Add, subtract, multiply decimals
Draw a shape and label its points on a coordinate grid
Line types
Make a Model
Make a Diagram
Write an Equation
Take Notes

Game pp. 31 and 39

Choice
A Whole in One or variation
Collect $10,000 or variation

Read and Reason p. 47

Factor numbers
Using inferred information
Attributes of prisms
Differentiating cubes from rectangular prisms

© Great Source. Copying is prohibited.

NUMBER NAMES TODAY'S NUMBER 0.20

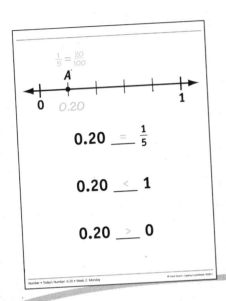

$$0.20 \underline{} \frac{1}{5}$$

$$0.20 \underline{\phantom{<}} 1$$

$$0.20 \underline{} 0$$

NUMBER Compare decimals

✎ *This number line has 5 equal parts between 0 and 1. How would you use a fraction to label Point A?* ($\frac{1}{5}$)

✎ *If there were 100 equal parts how many would be in one fifth?* (20, because 20 repeated 5 times equals 100) *How would you write 20 out of 100 as a fraction?* ($\frac{20}{100}$) *Decimal?* (0.20)

✎ *So, what can you tell about $\frac{1}{5}$, $\frac{20}{100}$, and 0.20?* (They are equal.) *Write the three names for Point A.* ($\frac{1}{5}$, $\frac{20}{100}$, 0.20)

REACHING ALL LEARNERS Shade 20 squares on the Blank Hundred Chart to help students see that $\frac{20}{100} = \frac{1}{5}$.

Math at Hand 031, 035

$$5 \times 0.20 = \underline{1}$$

$$20 \times 0.20 = \underline{4}$$

$$25 \times 0.20 = \underline{5}$$

Problem Solving:

sample answer: I know 10 times 20¢ equals $2; 5 times 20¢ equals $1; the sum is $3.

OPERATIONS Multiply by decimals

• *What is another way to describe multiplying 20 hundredths by a whole number?* (sample answer: add 20 hundredths that number of times)

✎ *What is another way to describe 5 × 0.20?* (sample answer: add 20 hundredths 5 times) *What is 5 × 0.20?* (1) *20 × 0.20?* (4) *25 × 0.20?* (5)

✎ **Problem Solving** *Carla is paid 20¢ each time she collects the mail for her neighbor. So far, she has collected the mail 15 times. How much money has she earned?* ($3) *Explain how you got the answer.* (see recording pad)

Math at Hand 142

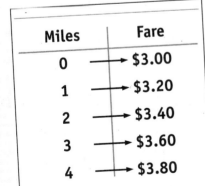

Miles	Fare
0 →	$3.00
1 →	$3.20
2 →	$3.40
3 →	$3.60
4 →	$3.80

Rule: The fare increases by 20¢, or $0.20, each mile.

PATTERNS AND ALGEBRA Number pattern

• **Problem Solving** *The meter on the taxi starts at $3.00. The recording pad shows the fare for a 4-mile ride.*

• *By how much is the fare increasing for each mile traveled?* (20¢ or $0.20)

✎ *What is a rule that describes the pattern?* (sample answer: the fare increases by 20¢, or $0.20, each mile)

REACHING ALL LEARNERS Use play money to model the increase in fare from $3.00 to $3.80.

Math at Hand 401

© Great Source. Copying is prohibited.

KEY ✎ = record on pad

GEOMETRY Lines

✎ *Parallel lines are always the same distance apart. Write* parallel *beneath the diagram of parallel lines.*

✎ *Intersecting lines cross each other. Write* intersecting *beneath each diagram of intersecting lines.*

✎ *Perpendicular lines cross each other and always form right angles. Write* perpendicular *beneath the diagram of perpendicular lines.*

• *Name some real-life examples of parallel, intersecting, and perpendicular lines.* (see recording pad)

Math at Hand 340–341

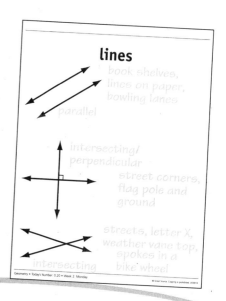

MEASUREMENT Metric length

• *A fingernail is about 1 centimeter wide. The distance from the floor to the doorknob is about 1 meter tall.*

✎ *Would you say the height of the rectangle is closer to 6 centimeters or 6 meters?* (6 centimeters) *Tell why.* (sample answers: 6 meters would be too tall; it is about 6 fingernails high)

✎ *Would you say the ceiling height is about 3 centimeters or 3 meters?* (3 meters) *Tell why.* (sample answers: it is more than 3 fingernails high; it is about 3 times the height of the doorknob)

Math at Hand 294

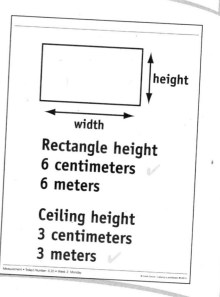

VOCABULARY *algebra*

• *Algebra is the way mathematicians describe how things are related.*

• *Tell a story that can use the algebraic expression, 3 times g, to describe a relationship or a rule.* (sample answer: The apple cider costs $3 a gallon. So, 3*g* is how you can find the total cost depending on the number of gallons you buy.)

• *Algebraic equations compare equal quantities. Tell a story that fits the equation 3g = 24.* (sample answer: There are 3 rows of seats in the section. If there are 24 seats in all, how many seats are in each row?)

Math at Hand 198, 516

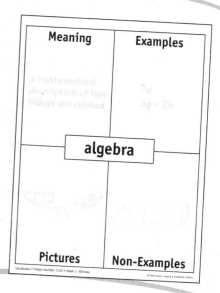

© Great Source. Copying is prohibited.

PRACTICE

Written Practice

CONCEPTS AND SKILLS

- Use $<$, $>$, or $=$ to compare
- Multiply by decimals
- Line geometry
- Review decimal standard form
- Problem Solving Strategies and Skills: *Act It Out, Make a Diagram, Make an Organized List; Solve in More Than One Way*

PREVIEW THE PRACTICE

- Draw a number line. Mark on it 0, 0.50, and 1. *Is 0.20 between 0 and 0.50, or 0.50 and 1?* (0 and 0.50) *What are different ways you can write 0.20 as a fraction?* (sample answers: $\frac{20}{100}$, $\frac{2}{10}$, or $\frac{1}{5}$)

SUPPORT THE PRACTICE

- Problems 1–6 compare 0.20 to whole numbers, decimals, and fractions. Refer students to the number line from the Preview.
- Problems 7–12 ask students to multiply by 0.20. Remind students they can think of 0.20 as $\frac{1}{5}$.
- Problems 13–15 apply line geometry to reading a street map. Revisit today's Geometry recording pad, if needed.
- Problems 16–19 review decimal place value and standard form. Use a decimal place value chart, if needed.

Name _____

NUMBER AND OPERATIONS

Use $<$, $>$, or $=$ to compare. ◄1–6. MAH 031, 035

1. $0.20 \underline{} = \underline{} \frac{20}{100}$
2. $0.20 \underline{} = \underline{} \frac{1}{5}$
3. $0.20 \underline{} < \underline{} 0.50$
4. $0 \underline{} < \underline{} 0.20$
5. $1 \underline{} > \underline{} 0.20$
6. $0.20 \underline{} = \underline{} \frac{2}{10}$

Multiply. ◄7–12. MAH 142

7. $40 \times 0.20 = \underline{} 8$
8. $10 \times 0.20 = \underline{} 2$
9. $50 \times 0.20 = \underline{} 10$
10. $55 \times 0.20 = \underline{} 11$
11. $100 \times 0.20 = \underline{} 20$
12. $60 \times 0.20 = \underline{} 12$

GEOMETRY

Use the map to answer the questions 13–15. ◄13–15. MAH 340–341

13. Which street is perpendicular to Blair Road?
   Royal Boulevard

14. Which street intersects Apple Lane?
   Queen Street

15. Which street is parallel to Apple Lane?
   Blair Road

Queen Street
Apple Lane
Blair Road
Royal Boulevard

REVIEW

Write in standard form. ◄16–19. MAH 012

16. five tenths _0.5_
17. eight hundredths _0.08_
18. twenty-two hundredths _0.22_
19. seventy-four hundredths _0.74_

© Great Source. Permission is granted to copy this page.

REACHING ALL LEARNERS

- Some students might benefit from having a number line to work with for Problems 1–6.
- Remind students that sometimes using a simpler number can help them recognize computation patterns. For example, in Problem 7, students can start with $4 \times 0.20 = 0.80$. Since 40×0.20 is 10 times greater, so the product is 8.

Math at Hand

If students need help, encourage them to refer to the MAH items shown on the student page.

© Great Source. Copying is prohibited.

Complete each step. ◄20. MAH 396

20. Mr. Tran changed the seating chart for his class. Layne now sits (behind Gordon) but (in front of Hyatt.) Rey sits (in front of Gordon) but (behind Yesenia.) If (Hyatt is in the last seat,) then who sits in the first seat?

   a. Underline the question you need to answer.

   b. Loop the words that help you understand position.

   c. Mark the strategy/strategies you will use.

   d. Solve the problem. Explain your thinking.

   _____

   _____

   _____

   _____

   _____

   _____

   _____

   _____

   e. Answer the question.

   Yesinia is in the first seat.

POSSIBLE STRATEGIES

- Act It Out
- Make a Diagram
- Make an Organized List

sample strategy:
Make an Organized List

Yesinia ◄— first seat
Rey
Gordon
Layne
Hyatt ◄— last seat

© Great Source. Permission is granted to copy this page.

PROBLEM SOLVING

Work in small groups of 3 or 4 students.

- Encourage students to find ways to identify needed information to solve the problem.
- *What information do you need to answer the question?* (the seating position of each student)
- *How can you use the information?* (to act it out, make a diagram, make an organized list)

SCORING

a. Question underlined: 1 pt

b. Position words circled: 1 pt

c. Choose and apply an appropriate strategy: 1 pt

d. Explanation of solution: 1 pt

e. Correct answer: 1 pt

GLOSSARY TO GO

Today's Vocabulary *algebra*

Have students complete an entry for today's vocabulary term in their Glossaries. Encourage students to use both words and drawings.

MATH JOURNAL

- *Write a problem like the one in Problem 20. Use the seating arrangement in your classroom as a guide.* (Check student's work.)

REACHING ALL LEARNERS

If students have difficulty with the problem, encourage them to act it out. Invite volunteers to assume the role of the students in the problem.

© Great Source. Copying is prohibited.

GAME

Active Practice

CONCEPTS AND SKILLS

- Review decimal place value
- Add decimals
- Subtract decimals

MATH TALK

Model the correct use of these words and encourage students to use them as they work.

- **difference** the amount that remains after one quantity is subtracted from another.
- **running total** the result of a quantity added to the previous sum
- **sum** the result of addition

MATERIALS

For each pair: two number cubes, 1–6 and 4–9; recording sheet (p. 32), pencils

GAME

A Whole in One

Object: Be the first to add decimal amounts to equal 1 whole, or greater.

MATERIALS

Two Number Cubes, 1–6 and 4–9; recording sheet (p. 32), pencils

DIRECTIONS

1. Use the recording sheet on p. 32.

2. Take turns tossing the number cubes. When it is your turn, write the rolled numbers in the *Numbers* column. Then write the sum of the digits as a number of hundredths in the *Sum* column. For example, if you roll a 3 and a 4, the sum is 0.03 + 0.04 = 0.07. The running total is 0.07.

   NOTE: If you roll a double, you get an extra turn!

3. At the beginning of your next turn, you must state the current *Running Total* and the amount you still need to make 1 whole. **(I have a running total of 18 hundredths, I still need 82 hundredths to reach 1 whole.)**

4. The first player to reach 1 whole or greater wins.

© Great Source. Permission is granted to copy this page.

A Whole in One

Numbers	Sum	Running Total	Still Need
3, 4	0.03 + 0.04 = 0.07	0.07	0.93
5, 6	0.05 + 0.06 = 0.11	0.07 + 0.11 = 0.18	0.82

REACHING ALL LEARNERS

Simplify Play with one 1–6 cube. Instead of hundredths, use tenths. The first roll will be the starting Running Total. The goal is to be the first to reach 3 wholes.

Variation Work with tenths and hundredths. Choose one number to be the tenths, and the other to be the hundredths.

Math at Hand

- Decimals: Place Value, 012
- Add Decimals, 125–126
- Subtract Decimals, 135

© Great Source. Copying is prohibited.

Day 1

REVIEW THE MATH

- Review how to align decimals when adding and subtracting.
- Talk about how to use a zero when a decimal is less than 10 hundredths. *How do you write 3 hundredths?* (0.03) *Can you tell why is there a zero between the decimal point and 3?* (The 0 is a placeholder for the tenths place.)

MODEL THE GAME

- Model how to write and read decimals and the correct use of the mathematical vocabulary while playing the game.
- Demonstrate how to add and subtract decimals using the recording sheet.
- Have volunteer play a demonstration game.

Day 2

PLAY THE GAME

- Review the directions for playing the game.
- Assign pairs of students to play together.

REFLECT ON THE MATH

Encourage students to ask themselves:

- *Did I line up the decimal points correctly?*
- *Did I add or subtract correctly?*
- *Does my answer make sense?*
- *How much of a lead do I have?*
- *What would I need to roll to catch up?*

MODEL THE GAME

Teacher: I just rolled a 3 and a 4. What next?

Student: Write them down in the Numbers column.

S: But, in the Sum column remember to write them as hundredths. So, write 0.03 for 3 and 0.40 for the 4 you rolled.

S: Then, you add the numbers. And write it in the Running Total column.

T: So, how much more do I need to reach 1 whole?

S: Just 93 hundredths.

T: How did you figure that?

S: Subtract the sum 0.07 from 1 to get 0.93.

T: Great. This time I roll a 5 and a 6. How do I figure out the new running total?

S: You add 0.06 and 0.05. The new running total is 0.18.

T: What do I still need?

S: You need 82 hundredths more to reach 1 whole.

ONGOING ASSESSMENT

If students need more help, use the hints below, or refer to the *Math at Hand* items shown to the left.

- **Are students having difficulty working with hundredths?** Remind students to think of hundredths in terms of money. For example, think of 0.65 as 65¢.

- **Are students having difficulty adding or subtracting?** Review regrouping strategies with whole numbers.

© Great Source. Copying is prohibited.

Additional Support

CONCEPTS AND SKILLS

- Read a table
- Make and interpret a bar graph
- Find range, mean, and median for a set of data
- Compare and summarize data in a table or graph

MATH TALK

Model the correct use of these words and encourage students to use them as they work.

- **mean** a number found by dividing the sum of two or more addends by the number of addends; the mean is often referred to as the *average*
- **median** the middle number of a set of numbers when the numbers are arranged from least to greatest; or, the mean of two middle numbers when the set has two middle numbers
- **range** the difference between the greatest and the least value in a set of data

MATERIALS

For each group of students: ruler*, calculator*

*Optional materials

GET STARTED

- Talk briefly with students about precipitation, precipitation in different parts of the country, and local precipitation.

DATA STUDY

Name _____

Making a Bar Graph

What is the range, median, and mean of the data?

READ THE TABLE

Complete the table. Round the decimals.

Average Annual Precipitation of 5 U.S. Cities

City	Inches of Precipitation	Round to Nearest Tenth of an Inch	Round to Nearest Whole Inch
Baltimore, Maryland	40.76	40.8	41
Mobile, Alabama	63.96	64.0	64
Jacksonville, Florida	51.32	51.3	51
Reno, Nevada	7.53	7.5	8
San Francisco, California	19.70	19.7	20

GRAPH THE DATA

- Choose whether you want to make a horizontal or vertical bar graph.
- Title your graph. Draw vertical and horizontal axes.
- Look at the whole-number data in the table to determine the scale for your graph. Start at 0. Label the axes.
- Use the data that is rounded to the nearest whole inch to draw a bar for each city.

ANALYZE THE DATA

1. Look at the graph. Which city has the most precipitation? __Mobile, Alabama__
   The least? __Reno, Nevada__

2. Look at the graph. About how much more precipitation does Baltimore get than San Francisco? __About 20 inches__

3. Use the data in the table. What is the range of the data? __63.96 in. − 7.53 in. = 56.43 in.__
   Median? __Median: 40.76 in.__ Mean? __Mean: 183.27 in. ÷ 5 = 36.654 in.__

© Great Source. Permission is granted to copy this page.

REACHING ALL LEARNERS

- Review comparing and ordering decimals to the hundredths' place.
- Review adding and subtracting decimals as well as dividing decimals by a whole number.
- Review rounding decimals to a designated place, using the same rounding rules for whole numbers.

Math at Hand

- Mean, 260–261
- Median, 261
- Range, 257
- Data in Tables, 267
- Making Graphs, 269

© Great Source. Copying is prohibited.

Day 1

Have students take turns reading the names of the cities and the decimals aloud in class. Reading decimals aloud may indicate their grasp or lack of understanding of decimal place value. Then have students round the decimals, first to the nearest tenth and next to the nearest whole number to complete the table.

Day 2

After students read the directions, work with them as needed to create an accurate graph of the data using the grid on the next page. Be sure they think about what information they want someone else to see when the graph is completed. Students may use rulers to draw the axes and bars in their graphs. Discuss as a group how to choose an appropriate scale for the axis that is to be used to indicate the number of inches of precipitation.

After students complete the graphing task, invite them to display their bar graphs to the class. Encourage them to talk about the scale they used and why they thought it was reasonable. Even though students may have used different scales, ask them to compare each other's graphs to see how they are similar or different.

Help students answer any of the questions at the bottom of student page, 33. Discuss the answers to all the questions, and especially have students share their comparison statements. Then have students consider the following questions:

- *How can you estimate the difference in precipitation by looking at the graph?* (Look at the tops of the bars of any two cities. Then subtract the numbers that the tops of the bars stand for.)

- **What if?** *Suppose we added the precipitation measurement for our city to this data in order from the greatest to the least number of inches of precipitation, between which two cities might it be listed? Would the range, median, and mean change?* (Answers will vary. The range will not change if the added measurement is between the least and the greatest amount in the table. But the median and the mean of all the data would change.)

Teacher: Read the title of the table. Look at the word precipitation. Can anyone tell me what that is?

Student: Does it mean rain? Why doesn't it just say rain?

S: Could it mean snow?

T: You're both correct. Precipitation includes rain, snow, sleet, or hail. If you look at the cities listed in the table, could some of them get snow and rain? Which ones?

S: I heard it's cold in Omaha. So, I think they get snow and rain.

T: What kinds of precipitation do we get in our state or in our city?

S: It usually rains in spring.

S: We got some hail last year. Our car got dented.

T: Do you think the precipitation in our town is similar to one of the cities listed in the table? How much precipitation do you think we get in a year?

Sample graph: Graphs will vary. Bars in graphs should correspond to data in table.

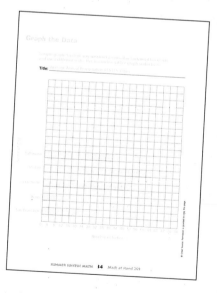

© Great Source. Copying is prohibited.

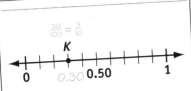

$$\frac{30}{100} = \frac{3}{10}$$

K

0   0.30 0.50   1

Fraction:

$\frac{30}{100}$ or $\frac{3}{10}$

Decimal:

0.30

Least to greatest:

0.20, 0.30, 0.50

NUMBER **Order decimals**

✎ *The number line has 10 equal parts. How would you use a fraction to label Point K?* ($\frac{3}{10}$)

• *Suppose there were 100 equal parts, which mark would be 30 hundredths?* (Point *K*) *How would you write 30 out of 100 as a fraction?* ($\frac{30}{100}$) *Decimal?* (0.30) *So, what can you tell about $\frac{3}{10}$, $\frac{30}{100}$, and 0.30?* (They are equal.)

✎ **Problem Solving** *How would you put 0.30, 0.20, 0.50 in order from least to greatest?* (0.20, 0.30, 0.50)

REACHING ALL LEARNERS Use the Blank Hundred Chart to help students visualize $\frac{3}{10}$ as $\frac{30}{100}$ or 0.30.

Math at Hand 018

$1 + 0.30 =$ ___1.30___

$1 - 0.30 =$ ___0.70___

$1 \times 0.30 =$ ___0.30___

$5 \times 0.30 =$ ___1.50___

OPERATIONS **Compute with decimals**

✎ *When you add 1 and 30 hundredths, is the sum equal to or less than 2?* (less than) *What is the sum?* (1.30) *When you subtract 0.30 from 1, what is the difference?* (0.70) *How do you know?* (30 + 70 is 100, and 100 hundredths is 1 whole)

✎ *If you multiply 1 by 0.30, is the product greater than or less than 1?* (less than) *Why is that?* (sample answer: 1 times any number is that number)

✎ *What is another way to describe 5 × 0.30?* (sample answer: find 3 tenths 5 times) *What is the answer?* (1.50)

Math at Hand 125–126, 135, 142–143

$0.30 + 0.30 = 0.60$
$0.60 + 0.30 = 0.90$
$0.90 + 0.30 = 1.20$
$1.20 +$ ___0.30___ $=$ ___1.50___

Rule: sample answer: Each sum is 0.30 more than the sum before.

PATTERNS AND ALGEBRA **Write a rule**

• *Look at the equations, how are they alike?* (sample answer: they are all addition) *Different?* (sample answers: the first addend is different; each has a different sum; each sum is 0.30 greater)

✎ **Problem Solving** *If the pattern continues, what is the next equation?* (sample answer: add 0.30 to 1.20) *What's the sum?* (1.50)

✎ *What is a rule that describes the pattern of the sums?* (sample answer: each sum is 0.30 more than the sum before)

Math at Hand 401

© Great Source. Copying is prohibited.

KEY ✎ = record on pad

GEOMETRY Interior angles of triangles

- *The sum of the interior angles of any triangle is 180 degrees.*
- *The little square is a symbol for a 90-degree angle. What is another name for this angle?* (right angle or square corner) *What is the symbol for degrees?* (the small circle)
- ✎ **Problem Solving** *Explain how you can find the measure of the third angle.* (sample answer: add what I know, then subtract from 180°) *What is the answer?* (60°)

Math at Hand 354

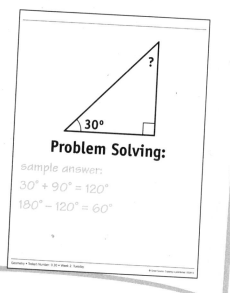

Problem Solving:

sample answer:

30° + 90° = 120°

180° − 120° = 60°

Geometry • Today's Number: 0.30 • Week 2: Tuesday

MEASUREMENT Time

- ✎ *How many minutes are in 1 hour?* (60)
- *If you broke 60 minutes into 10 equal parts, how many minutes would be in each part?* (6 minutes)
- ✎ **Problem Solving** *So, how would you find 3 tenths of 60 minutes?* (sample answers: add 6 minutes 3 times; multiply 6 minutes by 3) *What is the answer?* (18 minutes)

REACHING ALL LEARNERS Help students skip-count by 6.

Math at Hand 322

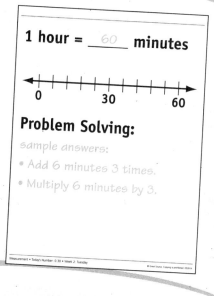

1 hour = ___60___ minutes

Problem Solving:

sample answers:

- Add 6 minutes 3 times.
- Multiply 6 minutes by 3.

Measurement • Today's Number: 0.30 • Week 2: Tuesday

VOCABULARY *equation*

- *When you write an equation, what symbol do you always need to include?* (an equal sign)
- *What is on both sides of an equation?* (equal values)
- *How would you define equation?* (a number sentence that shows 2 equal values)

Math at Hand 235, 523

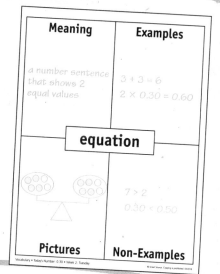

Meaning	Examples
a number sentence that shows 2 equal values	3 + 3 = 6 2 × 0.30 = 0.60

equation

Pictures	Non-Examples

7 > 2

0.30 < 0.50

Vocabulary • Today's Number: 0.30 • Week 2: Tuesday

© Great Source. Copying is prohibited.

PRACTICE

Written Practice

CONCEPTS AND SKILLS

- Order decimals
- Add, subtract, multiply decimals
- Patterns in equations
- Review coin values
- Problem Solving Strategies and Skills: *Make a Diagram, Make a Table, Write an Equation; Find Needed Information*

PREVIEW THE PRACTICE

- Use the number line on the student page. *Which decimal is closer to 0 — 0.40 or 0.70?* (0.40) *0.70 or 0.30?* (0.30) *Order the decimals from least to greatest.* (0.30, 0.40, 0.70)

SUPPORT THE PRACTICE

- Problems 1–4 provide practice ordering familiar decimals. Use the number line to help students position the decimals.
- Problems 5–10 work with 0.30. Help students see that Problems 8 and 9 compute with 1.30.
- Problems 11–12 examine patterns in equation format. Students analyze similarities and differences before articulating a rule. Revisit today's Patterns and Algebra recording pad, if needed.
- Problems 13–16 review decimals in the context of coin values. Use play coins or counters to help students find the total values.

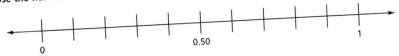

Name _____

NUMBER AND OPERATION

Use the number line to help you order from least to greatest. ◀1–4. MAH 018

```
←———|———|———|———|———|———|———|———|———|———|———→
    0                       0.50                    1
```

1. 0.60, 0.30, 0.70

0.30, 0.60, 0.70

2. 1, 0.30, 0.50

0.30, 0.50, 1

3. 0.40, 0.30, 0

0, 0.30, 0.40

4. 1, 0.30, 0

0, 0.30, 1

Compute. ◀5–10. MAH 125–126, 135, 142–143

5. 2 + 0.30 = ___2.30___ **6.** 8 − 0.30 = ___7.70___ **7.** 5 × 0.30 = ___1.50___

8. 2 + 1.30 = ___3.30___ **9.** 8 − 1.30 = ___6.70___ **10.** 10 × 0.30 = ___3___

PATTERNS AND ALGEBRA

Answer the questions. ◀11–12. MAH 401

11. 1.30 + 0.30 = 1.60
1.60 + 0.30 = 1.90
1.90 + 0.30 = 2.20

How are the equations alike?
add 0.30 in each equation

How are the equations different?
different addend and sum

What is a rule that describes the sums?
each sum is 0.30 more than the sum before

12. 1 × 0.30 = 0.30
2 × 0.30 = 0.60
3 × 0.30 = 0.90

How are the equations alike?
multiply by 0.30 in each equation

How are the equations different?
different multiplier and product

What is a rule that describes the products?
each equation is a multiple of 0.30

SUMMER SUCCESS: MATH **35** MAH: *Math at Hand*

© Great Source. Permission is granted to copy this page.

REACHING ALL LEARNERS

Help students recognize the similarity between Problems 5 and 8. Both are addition equations, except Problem 8 works with 1.30. Likewise, note the similarity in the subtraction in Problems 6 and 9.

Math at Hand

If students need help, encourage them to refer to the MAH items shown on the student page.

© Great Source. Copying is prohibited.

Write the total amount of each group of coins. ◀13–16. MAH 025

13. 6 quarters and 5 dimes

14. 17 nickels and 17 pennies

15. 3 dimes, 7 nickels, and 12 pennies

16. 2 quarters, 1 dime, 5 nickels, and 4 pennies

$2.00

$1.02

$0.77

$0.89

PROBLEM SOLVING • **UNDERSTAND** • **PLAN** • **TRY** • **LOOK BACK**

Complete each step. ◀17. MAH 396

17. Anita walks for an hour daily. She walks about 0.3 mile every 10 minutes. How far does Anita walk in one hour?

a. Underline the question you need to answer.

b. Loop the words that show a relationship between distance and time.

c. Mark the strategy/strategies you will use.

d. Solve the problem. Explain your thinking.

POSSIBLE STRATEGIES

• Make a Diagram
• Make a Table
• Write an Equation

sample strategy:
Make a Diagram

e. Answer the question.

Anita walks 1.8 miles in one hour.

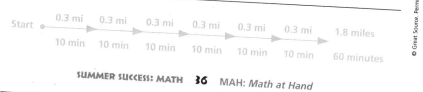

Start 0.3 mi 0.3 mi 0.3 mi 0.3 mi 0.3 mi 0.3 mi 1.8 miles
10 min 10 min 10 min 10 min 10 min 10 min 60 minutes

SUMMER SUCCESS: MATH   **36**   MAH: *Math at Hand*

© Great Source. Permission is granted to copy this page.

REACHING ALL LEARNERS

Refer students to an analog clock face. Help them recognize that there are 6 ten-minute intervals in one hour.

© Great Source. Copying is prohibited.

PROBLEM SOLVING

Work in small groups of 3 or 4 students.

• Encourage students to find ways to identify needed information to solve the problem.

• *What information do you need to answer the question?* (the distance Anita walks every 10 minutes)

• *How can you use the information?* (make a diagram to chart the distance covered in one hour)

SCORING

a. Question underlined: 1 pt

b. Time and distance words circled: 1 pt

c. Choose and apply an appropriate strategy: 1 pt

d. Explanation of solution: 1 pt

e. Correct answer: 1 pt

GLOSSARY TO GO

Today's Vocabulary *equation*

Have students complete an entry for today's vocabulary term in their Glossaries. Encourage students to use both words and drawings.

MATH JOURNAL

• *Write about a time when drawing a sketch helped you solve a problem.* (Check student's work.)

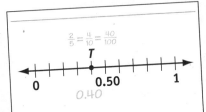

$\frac{2}{5} = \frac{4}{10} = \frac{40}{100}$

T

0   0.50   1
         0.40

0.40 rounds to ___0___

0.40 is closer to 0 than 1

NUMBER Round decimals

✎ *How would you use a fraction to label Point* T *on the 10-part number line?* ($\frac{4}{10}$)

✎ *If there were 100 equal parts, then Point* T *would be the 40th mark. How many ways can you name Point* T? ($\frac{40}{100}$, 0.40) *Some students might see that* $\frac{2}{5}$ *is also an answer.*

• *Is Point* T *closer to 0 or 1?* (0) *If you round to the nearest whole number, does 0.40 round to 0 or 1? Why?* (0.40 rounds to 0 because it is closer to 0.)

REACHING ALL LEARNERS Post the Blank Hundred Chart with 40 squares shaded.

Math at Hand 096

$1 + 0.40 =$ ___1.40___

$1 - 0.40 =$ ___0.60___

$1 \times 0.40 =$ ___0.40___

$10 \times 0.40 =$ ___4.00___

$100 \times 0.40 =$ ___40.00___

OPERATIONS Compute with decimals

✎ *Is the sum of 1 and 40 hundredths equal to or less than 2?* (less than) *What is the sum?* (1.40) *When you subtract 0.40 from 1, what is the difference?* (0.60) *How do you know?* (40 + 60 is 100, and $\frac{100}{100}$ is 1 whole)

✎ *If you multiply 1 by 0.40, is the product greater than or less than 1?* (less than) *Why is that?* (sample answer: 1 times any number is that number)

✎ *What is another way to describe 10 × 0.40?* (sample answer: find 4 tenths 10 times) *What is the answer?* (4.00) *What is the answer to 100 × 0.40?* (40.00)

Math at Hand 085, 125–126, 135, 142–143

Tom	Aimee
7	11
5	9
2	6
3	7

Equation: Tom + 4 = Aimee

PATTERNS AND ALGEBRA Function table

• *Tom is 4 years younger than Aimee. The function table lists examples of ages for Tom and Aimee.*

• *Are the numbers in any order?* (no) *Is it possible to see the relationship anyways?* (yes) *What is the relationship?* (Aimee is 4 years older.)

✎ **Problem Solving** *What equation describes the age relationship in the function table?* (Tom + 4 = Aimee) Invite a volunteer to fill in the blank.

Math at Hand 241

© Great Source. Copying is prohibited.

KEY ✎ = record on pad

GEOMETRY Coordinate grid

- *Suppose you want to graph Tom and Aimee's ages.*
- ✎ *If you list the ages in the form (Tom, Aimee), what would they be?* (7, 11), (5, 9), (2, 6), (3, 7)
- ✎ The math name for pairs of numbers that can be positioned on a grid is *ordered pair*. The first number tells how many spaces across. The second number tells how many spaces up. ***Where would plot point (2, 6)?*** (see recording pad)
- Invite volunteers to plot the other points from today's Patterns and Algebra recording pad.

Math at Hand 265–266

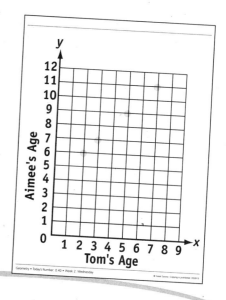

MEASUREMENT Customary weight

- *Would you use ounces, pounds, or tons to describe the weight of a letter?* (ounces) *Tell why.* (because it is light)
- *When would you use pound to weigh an item?* (when the item is at least 16 ounces) *Example?* (sample answers: box of books; bag of potatoes; suitcase)
- *When would you use ton to measure an item?* (when it is a very heavy item) *Example?* (a car; a ship; pieces of iron)
- ✎ *Write the unit that best fits the weight of the item.*

Math at Hand 317

VOCABULARY *expression*

- *An expression names a number. When you write an expression, do you use an equal sign?* (no)
- *An expression can include an operation. Can you give an example?* (sample answers: 6 + n; 0.40 × 5, (2 + 3) −1)
- *How would you use an expression to write: a full bag of apples plus 2 more?* (sample answers: apples + 2; a + 2)

Math at Hand 237–238, 523

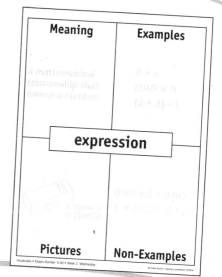

© Great Source. Copying is prohibited.

PRACTICE

Written Practice

CONCEPTS AND SKILLS

- Round decimals
- Add, subtract, multiply decimals
- Coordinate grid and ordered pairs
- Review ordering decimals
- Problem Solving Strategies and Skills: *Act It Out, Make a Model, Make a Diagram; Find Needed Information*

PREVIEW THE PRACTICE

- Write on the board, 0.70. *Is 0.70 closer to 0 or 1?* (1) *Is 0.70 greater than or less than 0.50?* (greater than) *Would you round UP to 1 or DOWN to 0?* (UP to 1)

SUPPORT THE PRACTICE

- Problems 1–6 use a number line to help students round decimals to 0 or 1. Help students decide whether the decimal is less than, equal to, or greater than 0.50.
- Problems 7–12 work with 0.40. Help students see that Problem 11 computes with 2.40.
- Problems 13–17 ask students to choose the best unit for measuring the weight of various objects. Refer to today's Measurement recording pad, if needed.
- Problems 18–19 review ordering decimals from least to greatest. Use a number line to help students position the numbers.

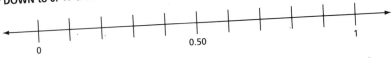

PRACTICE TODAY'S NUMBER **0.40**

Name _____

NUMBER AND OPERATIONS

Use the number line to tell whether the number rounds UP to 1 or DOWN to 0. ◄1–6. MAH 096

0   0.50   1

1. 0.40 rounds ___down___ to 0
2. 0.75 rounds ___up___ to ___1___
3. 0.30 rounds ___down___ to ___0___
4. 0.50 rounds ___up___ to ___1___
5. 0.20 rounds ___down___ to ___0___
6. 0.25 rounds ___down___ to ___0___

Compute. ◄7–12. MAH 085, 125, 135

7. $0.40 + 2 =$ ___2.40___
8. $2 - 0.40 =$ ___1.60___
9. $10 \times 0.40 =$ ___4.00___
10. $0.40 + 6 =$ ___6.40___
11. $2.40 - 2 =$ ___0.40___
12. $100 \times 0.40 =$ ___40.00___

MEASUREMENT

Fill in the blank. Write *ounce(s), pound(s),* or *ton(s)* to describe the most likely unit of weight for the object. ◄13–17. MAH 317

13. A can of soup weighs about 1 ___pound___.
14. A pencil weighs about 1 ___ounce___.
15. A bag of apples weighs about 5 ___pounds___.
16. An elephant weighs about 4 ___tons___.
17. A box of markers weighs about 5 ___ounces___.

REVIEW

Order from least to greatest. ◄18–19. MAH 018

18. 0.60, 0.30, 0.70, 0.40
___0.30, 0.40, 0.60, 0.70___

19. 1, 0.30, 0.50, 0.40
___0.30, 0.40, 0.50, 1___

© Great Source. Permission is granted to copy this page.

REACHING ALL LEARNERS

Label or invite volunteers to label assorted objects in the room with the words *ounces* or *pounds*. No object inside the room will weigh a ton, but 20 hundred-pound students would be a good image of a ton.

Math at Hand

If students need help, encourage them to refer to the MAH items shown on the student page.

© Great Source. Copying is prohibited.

Complete each step. ◄20. MAH 396

20. Maggie draws 2 horizontal lines that are also parallel. Next, she draws two more parallel lines that are perpendicular to the first two lines. What type of figure did she make?

   a. Underline the question you need to answer.

   b. Loop the types of lines Maggie draws.

   c. Mark the strategy/strategies you will use.

   d. Solve the problem. Explain your thinking.

POSSIBLE STRATEGIES

- Act It Out
- Make a Model
- Make a Diagram

sample strategy:
Make a Diagram

_____

_____

_____

_____

_____

_____

_____

_____

   e. Answer the question.

   Sample answer: She made a rectangle.

© Great Source. Permission is granted to copy this page.

PROBLEM SOLVING

Work in small groups of 3 or 4 students.

- Encourage students to find ways to identify needed information to solve the problem.
- *What information do you need to answer the question?* (the types of lines being drawn)
- *How can you use the information?* (make a diagram)

SCORING

   a. Question underlined: 1 pt

   b. Types of lines circled: 1 pt

   c. Choose and apply an appropriate strategy: 1 pt

   d. Explanation of solution: 1 pt

   e. Correct answer: 1 pt

GLOSSARY TO GO

Today's Vocabulary *expression*

Have students complete an entry for today's vocabulary term in their Glossaries. Encourage students to use both words and drawings.

MATH JOURNAL

- *Use words to describe how to draw a right triangle.* (Check to be sure students use words such as *perpendicular, intersect, 90° angle,* or *square corner.*)

REACHING ALL LEARNERS

For students having difficulties with Problem 20, revisit the Geometry recording pad for this week Monday.

© Great Source. Copying is prohibited.

GAME

Active Practice

CONCEPTS AND SKILLS

- Review place value to 10 thousands
- Add and subtract 3- and 4-digit numbers
- Read and write 4-digit numbers

MATH TALK

Model the correct use of these words and encourage students to use them as they work.

- **difference** the amount that remains after one quantity is subtracted from another
- **sum** the result of addition

MATERIALS

For each pair: Play Money I Cards (33 of the $100 bills), Play Money II Cards (11 of the $100 bills, 20 of the $1,000 bills, and 2 of the $10,000 bills), two 4–9 Number Cubes, pencils

GAME

Collect $10,000

Object: Be the first to collect $10,000, or more.

MATERIALS

Play Money I Cards (33 of the $100 bills), Play Money II Cards (11 of the $100 bills, 20 of the $1,000 bills, and 2 of the $10,000 bills), two 4–9 Number Cubes, pencils

DIRECTIONS

1. Use p. 40 to make a recording sheet like this one.
2. In this game you and your partner must have the same number of turns.
3. You roll the cubes, take the sum in $100 bills, and write the amount of money on the recording sheet. Your partner does the same.
4. Take turns rolling the cubes. The sum collected for each turn is added to the amount shown on the recording sheet. You and your partner must state your total and how much more money you need to reach $10,000 before taking each turn. **(It's my turn. I have $2,100. I still need $7,900 to reach $10,000.)**
5. Whenever possible, trade for the next-higher denomination bill. For example, when you have ten $100 bills, trade them for a $1,000 bill.
6. The first player to collect at least $10,000 is the winner. If you and your partner reach $10,000 in the same round, the player with the greater amount of money is the winner.

Collect $10,000	
Player 1	Player 2
$600	$900
+ $700	+ $500
$1,300	$1,400

It's my turn. I have $2,100. I still need $7,900 to reach $10,000.

REACHING ALL LEARNERS

Simplify Eliminate the rule that requires the player to state the amount still needed to reach $10,000.

Variation If a student fails to exchange the smaller denominations for a larger denomination, the opposing player may call "exchange" and take the equivalent denomination as a bonus. For example, when a player neglects to exchange 10 hundreds for $1,000, the opposing player points out the error and takes $1,000.

Math at Hand

- Read and Write Large Numbers, 005
- Adding with Whole Numbers, 119–124

© Great Source. Permission is granted to copy this page.

© Great Source. Copying is prohibited.

Day 1

- Use a place value chart to review place value to 10 thousand.
- Write the number 36,829 on the chalkboard. *Who can tell me what is the place value of the digit 6?* (thousand) *The digit 3?* (ten thousand) *How about the digit 2?* (ten)

- Show how to play the game and how to keep score.
- Have volunteers play a demonstration game.
- Model how to read large numbers.
- Model how to find the difference from $10,000 using mental math.

Day 2

- Review the directions for playing the game.
- Assign partners to play the game.

Encourage students to ask themselves:

- *How many more do I need to reach $10,000?*
- *Did I add the numbers correctly?*
- *Did I make the correct trade?*

Teacher: I just rolled a 5 and a 6. How many bills should I take and what amount should I write on the recording sheet?

Student: You have a total of 11. Take eleven $100 bills, and write $1,100.

T: Then what?

S: You should trade ten $100 bills for one $1,000 bill.

T: Before my next turn, I have to tell everybody that I have $1,100. How much more money do I need to reach $10,000?

S: You need $8,900 more to reach $10,000.

T: How did you figure that?

S: If I have $1,000, I'd need $9,000. Since I have $1,100, I'd need $100 less than $9,000. That's $8,900.

T: If I roll a 6 and an 8 on my next turn, what will I put down on the recording sheet?

S: You should record $1,400 because 6 plus 8 equals 14.

T: What will be my new total?

S: You'll have $2,500.

If students need more help, use the hints below, or refer to the *Math at Hand* items shown to the left.

- **Can students set up an addition sentence and compute?** If students have difficulty with the addition portion of the game, review regrouping with whole numbers.
- **Can students work with large numbers?** Review how to read and write large numbers.

© Great Source. Copying is prohibited.

CONCEPT BUILDER
MAKE & TAKE

Additional Support

CONCEPTS AND SKILLS

- Practice adding decimals
- Review place value of decimals
- Verbalize and visualize decimal amounts
- Estimate reasonable sums
- Use mental math

MATH TALK

Model the correct use of these words and encourage students to use them as the work.

- **decimal number** a number written using base ten
- **hundredths** 100 equal pieces
- **tenths** 10 equal pieces

MATERIALS FOR DAY 1

Decimal Kit Pieces (SE page 41), 1–9 Digit Cards (SE page 41A), scissors, paper, pencils, bags

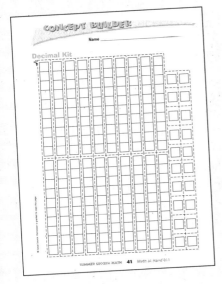

Decimal Kit **Day 1**

GET READY

Follow the instruction below to prepare a sample Decimal Kit to use for demonstration..

BUILD THE DECIMAL KIT

1. Have students cut out the Decimal Kit Pieces and the 1–9 Digit Cards on pages 41 and 41A of their books.

2. Have students make a place-value mat like the one shown.

3. Students should write their names or initials on the Decimal Kit Pieces, the 0-9 Digit Cards, the place-value mat, and the storage bag.

Tenths	Hundredths

4. Have students keep all the pieces in the storage bags until tomorrow.

FOCUS ON THE MATH

- *What is the smallest unit in the Decimal Kit?* (hundredths) *What is the largest unit in the Decimal Kit?* (tenths) *How would 0.36 be represented with the Decimal Kit?* (3 rods and 6 units, or 3 tenths and 6 hundredths) *How would 0.8 be represented with the Decimal Kit?* (8 rods, or 8 tenths)

- *How many hundredths are equal to one whole?* (100) *How many hundredths are equal to one tenth?* (10) *What fraction and decimal represents one hundredths?* ($\frac{1}{100}$, 0.01) *How many tenths are equal to one whole?* (10) *What fraction and decimal represents one tenths?* ($\frac{1}{10}$, 0.1)

- The Decimal Kit represents the decimal system, which is also the foundation of the metric system. *How many centimeters are in a meter?* (100) *What is equivalent to 1 centimeter in the Decimal Kit?* (1 hundredths) *How many decimeters are in a meter?* (10) *What is equivalent to 1 decimeter in the Decimal Kit?* (1 tenths)

© Great Source. Copying is prohibited.

Decimal Kit **Day 2**

Explain how to play a game using the Decimal Kit.

1. The object of the game is to be the first player to collect one whole using hundredths and tenths.

2. Shuffle the 1–9 Digit Cards and place them facedown on the table.

3. Player 1 draws two cards, adds the numbers, and collects that many hundredths squares or combinations of tenth strips and hundredths squares. The pieces are placed in the correct places on the place-value mat.

4. Player 2 follows the same steps. Throughout the game, hundredths squares are traded for tenth strips whenever possible.

5. Before each turn, players must state the total value of the pieces displayed on their place-value mats. Then they must say how much more is needed to make 1 whole.

6. The player who is first to collect 10 tenth strips (one whole) is the winner.

MODEL THE ACTIVITY

Be sure students understand the representation of *tenths* and *hundredths*. Display the representation of both values using the Decimal Kit.

Model how to express a decimal using the Decimal Kit Pieces. Emphasize the representations for decimals such as 0.8 and 0.80. Draw an analogy between the decimal representation and the expression of the same value using money. Eighty cents can be represented with 8 dimes or 80 pennies. While the representation changes, the value does not change.

REFLECT ON THE MATH

Encourage students to ask themselves:

- *Am I reading the place value chart correctly?*
- *Did I line up the decimals correctly before adding?*
- *Is this a good time to make a trade?*

REACHING ALL LEARNERS

Alternate between having the students represent decimals using the Decimal Pieces Kit and play or real money.

Math at Hand
Decimals, 011–013

© Great Source. Copying is prohibited.

Decimal Kit pieces, 1–9 Digit Cards, and place-value mat assembled previously

Note: Send these materials home with the Newsletter at the end of the week.

Tenths	Hundredths

ONGOING ASSESSMENT

If students need more help, use the hints below, or refer to the *Math at Hand* items shown to the left.

- **Are students able to express decimal values using the Decimal Kit pieces?** Ask students to think of the numerical or concrete representation in terms of money. If necessary, label the place-value mat with dual headings: tenths/dime and hundredths/penny.

- **Are students able to read decimal representations correctly?** Work on tenths in isolation before incorporating hundredths.

NUMBER NAMES TODAY'S NUMBER 0.60

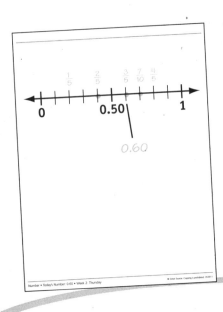

NUMBER Comparing decimals

- **Problem Solving** *I am a hundredths decimal, with a digit that is not zero. I am less than $\frac{7}{10}$. I am between 0.50 and 1 on the number line. If you label fifths you label me. What decimal number am I?*

✎ *Show $\frac{7}{10}$ on the number line.* (see recording pad)

✎ *Which point shows fifths?* (see recording pad)

✎ *What is the decimal number?* (0.60)

REACHING ALL LEARNERS Shade $\frac{4}{5}$ of the squares on the Blank Hundred Chart. Count 60 squares.

Math at Hand 012, 031

---

1 + 0.60 = 1.60

1 − 0.60 = 0.40

1 × 0.60 = 0.60

10 × 0.60 = 6.00

100 × 0.60 = 60.00

OPERATIONS Compute with decimals

✎ *Is the sum of 1 and 60 hundredths equal to or less than 2?* (less than) *What is the sum?* (1.60) *When you subtract 0.60 from 1, what is the difference?* (0.40) *How do you know?* (60 + 40 is 100, and $\frac{100}{100}$ is 1 whole)

✎ *If you multiply 1 by 0.60, is the product greater than or less than 1?* (less than) *Why is that?* (sample answer: 1 times any number is that number)

✎ *What is another way to describe 10 × 0.60?* (sample answer: find 6 tenths 10 times) *What is the answer?* (6.00) *What is the product of 100 × 0.60?* (60.00)

Math at Hand 085, 125–126, 135, 142–143

Hours Worked	Amount Earned
3	→ $12
5	→ $20
2	→ $8
6	→ $24

Equation:

Hours worked × $4 = Amount earned

PATTERNS AND ALGEBRA Function table

- *Joey earns $4 an hour babysitting. The table lists the number of hours he worked during spring break.*

- *Are the numbers in any order?* (no) *Is that okay?* (yes) *Tell why.* (sample answer: what Joey earns an hour doesn't change)

✎ **Problem Solving** *How would you use a multiplication equation to describe the relationship in the function table?* (Hours Worked × $4 = Amount Earned) Invite a volunteer to fill in the blank.

Math at Hand 241

© Great Source. Copying is prohibited.

KEY ✎ = record on pad

GEOMETRY Angles

✎ *Angles less than 90° are called* acute. *Which angle is* acute? (see recording pad)

✎ *Angles that measure exactly 90° are called* right *or* square. *Which angle is it?* (see recording pad)

✎ *Angles greater than 90° but less than 180° are called* obtuse. *Which angle is* obtuse? (see recording pad)

✎ *Angles that measure exactly 180° are called* straight. *Which angle is it?* (see recording pad)

Math at Hand 347

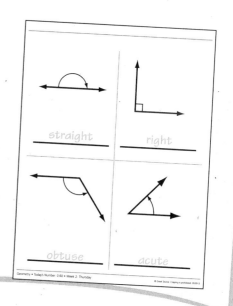

MEASUREMENT Metric mass

• *Would you use grams or kilograms to describe the mass of a feather?* (grams) *Tell why.* (because it is light) *Other examples?* (sample answers: sheet of paper, a pencil, shoelace, a postage stamp)

• *When would you use kilogram to describe the mass of an item?* (to find heavier masses) *Example?* (sample answers: sack of rice; a fifth grader; suitcase; watermelon)

✎ *Write the unit that best fits the mass of the item.*

REACHING ALL LEARNERS Remind students that mass measures the amount of matter in an object.

Math at Hand 318

VOCABULARY variable

• *What does it mean when you say something varies?* (it changes)

• *Which is the variable in the expression b + 0.60?* (b)

• *How would you define variable?* (a quantity that can change)

Math at Hand 236, 537

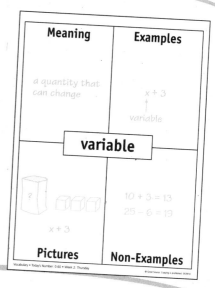

© Great Source. Copying is prohibited.

PRACTICE

Written Practice

CONCEPTS AND SKILLS

- Decimal place value
- Add, subtract, multiply decimals
- Function table and equations
- Review using symbols to compare numbers
- Problem Solving Strategies and Skills: *Make a Model, Make a Diagram, Write an Equation; Ignore Unneeded Information*

PREVIEW THE PRACTICE

- *What is a fraction name for 0.50?* (sample answers: $\frac{50}{100}$, $\frac{5}{10}$, or $\frac{1}{2}$)
- *A hundredths decimal shows how many decimal places?* (2)

SUPPORT THE PRACTICE

- Problems 1–2 use place value words to name a number. Students work with whole numbers, decimals, and fractions. Revisit today's Number recording pad, if needed.
- Problems 3–8 work with 0.60. Help students see that Problem 7 computes with 1.60.
- Problems 9–10 focus on numbers in a function table and the equation that describes the pattern. Remind students to first find the relationship between the numbers.
- Problems 11–16 review using symbols to compare numbers. Use a number to position the numbers, if needed.

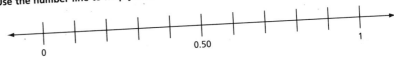
Name _____

NUMBER AND OPERATION

Use the number line to help you name the decimal number. ◄1–2. MAH 012, 031

```
←———+——+——+——+——+——+——+——+——+——+——→
    0              0.50                1
```

1. I am a hundredth decimal with one digit that is not zero. I am less than $\frac{6}{10}$, but greater than 0.30. I am between 0.50 and 0 on the number line. What decimal number am I?

   _____0.40_____

2. I am a hundredth decimal with one digit that is not zero. I am less than $\frac{9}{10}$, but greater than 0.40. I am between 0.50 and 1 on the number line. I am midway between two other decimals. What decimal number am I?

   _____0.70_____

Compute. ◄3–8. MAH 085, 125, 135

3. $0.60 + 2 =$ ___2.60___   4. $2 - 0.60 =$ ___1.40___   5. $10 \times 0.60 =$ ___6.00___

6. $0.60 + 6 =$ ___6.60___   7. $2 - 1.60 =$ ___0.40___   8. $100 \times 0.60 =$ ___60.00___

PATTERNS AND ALGEBRA

Complete the table. Write an equation to describe the pattern. ◄9–10. MAH 241

9.

Hours Parked	Meter Amount
3 hours →	$1.80
5 hours →	$3.00
2 hours →	$1.20
6 hours →	$3.60

Equation:
Hours Parked × $0.60 = Meter Amount

10.

Tables	Chairs
10 →	60
2 →	12
3 →	18
5 →	30

Equation:
Tables × 6 = Chairs

SUMMER SUCCESS: MATH   **43**   MAH: *Math at Hand*

© Great Source. Permission is granted to copy this page.

REACHING ALL LEARNERS

Help students articulate the number relationship in Problems 9–10. For example, in Problem 9, guide students to the value 2 in the Hours Parked column. *What number times 2 equals $1.20?* ($0.60) *Does this factor work with the other numbers in the table?* (yes)

Math at Hand

If students need help, encourage them to refer to the MAH items shown on the student page

© Great Source. Copying is prohibited.

Use <, >, or = to compare. ◀10–15. MAH 031, 035

11. 0.30 ____ $=$ ____ $\frac{30}{100}$ **12.** 0.40 ____ $=$ ____ $\frac{2}{5}$

14. 1 ____ $>$ ____ 0.40 **15.** 1 ____ $>$ ____ 0.30

13. 0.60 ____ $>$ ____ 0.50

16. 0.20 ____ $=$ ____ $\frac{2}{10}$

PROBLEM SOLVING · **UNDERSTAND** · **PLAN** · **TRY** · **LOOK BACK**

Complete each step. ◀17. MAH 396

17. The Hardin family is building a rectangular deck. It will extend into the backyard, which now measures 60 feet by 21 feet. The dimensions of the deck will be (10 feet by 30 feet.) What is the perimeter of the deck?

a. Underline the question you need to answer.

b. Loop the information used to find the dimensions.

c. Mark the strategy/strategies you will use.

d. Solve the problem. Explain your thinking.

POSSIBLE STRATEGIES

- Make a Model
- Make a Diagram
- Write an Equation

sample strategy:
Make a Diagram

30 feet

10 feet

e. Answer the question.

The perimeter of the deck will be 80 feet.

© Great Source. Permission is granted to copy this page.

REACHING ALL LEARNERS

Help students recognize that the dimensions of the backyard are not needed to solve the problem. They can just ignore it.

© Great Source. Copying is prohibited.

PROBLEM SOLVING

Work in small groups of 3 or 4 students.

- Encourage students to find ways to identify needed information to solve the problem.
- *What information do you need to answer the question?* (the deck dimensions)
- *What information can you ignore?* (the back yard dimensions)
- *How can you use the information?* (make a diagram)

SCORING

a. Question underlined: 1 pt

b. Deck dimensions circled: 1 pt

c. Choose and apply an appropriate strategy: 1 pt

d. Explanation of solution: 1 pt

e. Correct answer: 1 pt

GLOSSARY TO GO

Today's Vocabulary *variable*

Have students complete an entry for today's vocabulary term in their Glossaries. Encourage students to use both words and drawings.

MATH JOURNAL

- *Explain why you can't always use 2 × (length + width) to find the perimeter of a quadrilateral. Draw an example.* (sample answer: some quadrilaterals have uneven sides)

NUMBER NAMES TODAY'S NUMBERS Review

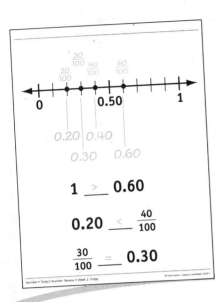

$$1 \underline{\ >\ } 0.60$$

$$0.20 \underline{\ <\ } \frac{40}{100}$$

$$\frac{30}{100} \underline{\ =\ } 0.30$$

NUMBER Decimals and fractions

✎ *Let's review the numbers we've learned this week. How would you use decimals to label the points on the number line?* (0.20, 0.30, 0.40, 0.60)

✎ *Using decimals is one way to label the points. How would you use fractions?* ($\frac{20}{100}$, $\frac{30}{100}$, $\frac{40}{100}$, $\frac{60}{100}$) Some students might recognize equivalents such as $\frac{2}{10}$, $\frac{3}{10}$, $\frac{4}{10}$, $\frac{6}{10}$, or $\frac{1}{5}$, $\frac{2}{5}$, $\frac{3}{5}$.

✎ *Can you use the fraction $\frac{1}{5}$ instead of $\frac{20}{100}$?* (yes) *Why?* (sample answer: $\frac{1}{5}$ is another name for $\frac{20}{100}$) Complete the comparisons.

Math at Hand 019

---

mental math

$$100 \times \$0.60 = \$\underline{\ 60.00\ }$$

$$50 \times \$0.60 = \$\underline{\ 30.00\ }$$

$$100 \times 0.40 = \underline{\ 40.0\ }$$

$$50 \times 0.40 = \underline{\ 20.0\ }$$

$$25 \times 0.40 = \underline{\ 10.0\ }$$

OPERATIONS Mental math

- **Problem Solving** *Your class is selling "Summer School Success!" buttons for $0.60 each. If you sell 100 buttons, how much money is that?*

- *Explain how you can solve this problem using mental math.* (sample answer: I know 100 times 6¢ is $6, so 100 times is 60¢ is $60.)

✎ Invite volunteers to explain their mental math strategies for the other computations. Accept all reasonable methods.

Math at Hand 083

Equations

Left	Right
1.20 →	1.00
7.60 →	7.00
2.40 →	2.00
3.30 →	3.00
8.30	8.00

Equation: *sample answer:*

Left – decimal part = Right

PATTERNS AND ALGEBRA Equations

- *Are the numbers in the Left column in any order?* (no) *In the Right column?* (no) *What do you think is the relationship between the numbers in the two columns?* (sample answer: the number in the Right column is the whole number without the decimal number in the Left column)

✎ *Do you think 8.30 or 8.00 could be the next term in the Left column?* (8.30) *Tell why.* (sample answer: all the other numbers in the column have a decimal part) *What would be the term in the Right column?* (8.00)

✎ *What's an equation that describes the relationship?* (see recording pad)

Math at Hand 241

© Great Source. Copying is prohibited.

KEY ✎ = record on pad

GEOMETRY Coordinate grid

- *On a coordinate grid, number pairs are used to name points. The pair is always named in order (first x, then y) or (first across, then up).*
- ✎ *Label the 4 corner points of the rectangle.* (see recording pad)
- ✎ **Problem Solving** *Draw and label 4 other points that can be corners of another quadrilateral.* (see recording pad for a sample quadrilateral)

REACHING ALL LEARNERS Remind students that a quadrilateral can have different lengths for each side.

Math at Hand 265–266, 364

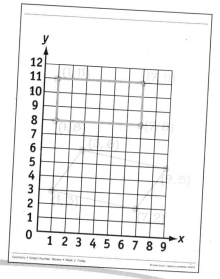

MEASUREMENT Time

- **Problem Solving** *Nancy wants to record the special report on TV. The cassette tape has 45 minutes left. The special report runs $\frac{6}{10}$ of an hour. Can she use the cassette tape to record the entire program?*
- *Tell how you can help Nancy figure this out.* (sample answer: $\frac{1}{10}$ of 60 minutes is 6 minutes, so $\frac{6}{10}$ is 36 minutes)
- *Does the cassette tape have enough time to record the program?* (yes)

REACHING ALL LEARNERS Help students skip-count by 6.

Math at Hand 322

Problem solving:

1 hour = _____ minutes

$\frac{1}{10}$ of 1 hour
        = _____ minutes

$\frac{6}{10}$ of 1 hour
        = _____ minutes

VOCABULARY Review

Let's work together to do today's matching exercise. Draw a line to match each word with an example that describes it

- *Geometry is the study of shapes and figures. What is the study of relationships in math?* (algebra)
- *What can you use to represent a quantity that changes?* (a variable)
- *What does an equation show you that an expression doesn't?* (2 equal values)

Math at Hand 198, 235–238

Match

_____ algebra
_____ equation
_____ expression
_____ variable

A. something that changes
B. 0.20 + *m*
C. equations or expressions
D. 0.60 + *d* = 2

© Great Source. Copying is prohibited.

PRACTICE

Written Practice

CONCEPTS AND SKILLS

- Write decimal and fraction names for points on a number line
- Add, subtract, multiply decimals
- Draw a shape and label its points on a coordinate grid
- Review line types
- Problem Solving Strategies and Skills: *Make a Model, Make a Diagram, Write an Equation; Take Notes*

PREVIEW THE PRACTICE

- Look at the number line on the student page. *The points are between which two whole numbers?* (0 and 1) *The number line is divided into how many equal parts?* (10)

SUPPORT THE PRACTICE

- Problems 1–4 ask students to provide a decimal and a fraction name for points on a number line. Remind students that 0.5 and 0.50 are equal.
- Problems 5–9 allow students to play the role of the teacher. Help students articulate a comment for Problem 9.
- Problem 10 directs students to draw any 5-sided shape on the coordinate grid. Some students might need a ruler to complete the shape.
- Problems 11–13 revisit the names of line types. Remind students that perpendicular lines are limited to those that cross and form 90° angles.

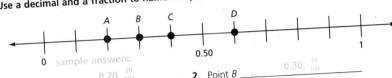

Name _____

NUMBER AND OPERATION

Use a decimal and a fraction to name the point on the number line. ◄1–4. MAH 019

sample answers:

1. Point A ___ 0.20, $\frac{20}{100}$
2. Point B ___ 0.30, $\frac{30}{100}$
3. Point C ___ 0.40, $\frac{40}{100}$
4. Point D ___ 0.60, $\frac{60}{100}$

Help the teacher correct this paper. Write a note to the student.

Compute. ◄5–9. MAH 083

5. $1.60 - 0.60 =$ ___ 1 ✓

6. $2 + 0.40 =$ ___ 2.40 ✓

7. $100 \times \$0.40 =$ ___ \$4 ✗

8. $10 \times 0.30 =$ ___ 3 ✓

9. Comment: Use mental math to check your answer. In #7, you know 100 times 4¢ is \$4, so 100 times 40¢ is \$40.

GEOMETRY

Draw and label a 5-sided shape. ◄10. MAH 265–266, 357

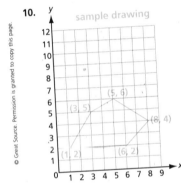

10. sample drawing

(3, 5) (5, 6) (8, 4) (1, 2) (6, 2)

© Great Source. Permission is granted to copy this page.

SUMMER SUCCESS: MATH **45** MAH: *Math at Hand*

REACHING ALL LEARNERS

Remind student that ordered pairs of numbers are always listed in the format (*x, y*) or (across, up).

Math at Hand

If students need help, encourage them to refer to the MAH items shown on the student page.

© Great Source. Copying is prohibited.

Loop the name that *best* describes the lines. ◄11–13. MAH 347

11. 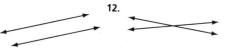 **12.** **13.**

11.
(parallel lines)
perpendicular lines
intersecting lines

12.
parallel lines
perpendicular lines
(intersecting lines)

13.
parallel lines
(perpendicular lines)
intersecting lines

PROBLEM SOLVING • **UNDERSTAND** • **PLAN** • **TRY** • **LOOK BACK**

Complete each step. ◄14. MAH 396

14. At the Garden Center there is a (5-sided) gazebo. (One side measures 4 meters) and the (other sides measure 3 meters each.) What is the perimeter of the gazebo?

a. Underline the question you need to answer.

b. Loop all the information about the gazebo.

c. Mark the strategy/strategies you will use.

d. Solve the problem. Explain your thinking.

Perimeter = 4 m + (4 × 3 m) = 4 m + 12 m = 16 m

_____

_____

_____

_____

e. Answer the question.

The perimeter of the gazebo is 16 m.

POSSIBLE STRATEGIES

- Make a Model
- Make a Diagram
- Write an Equation

sample strategy:
Write an Equation

© Great Source. Permission is granted to copy this page.

REACHING ALL LEARNERS

If students are stymied by not knowing the word gazebo, point out that they can solve the problem without knowing the word. However, you might explain that a gazebo is like an outdoor playhouse without walls.

© Great Source. Copying is prohibited.

PROBLEM SOLVING

Work in small groups of 3 or 4 students.

- Encourage students to find ways to identify needed information to solve the problem.

- *What information do you need to answer the question?* (the lengths of the 5 sides of the gazebo)

- *How can you use the information?* (use the lengths with the equation for Perimeter)

SCORING

a. Question underlined: 1 pt

b. Gazebo information words circled: 1 pt

c. Choose and apply an appropriate strategy: 1 pt

d. Explanation of solution: 1 pt

e. Correct answer: 1 pt

GLOSSARY TO GO

Today's Vocabulary Review

Have students review and share the entries they made for this week's vocabulary words, *algebra*, *equation*, *expression*, and *variable*. Ask students to add more words and/or drawings to the maps if they can.

MATH JOURNAL

- *Name some examples of when mental math can come in handy.* (sample answers: when I don't have anything to write with; when the calculator is dead; when I need to check my work)

READ AND REASON

Additional Support

CONCEPTS AND SKILLS

- Factor numbers
- Using inferred information

MATH TALK

Model the correct use of these terms and encourage students to use them as they work.

- **factor** a number that divides evenly into another number with a quotient that is not a decimal
- **multiple** the product of a whole number and any other whole number

SUPPORT PROBLEM 1

Read the problem aloud once, and then have a volunteer read the problem again.

- *What is the story about?* (how to group people)
- *What is the math about?* (factors of 24) *How many students are at the party?* (24)
- *Where do you think we should start?* (Answers will vary.)
- *Are there any answers you can rule out?* (18 and 9) *Why?* (18 because it was too big; 9 because no multiple of 9 equals 24)

READ AND REASON

Name _____

Complete the sentences with answers so this story makes the *most* sense. Do not use an answer more than once.

1. Vicki and Mike are planning a party with games for 22 guests and themselves. They know that they can play games in pairs because there will be __12__ groups of __2__. Also, they could play games in groups of four, because they can have __6__ groups. Vicki says that they can even have __8__ groups of three friends playing. The kids are pleased that no one will be left out of any games.

© Great Source. Permission is granted to copy this page.

ANSWER CHOICES

- 18
- 12
- 6
- 9
- 2
- 8

Explain your thinking.

a. How did you begin?

Example: I remembered to add the two hosts to get 24. I knew how to factor 24 and that helped me figure out the numbers.

b. Which answers did you rule out?

I ruled out 18 because it was too big and 9 because you cannot multiply 9 by anything to get 24.

c. How are you sure that your answers make sense in the story?

I read the story again and it sounded okay.

SUMMER SUCCESS: MATH **47**

REACHING ALL LEARNERS

- You might need to draw a picture to help some students see the different groups.
- Remind students that Mike and Vicki should be included in the total count of 24.

Math at Hand

- Factors, p.051
- Prisms, p. 383

© Great Source. Copying is prohibited.

Complete the sentences with answers so the story below makes the *most* sense. Do not use an answer more than once.

2. When you look at a cereal box, you can see that it has three pairs of _____rectangular_____ faces that are _____parallel_____ to one another. It is not like a cube, which has _____six_____ square faces that are _____congruent_____. A cereal box is not a _____cube_____.

ANSWER CHOICES

- rectangular
- parallel
- sphere
- congruent
- cube
- six

Explain your thinking.

a. How did you begin?
    Example: I drew a picture of a cereal box.
    _____

b. What answers did you rule out?
    Example: I ruled out sphere because cereal boxes are not in that shape.
    _____

c. How are you sure that your answers make sense in the story?
    Example: The faces on the cereal box are rectangles, so I put that in the first blank.
    _____

© Great Source. Permission is granted to copy this page.

© Great Source. Copying is prohibited.

CONCEPTS AND SKILLS

- Attributes of prisms
- Differentiating cubes from rectangular prisms

MATH TALK

Model the correct use of these terms and encourage students to use them as they work.

- **congruent** having exactly the same shape and size
- **cube** a solid with 6 square faces
- **face** a flat shape that is one of the sides of a solid figure
- **prism** a solid figure with 2 identical parallel bases and also faces that are parallelograms

SUPPORT PROBLEM 2

Read the problem aloud, and then have a volunteer read the problem again.

- *What is the story about?* (looking at a cereal box and a cube)
- *What is the math about?* (congruent faces of a rectangular prism and cube)
- *What does congruent mean?* (same size and shape)
- *Where do you think we should start?* (Answers will vary.)
- *Are there any answers you can rule out?* (sphere) *Why?* (because a cereal box is not round like a ball)

REACHING ALL LEARNERS

You might use a cereal box and a cube to compare and contrast the two solids.

Math at Hand

- Solid Figures, 382
- Prisms, 383

NEWSLETTER

This Newsletter is designed to be sent home with students at the end of the week along with the completed *Decimal Kit* Concept Builder materials.

The first page suggests a simple way for students to share with their parent or guardian basic math skills they have been practicing in class.

NEWSLETTER

Summer Success: Math

Another fantastic week in summer school! Your child has worked hard and reviewed a lot of math topics.

Earlier in the week, your child graphed ordered pairs on a coordinate grid. Here is an activity to encourage your child to share with you what they've learned in summer school.

- What do you call the paired numbers on the graph? (ordered pairs)
- What is special about these numbers? (you can locate them on the grid)
- Look at (4, 7). How do you locate the first number? (start at the bottom of the grid, go 4 spaces across) The second number? (from the 4th place on the bottom, go up the grid 7 spaces)
- Are (6, 2) and (2, 6) the same? (no) Tell how you know. (They are in different locations on the grid.)

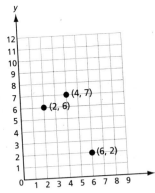

On the back of this page are directions for using the project called *Decimal Kit* that your child built this week. Invite your child to share this fun activity with you.

 Enjoy the time with your child, and thank you for helping to strengthen the mathematical tie between home and school.

© Great Source. Permission is granted to copy this page.

© Great Source. Copying is prohibited.

NEWSLETTER

Sharpen Decimal Skills with Decimal Kit

We have been working on writing, comparing, and computing with decimals this week. Play *Decimal Kit* with your child to practice adding hundredths.

1. The object of the game is to be the first player to collect 1 whole using hundredths and tenths.

2. You will need to make a Place-Value Mat like your child's.

3. Shuffle the 1–9 Digit Cards and place them facedown on the table.

4. Player 1 draws two cards, adds the numbers, and collects that many hundredths squares or combinations of tenth strips and hundredths squares. The pieces are placed in the correct places on the Place-Value Mat.

5. Player 2 follows the same steps. Throughout the game, hundredths squares are traded for tenth strips whenever possible.

6. Before each turn, players must state the total value of the pieces displayed on their Place-Value Mats. Then they must say how much more is needed to make one whole.

7. The player who is first to collect 10 tenth strips (1 whole) is the winner.

Tenths	Hundredths

You can make a variation of this game by using pennies and dimes, making the object of the game to be the first player to collect 1 dollar.

 Enjoy exploring decimals using the *Decimal Kit* with your child. Continue to look for opportunities to use math with your child as you go about your daily activities. Thank you again for your participation in these home math activities.

© Great Source. Permission is granted to copy this page.

The back side of this week's Newsletter includes instructions for the parent or guardian to help their student demonstrate the *Decimal Kit* Concept Builder activity at home.

© Great Source. Copying is prohibited.

Materials Read across to find materials needed for this week's daily activities.

*Optional materials

Game 1 sheet each of 0–9 Digit Cards, paper, pencil
Data Study straightedge or ruler*

Game 0–9 Digit Cards, paper, pencil
Data Study straightedge or ruler*

NUMBER NAMES *Instruction: 20–30 min*

Number Fractions, Equivalent fractions and decimals, Order fractions
Operations Compute with fractions
Patterns and Algebra Numeric patterns, Prediction, Write a rule, Order of Operations
Geometry Solids, Nets
Measurement Area, Time, Customary capacity and length, Circumference
Vocabulary Geometry terms

Number Names p. 50C
Today's Number: $\frac{1}{2}$
Fractions
Add fractions
Fraction patterns
Solid figures
Area
geometry

Number Names p. 56A
Today's Number: $\frac{1}{4}$
Equivalent fractions and decimals
Subtract fractions
Predict a number
Pyramids and cones
Time
solid figures

PRACTICE *Written Practice: 20–30 min*

Number and Operations Fraction concepts, Compute with fractions, Use symbols, Fractions on number lines
Patterns and Algebra Number patterns and rules
Geometry Solids, Nets
Measurement Area of rectangle, triangle, Fractions and time
Review Function table, equations, Solid figures, Area of rectangle, triangle, Modeling fractions
Problem Solving Strategies and skills

Practice p. 51

Fraction concepts
Compute with $\frac{1}{2}$
Area of rectangle, triangle
Function table, equations
Guess, Check, and Revise
Make a Table
Make an Organized list
Use Logical Reasoning

Practice p. 57

Use =, <, or >
Compute with $\frac{1}{4}$
Fractions and time
Solid figures
Make a Table
Make an Organized list
Write an Equation
Check for Reasonableness

GAME *Active Practice: 20–30 min*

Estimate quotients, Whole number division, Remainders, Compare mixed numbers, Factors and products, Multiplication and division facts

Game p. 53

Division Estimation
Estimate quotients
Whole number division
Remainders
Compare mixed numbers

Game p. 53

Division Estimation
Estimate quotients
Whole number division
Remainders
Compare mixed numbers

FOCUS *Additional Support: 20–30 min*

Use a table, Make a line graph, Data Metric units in decimal or fraction form Multiplication, Volume concept, Elapsed time, Compute with units of time

Data Study p. 55

Making a Line Graph
Use a table
Make a line graph
Compare and summarize data

Data Study p. 55

Making a Line Graph
Use a table
Make a line graph
Compare and summarize data

© Great Source. Copying is prohibited.

PLANNER

Game 1–6 and 4–9 number cubes, paper, pencil
Concept Builder Centimeter Strip, scissors, tape or glue, crayons or markers, adding machine tape

Game 1–6 and 4–9 number cubes, paper, pencil
Concept Builder materials previously prepared

Game see Tuesday and Thursday
Newsletter SE p. 71 (Send home with the Concept Builder materials.)

Number Names p. 58A

Today's Number: $\frac{3}{4}$
Equivalent fractions and decimals
Compute with $\frac{3}{4}$
Write a rule
Prisms
Customary capacity
prism

Number Names p. 64A

Today's Number: $\frac{1}{3}$
Equivalent fractions
Compute with $\frac{1}{3}$
Write a rule
Geometric nets
Circumference
net

Number Names p. 66A

Today's Number: Review
Order fractions
Compute with fractions
Order of Operations
Solids and nets
Customary length
Vocabulary review

Practice p. 59

Use pictorial fraction models
Compute with $\frac{3}{4}$
Numeric patterns and rules
Area of rectangle, triangle
Make a Table
Make an Organized List
Write an Equation
Solve in More Than One Way

Practice p. 65

Fractions on a number line
Compute with $\frac{1}{3}$
Geometric nets and solids
Modeling fractions
Make a Model
Make a Diagram
Write an Equation
Use Logical Reasoning

Practice p. 67

Order fractions
Fractions on a number line
Compute with fractions
Geometric nets and solids
Look for a Pattern
Make a Diagram
Write an Equation
Take Notes

Game p. 61

Factor Frenzy
Factors and products
Multiplication and division facts

Game p. 61

Factor Frenzy
Factors and products
Multiplication and division facts

Game pp. 53 and 61

Choice
Division Estimation or variation
Factor Frenzy or variation

Concept Builder p. 63

Make & Take:
Meter Measuring
Metric units
Relate centimeter to meter in decimal or fraction form

Concept Builder p. 63

Make & Take:
Meter Measuring
Metric units
Relate centimeter to meter in decimal or fraction form

Read and Reason p. 69

Multiplication
Volume concept
Elapsed time
Compute with units of time

© Great Source. Copying is prohibited.

NUMBER NAMES TODAY'S NUMBER $\frac{1}{2}$

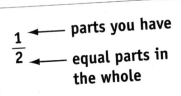

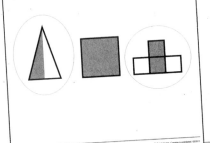

NUMBER Fractions

✎ *A fraction is a number that tells how many equal parts something has been divided into, and how many of those parts you are looking at.*

- *What does $\frac{1}{2}$ tell you?* (one part of 2 equal parts)

✎ *Circle the diagrams that show $\frac{1}{2}$. Describe the equal part of each diagram you circle.* (sample answers: the triangle is split in two equal parts; 2 shaded squares out of 4 is equal to $\frac{1}{2}$ of the 4 squares)

Math at Hand 028–029

$\frac{1}{2} + \frac{1}{2} + \frac{1}{2} =$ _____ $\frac{3}{2}$

$\frac{3}{2}$ __>__ 1 whole

$\frac{3}{2}$ __<__ 2 wholes

OPERATIONS Add fractions

✎ **Problem Solving** *A recipe calls for $\frac{1}{2}$ cup of brown sugar, $\frac{1}{2}$ cup of white sugar, and $\frac{1}{2}$ of powdered sugar. How many cups of sugar is that?* ($\frac{3}{2}$)

✎ *Tell how you know the total amount of sugar is more than 1 whole cup?* (sample answer: I know two $\frac{1}{2}$ cups make 1 whole cup)

✎ *Is the total amount of sugar more than 2 whole cups?* (no) *Tell how you know.* (sample answer: you need one more $\frac{1}{2}$ cup to make 2 cups)

Math at Hand 157–159

$5, 5\frac{1}{2}, 6, 6\frac{1}{2}, 7, 7\frac{1}{2},$

_8_ , _$8\frac{1}{2}$_ , _9_

Rule: Add $\frac{1}{2}$ to the term before.

PATTERNS AND ALGEBRA Fraction pattern

- *What pattern do you see?* (sample answer: whole number, fraction, whole number, fraction and so on)

- *Can you tell how the numbers change starting with 5?* (sample answer: each number after 5 is $\frac{1}{2}$ more than the one before)

✎ *What are the next three terms in the pattern?* ($8, 8\frac{1}{2}, 9$)

✎ *How would you write a rule that describes the pattern?* (sample answer: add $\frac{1}{2}$ to the term before)

Math at Hand 401

KEY ✎ = record on pad

© Great Source. Copying is prohibited.

GEOMETRY Solid figures

- *How are the figures on the left side different from those on the right side?* (3-dimensional, or solid, figures are on the left and 2-dimensional flat plane figures are on the right)

✎ *Solid figures have 3-dimensions. Can you describe or name the dimensions?* (length, width, height)

- *What are some differences between solid and plane figures?* (sample answers: some solids roll, plane figures don't; solids have volume, plane figures don't)

REACHING ALL LEARNERS Use cardstock solids or familiar objects such as tissue boxes, soup cans, cereal boxes to show the 3-dimensions.

Math at Hand 382

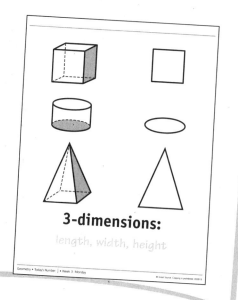

3-dimensions:
length, width, height

Geometry • Today's Number • Week 3: Monday

MEASUREMENT Area

✎ *Area is the number of square units needed to cover a shape. Tell how you would find the area of the rectangle.* (count the number of units in the shape) *Is there a shortcut?* (number of units in one row times the number of rows) *What is the area?* ($5 \times 10 = 50$; 50 square units)

✎ **Problem Solving** *Suppose you want to find the area of a triangle. The shape measures 10 units wide and 5 units tall. How would you find the area?* (sample answer: since the triangle is half the rectangle, divide the area of the rectangle in half) *What is the area?* (25 square units)

Math at Hand 299, 303

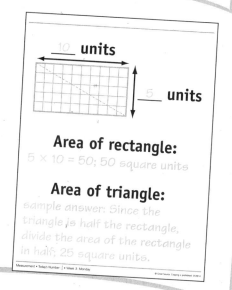

10 units

5 units

Area of rectangle:
$5 \times 10 = 50$; 50 square units

Area of triangle:
sample answer: Since the triangle is half the rectangle, divide the area of the rectangle in half; 25 square units.

Measurement • Today's Number • Week 3: Monday

VOCABULARY *geometry*

- *When do we use geometry in real life?* (sample answer: when we give directions, draw pictures, or build something)

- *What kinds of words do we use to describe or talk about geometric ideas?* (sample answer: *straight, curved, turn, round, line, parallel, intersect, solid, flat*)

- *What is* geometry? (The study of shapes, solids, position, and direction.)

Math at Hand 333, 524

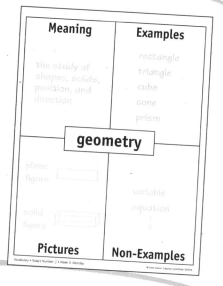

Meaning	Examples
the study of shapes, solids, position, and direction	rectangle triangle cube cone prism

geometry

plane figure	
solid figure	variable equation

| Pictures | Non-Examples |

Vocabulary • Today's Number • Week 3: Monday

© Great Source. Copying is prohibited.

PRACTICE

Written Practice

CONCEPTS AND SKILLS

- Fraction concepts
- Compute with $\frac{1}{2}$
- Area of rectangle and triangle
- Review function table and equations
- Problem Solving Strategies and Skills: *Guess, Check, and Revise, Make a Table, Make an Organized List; Use Logical Reasoning*

PREVIEW THE PRACTICE

- *What do the two numbers in a fraction tell us?* (sample answer: the top shows the parts you have, the bottom shows how many parts in the whole)

SUPPORT THE PRACTICE

- Problems 1–4 ask students to select the model for $\frac{1}{2}$. Remind students that fractions can represent part of a whole or part of a set.
- Problems 5–8 work on fraction computation and number sense. Revisit today's Operations recording pad, if needed.
- Problems 9–10 focus on area of rectangle and triangle. Students recognize the area of a triangle is one-half of a related rectangle.
- Problems 11–12 review function table and writing an equation to describe the pattern. Help students identify the pattern by focusing on smaller numbers.

PRACTICE TODAY'S NUMBER $\frac{1}{2}$

Name _____

NUMBER AND OPERATIONS

Circle the diagram that shows $\frac{1}{2}$. ◄1–4. MAH 028–029

1.   2.

3.   4.

Write *true* or *false*. ◄5–8. MAH 157–159

5. $\frac{1}{2} + \frac{1}{2} + \frac{1}{2} = 1$ ___false___   6. $\frac{1}{2} + \frac{1}{2} + \frac{1}{2} + \frac{1}{2} = 2$ ___true___

7. $\frac{1}{2} + \frac{1}{2} > 1$ ___false___   8. $\frac{1}{2} + \frac{1}{2} + \frac{1}{2} < 2$ ___true___

MEASUREMENT

Compute the area of the shaded figures. ◄9–10. MAH 299, 303

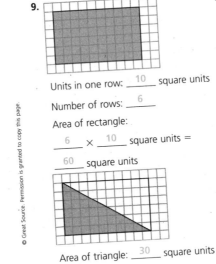
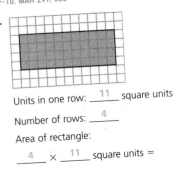
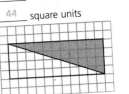

9.

Units in one row: __10__ square units

Number of rows: __6__

Area of rectangle:

__6__ × __10__ square units =

__60__ square units

Area of triangle: __30__ square units

10.

Units in one row: __11__ square units

Number of rows: __4__

Area of rectangle:

__4__ × __11__ square units =

__44__ square units

Area of triangle: __22__ square units

© Great Source. Permission is granted to copy this page.

SUMMER SUCCESS: MATH   **51**   MAH: *Math at Hand*

REACHING ALL LEARNERS

Use different examples to show that fractions can name part of one thing or part of a collection. *Is half a watermelon, part of one thing or part of a collection?* (one thing) *Is half a dozen eggs part of one thing or part of a collection?* (collection)

Math at Hand

If students need help, encourage them to refer to the MAH items shown on the student page.

© Great Source. Copying is prohibited.

Complete the table. Write an equation to describe the pattern. ◄11–12. MAH 241

11.

Hours Worked	Amount Paid
3 hours	$15
5 hours	$25
2 hours	$10
6 hours	$30

Equation: _Hours Worked × $5 = Amount Paid_

12.

Number of Tricycles	Number of Wheels
10	30
2	6
3	9
5	15

Equation: _Tricycles × 3 = No. Wheels_

PROBLEM SOLVING · **UNDERSTAND** · **PLAN** · **TRY** · **LOOK BACK**

Complete each step. ◄13. MAH 396

13. Dione is exploring probability with a number cube that has only 1s and 2s marked on the faces. He rolls the cube 10 times. Dione records a total score of 17 points. He rolls more 2s than 1s. How many 1s and how many 2s does Dione roll?

POSSIBLE STRATEGIES

- Guess, Check, and Revise
- Make a Table
- Make an Organized List

a. Underline the question you need to answer.

b. Loop the details about the number cubes.

c. Mark the strategy/strategies you will use.

d. Solve the problem. Explain your thinking.

_____

_____

_____

_____

sample strategy:
Make an Organized List

roll 1	2
roll 2	2
roll 3	2
roll 4	2
roll 5	2
roll 6	2
roll 7	2
roll 8	1
roll 9	1
roll 10	+ 1
total score	17

e. Answer the question.

He rolls three 1s and seven 2s.

© Great Source. Permission is granted to copy this page.

SUMMER SUCCESS: MATH **52** MAH: *Math at Hand*

© Great Source. Copying is prohibited.

REACHING ALL LEARNERS

Encourage students to make guesses. Then, model how to check the guesses to see if they fulfill all of the conditions outlined in the problem.

PROBLEM SOLVING

Work in small groups of 3 or 4 students.

- Encourage students to find ways to identify needed information to solve the problem.
- *What information do you need to answer the question?* (the number of times Dione rolls the number cube, Dione's score, the digits on the number cubes)
- *Is it important to know that Dione rolls more 2s than 1s?* (yes) *Why?* (it tells me the number of 2s needs to be greater than 1s)
- *How can you use the information?* (to guess, check, and revise, to make a table, to make an organized list)

SCORING

- **a.** Last sentence underlined: 1 pt
- **b.** Number cube details circled: 1 pt
- **c.** Choose and apply an appropriate strategy: 1 pt
- **d.** Explanation of solution: 1 pt
- **e.** Correct answer: 1 pt

GLOSSARY TO GO

Today's Vocabulary *geometry*

Have students complete an entry for today's vocabulary term in their Glossaries. Encourage students to use both words and drawings.

MATH JOURNAL

- *What is the difference between finding the perimeter and the area of a shape?* (sample answer: perimeter is the distance around the outside of a shape, area is the space inside a shape)

GAME

CONCEPTS AND SKILLS

- Estimate quotients
- Whole number division
- Write remainders as fractions
- Compare mixed numbers

MATH TALK

Model the correct use of these words and encourage students to use them as they work.

- **dividend** a quantity to be divided
- **divisor** the quantity by which another quantity is to be divided
- **quotient** the result of division
- **remainder** in whole number division, the amount left over that cannot be divided evenly by the divisor

MATERIALS

For each pair: two sets of 0–9 Digit Cards, paper, pencils

GAME

Division Estimation

Object: To create a division problem with a quotient as close to 25 as possible (either greater than 25 or less than 25).

> I know 3 times 25 equals 75. So the 3, 5, 8 cards will work best.

MATERIALS

Two sets of 0–9 Digit Cards, paper, pencils

DIRECTIONS

1. Make a recording sheet like this one.
2. This game is for groups of 2 to 4 players.
3. Shuffle the digit cards and place them face down in a draw pile.
4. Draw 4 cards, but only use 3 of the cards to create your division problem.
5. To create a division problem with a quotient as close to 25 as possible, use mental math and estimation to think of the best 3 digit cards to use. Then, throw out the digit card that seems least helpful. Before you can discard, explain why **(I know 3 times 25 equals 75. So the 3, 5, 8 cards will work best.)**
6. Write your division problem and its quotient on the recording sheet. Write any remainder as a fraction.
7. Compare the quotients. Circle on the recording sheet the quotient that is closest to 25.
8. After five rounds, the player with most quotients circled wins.

© Great Source. Permission is granted to copy this page.

Division Estimation

Name			
	Digit Cards Chosen	Division Problem	Quotient
Example:	5, 3, 8	$\begin{array}{r} 28\,R1 \\ 3\overline{)85} \\ -60 \\ \hline 25 \\ -24 \\ \hline 1 \end{array}$	$28\frac{1}{3}$
Round 1			
Round 2			

REACHING ALL LEARNERS

Simplify Ask students to create a 2-digit by 1-digit division problem with a quotient as close to 10 as possible.

Variation Change the focus to multiplication to create a multiplication problem that will yield a product as close to 500 as possible.

Math at Hand

- Estimate Quotients, 113–114
- Dividing with Whole Numbers, 146–148
- Ordering Fractions and Mixed Numbers, 042

© Great Source. Copying is prohibited.

Day 1

- Review the words used to discuss division: dividend, divisor, quotient, and remainder. Write a problem with a remainder on the chalkboard and label each of the components of the division.

- Invite students to show how they would estimate the answer to a division problem. *What are some ways to estimate?* (sample answers: you can round up or down; you can use front-end)

- Demonstrate with a student volunteer. Take turns to show how to play the game and how to keep score.

- Model writing a division problem, and how to find the answer.

Day 2

- Review the directions for playing the game.
- Assign partners to play the game.

Encourage students to ask themselves:

- *What estimation strategy can I use to get a quotient close to 25?* (One strategy I can use is to pick the divisor card, then estimate what is 20 times that number. Then see whether the remaining number cards can be grouped to make a 2-digit number close to that product.)

- *Which combinations of digits make it difficult for me to get a quotient of 25?* (If I get all high digits or all low digits, it is difficult to get a quotient of 25.)

Teacher: I got the digits 0, 8, 5, and 3. Which cards should I use?

Student: You should first multiply each number by 20.

T: Great. Get a ballpark figure first.

S: That way you'll know which 3 cards to keep.

S: You can even do the math in your head.

T: Show me how.

S: Okay. So, I figure 5 times 20. That's 100. I don't have the cards to make 100, so I go on.

S: 8 times 20 is 160. No good.

S: 3 times 20 is 60. Yes! You can use the 5 and 8 to make 85. And, throw out the 0 card.

S: Why didn't you keep the 0 card? Isn't 70 closer to 60?

S: Yes, but you want the answer to be as close to 25 as possible, so use the bigger number.

T: Terrific! Now let's see what you get. 85 divided by 3 equals 28 with a remainder 1.

S: Yes!

If students need more help, use the hints below, or refer to the *Math at Hand* items shown to the left.

- **Do students estimate successfully?** Ask students to explain how to round a number to a specific place value. Or, how to estimate using the front-end method.

- **Do students know how to set up a division problem?** Have students talk to you about how to set up a division problem.

- **Can students name the parts of a division problem?** Ask students to point to the different parts of the division problem.

© Great Source. Copying is prohibited.

DATA STUDY

Additional Support

CONCEPTS AND SKILLS

- Use a table
- Make a line graph
- Compare and summarize data

MATH TALK

- **decrease** to go down
- **increase** to go up
- **line graph** a graph that shows changes over time

MATERIALS

straightedges or rulers*
*Optional materials

GET STARTED

- Read and discuss the directions on page 55 with students.
- Assign partners to work together.

DATA STUDY

Name _____

Making a Line Graph

Which day was the warmest?

READ THE TABLE

Temperatures for 5 Days in January

Day of the Week	Lowest Temperature (°F)	Highest Temperature (°F)
Monday	24	37
Tuesday	28	34
Wednesday	20	28
Thursday	26	37
Friday	32	39

GRAPH THE DATA

- Choose whether you want to make a graph of the lowest or highest daily temperatures. Title your graph.
- Look at the data to determine the scale for your graph. Start at 0. Label the axes.
- Graph the data. Make sure you read the correct column of data in the table.

ANALYZE THE DATA

1. Which day of the week had the highest temperature? ___Friday___
   Lowest temperature? ___Wednesday___

2. Which days of the week had the same high temperature? ___Monday, Thursday___

3. What is the range and mean for the set of highest temperatures? Lowest temperatures? ___range: 39°F − 28°F = 11°F, mean: 175°F ÷ 5 = 35°F; range: 32°F − 20°F = 12°F, mean: 130°F ÷ 5 = 26°F___

4. Between which two days was there the greatest increase for the set of highest temperatures? ___28°F on Wednesday to 37°F on Thursday; no other pairs of consecutive days had a greater difference in temperatures for an increase.___

5. Write two comparison statements about the data in the graph. Use the word decrease in one of the statements. ___Answers will vary.___

© Great Source. Permission is granted to copy this page.

REACHING ALL LEARNERS

- Make sure students can read a table. Ask them about some data in a row or column.
- Review comparing whole numbers as needed.
- Review the different parts of a line graph.

Math at Hand

- Data in Tables, 267
- Making Graphs, 269
- Labeling the Axes, 270
- Choosing the Scales, 270
- Graphs That Show Change Over Time, 277–279

© Great Source. Copying is prohibited.

Day 1

READ THE TABLE

You may wish to talk briefly with students about temperature using a Fahrenheit scale. Here are some benchmarks: Water freezes at 32°F, room temperature is about 70°F, a very hot day is about 95°F, and water boils at 212°F.

GRAPH THE DATA

Work with students as needed to help them create an accurate graph of the data. Since a line graph shows how data change over time, one axis will represent time.

Discuss how to choose an appropriate scale for degrees Fahrenheit for the other axis. Also discuss how to locate points on the graph and connect them.

Allow students to use straightedges or rulers to draw their line segments between points as straight as possible. Remind them to check the points on their graphs to make sure they correspond to the temperatures listed in only one of the columns in the table.

Day 2

ANALYZE THE DATA

Help students answer any of the questions at the bottom of student page 55. Before discussing the answers to the questions, invite students to share their line graphs with the class. Encourage them to talk about which set of data they graphed and the scale they used. Then have them consider the following questions:

- *How do your graphs compare?* (The graph using a scale of 4s looks flatter than the graph using a scale of 2s.)

- *Which graph shows the increases or decreases in temperature a little more distinctly?* (The graph whose scale increases by 2s.)

- **What if?** *Suppose you wanted to compare highest and lowest temperatures at the same time using a graph. What would you do?* (Graph both sets of data on the same grid using 2 different lines.) *How would anyone reading your graph be able to tell the lines apart?* (Use a different color for each line and make a key at the bottom of the graph.)

- *Using a double-line graph, would it be possible to tell whether some of the highest temperatures are lower than some of the lowest temperatures during the week?* (You could see the high and low points for each set of data on the same graph.)

© Great Source. Copying is prohibited.

READ THE TABLE

Teacher: Look at the table. What information do you see?

Student: The high and low temperatures for 5 days in January.

T: What are some highs?

S: 39 degrees on Friday.

S: 34 degrees on Tuesday.

T: How about a low temperature?

S: 20 degrees on Wednesday.

GRAPH THE DATA

T: Look at the data in the table. What are the time units?

S: The days of a school week.

T: Now look at the grid. Where might you indicate the days of the week?

S: I can write M, T, W, Th, and F for each day. And, use a label like *Days of the Week* along the bottom of the graph.

Sample graph:

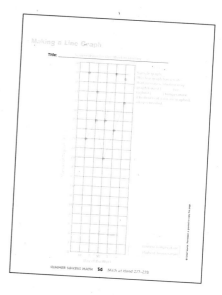

NUMBER NAMES TODAY'S NUMBER $\frac{1}{4}$

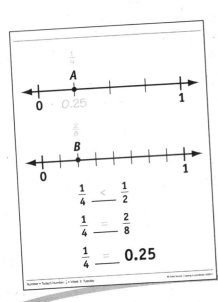

NUMBER Equivalent fractions and decimals

✎ *The top number line has 4 equal parts between 0 and 1. How would you use a fraction to label Point A?* $(\frac{1}{4})$ *A decimal?* (0.25)

✎ *The second number line has 8 equal parts between 0 and 1. How would you label Point B?* $(\frac{2}{8})$ *What is special about* $\frac{1}{4}, \frac{2}{8},$ *and 0.25?* (They're equal.)

✎ *How do you know* $\frac{1}{4}$ *is less than* $\frac{1}{2}$*?* (sample answer: If you cut something into 4 equal parts, each part is smaller than if you cut it into 2 equal parts.) Complete the comparisons.

Math at Hand 031, 035

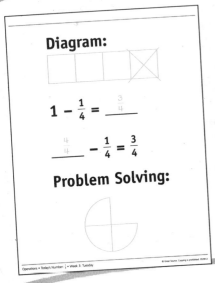

OPERATIONS Subtract fractions

• *If you have 1 whole and you subtract* $\frac{1}{4}$*, will the difference be greater than or less than 1?* (less than)

✎ *Draw a diagram to show* $1 - \frac{1}{4}$*.* (see recording pad for sample diagram) *What is 1 whole minus* $\frac{1}{4}$*?* $(\frac{3}{4})$

✎ **Problem Solving** *The pizza is cut into 4 slices. You eat one slice for snack. How many quarters are left?* (3)

REACHING ALL LEARNERS Use a diagram to help students see that each slice is one quarter of the whole. Ask students to recall when they had to cut something into 4 equal pieces and describe how they did it.

Math at Hand 163–164

PATTERNS AND ALGEBRA Predict a number

	Left	Right
1st term:	$1\frac{1}{4}$	2
2nd term:	$2\frac{1}{4}$	3
3rd term:	$3\frac{1}{4}$	4
4th term:	$4\frac{1}{4}$	5
10th term:	$10\frac{1}{4}$	11
20th term:	$20\frac{1}{4}$	21

• *What do you see in the table?* (sample answer: columns of numbers, fractions, and whole numbers)

• *How do the numbers change from Left to Right?* (the Right side lists the next greater whole number) *From top to bottom?* (increase by 1 whole)

• *Can you predict the 10th term in the table?* $(10\frac{1}{4}, 11)$ *The 20th term?* $(20\frac{1}{4}, 21)$

REACHING ALL LEARNERS Help students recognize that in the Left column, the term number is the whole number part of the fraction. So, any term is that number and $\frac{1}{4}$.

Math at Hand 401

© Great Source. Copying is prohibited.

KEY ✎ = record on pad

© Great Source. Copying is prohibited.

GEOMETRY Pyramids and cones

✎ *How are these solids alike?* (sample answers: they both come to a point or vertex; they can stand) *How are they different?* (sample answers: one solid has a round bottom, the other has a rectangle; one has a curved side, one has flat faces)

✎ *A pyramid has a base and a face for each edge of the base. Loop the pyramid. How many faces do you see?* (5)

• *What type of base does a cone have?* (a circle)

REACHING ALL LEARNERS Some students might say that a pyramid can have a square or a rectangular base. Use the solids in the kit. Let students count the sides, faces, corners (vertices).

Math at Hand 382, 386, 390

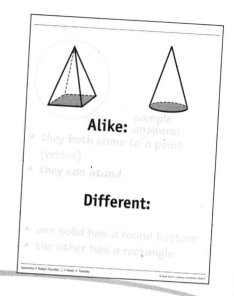

MEASUREMENT Time

✎ *What is another way to describe $\frac{1}{4}$-hour?* (15 minutes) *How many quarter hours are in 1 hour?* (4)

• *How can you use mental math to add 15 minutes to 11:30?* (sample answer: I can skip count by 5s from 11:30)

✎ **Problem Solving** *The park is $\frac{1}{4}$ hour away by bus. If you get on the bus at 11:30 A.M., will you arrive by noon?* (yes) *How can you show the time on the clock face?* (see recording pad)

REACHING ALL LEARNERS Use a clock face to show the start and end times. Count aloud the 5-minute increments from 11:30.

Math at Hand 322

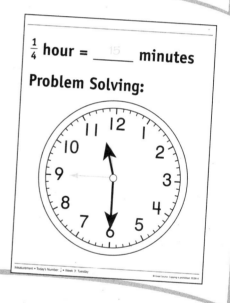

VOCABULARY solid figures

• *What does* solid *mean in geometry?* (3-dimensional)

• *Name some solid figures in the classroom.* (sample answers: tissue box, trash can, globe)

• *How are all solid figures alike?* (sample answers: they have length, width, and height; you can pick them up; you can stack some, roll others, or do both)

• *Is a square a solid figure?* (no) *Tell why.* (sample answers: it is a polygon or plane figure; it has only 2 dimensions—length and width)

Math at Hand 382, 534

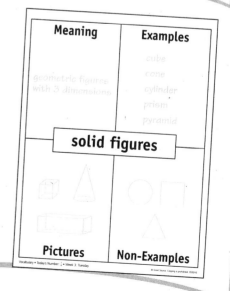

PRACTICE

Written Practice

CONCEPTS AND SKILLS

- Use = , < , or >
- Work with $\frac{1}{4}$
- Work $\frac{1}{4}$ hour
- Review solid figures
- Problem Solving Strategies and Skills: *Make a Table, Make an Organized List, Write an Equation; Check for Reasonableness*

PREVIEW THE PRACTICE

- *How many fourths make 1 whole?* (4) Draw a rectangle. Divide it into fourths. Invite a student to shade and label $\frac{1}{4}$.

SUPPORT THE PRACTICE

- Problems 1–6 compare numbers. Point out that the number line is divided into fourths between 0 and 1.

- Problems 7–9 work with the subtraction sentence $1 - \frac{1}{4} = \frac{3}{4}$. Students fill in the blank for the missing number/fraction. Some students might need to read aloud, using *what number* for the blank.

- Problems 10–12 work with elapsed time. Students can use the clock face to help them compute.

- Problems 13–15 review diagrams of plane and solid figures. Revisit Monday's Geometry recording pad, if needed.

PRACTICE TODAY'S NUMBER $\frac{1}{4}$

Name _____

NUMBER AND OPERATIONS

Use the number line to help you compare. Write =, <, or >. ◄1–6. MAH 031, 035

1. $\frac{1}{4}$ __=__ 0.25

2. $\frac{1}{4}$ __<__ 1

3. $\frac{1}{4}$ __>__ 0

4. $\frac{1}{4}$ __=__ $\frac{2}{8}$

5. $\frac{1}{4}$ __<__ 0.50

6. $\frac{2}{8}$ __=__ 0.25

Fill in the blank. ◄7–9. MAH 163–164

7. $1 - \frac{1}{4} = $ _____ $\frac{3}{4}$

8. $1 - $ _____ $ = \frac{3}{4}$

9. _____ $- \frac{1}{4} = \frac{3}{4}$

MEASUREMENT

What is $\frac{1}{4}$-hour from the start time? Use the clock face, if needed. ◄10–12. MAH 322

10. Start: 10:00

    End: _____ 10:15 _____

11. Start: 2:15

    End: _____ 2:30 _____

12. Start: 6:20

    End: _____ 6:35 _____

REVIEW

Loop *solid* or *not solid*. ◄13–15. MAH 382

13. *solid* (*not solid*)

14. (*solid*) *not solid*

15. (*solid*) *not solid*

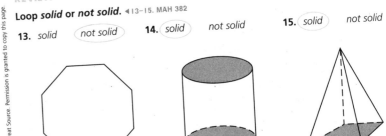

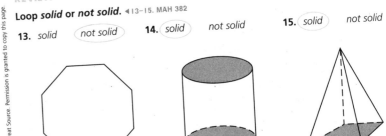

SUMMER SUCCESS: MATH **57** MAH: *Math at Hand*

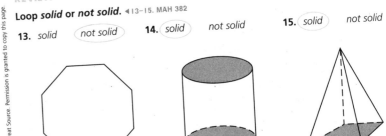© Great Source. Permission is granted to copy this page.

REACHING ALL LEARNERS

Help students recall that $\frac{1}{4}$ and $\frac{2}{8}$ name the same point on the number line. Show a number line divided into fourths. Then divide that line again into eighths. The total length of the line has not changed, just the number of equal parts between 0 and 1.

Math at Hand

If students need help, encourage them to refer to the MAH items shown on the student page.

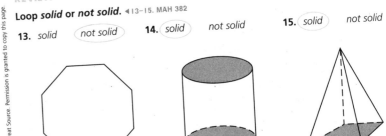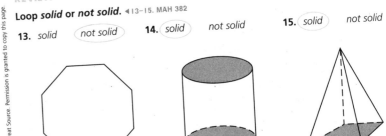© Great Source. Copying is prohibited.

 © Great Source. Copying is prohibited.

Complete each step. ◄16. MAH 396

16. Lynette works the night shift at the hospital. Her shift begins at 7:30 P.M. and ends at 3:45 A.M. When Lynette gets home, she sleeps from 5:00 A.M. until noon. Does Lynette spend more time working or sleeping? How much more time?

    a. Underline the questions you need to answer.

    b. Loop the details involving time.

    c. Mark the strategy/strategies you will use.

    d. Solve the problem. Explain your thinking.

    7:30 P.M. to 3:45 A.M. is $8\frac{1}{4}$ hours

    5:00 A.M. until noon is 7 hours

    _____

    _____

    _____

    _____

    _____

    _____

    _____

    _____

    _____

    _____

    e. Answer the question.

    Lynette spends $1\frac{1}{4}$ hours more working than sleeping.

    _____

    _____

POSSIBLE STRATEGIES

- Make a Table
- Make an Organized List
- Write an Equation

sample strategy:
Make an Organized List

© Great Source. Permission is granted to copy this page.

PROBLEM SOLVING

Work in small groups of 3 or 4 students.

- Encourage students to find ways to identify needed information to solve the problem.

- *What information do you need to answer the question?* (the beginning and ending times Lynette works and sleeps)

- *How can you use the information?* (to write an equation, to make a table, to make an organized list)

SCORING

a. Last sentence underlined: 1 pt

b. Starting and ending times circled: 1 pt

c. Choose and apply an appropriate strategy: 1 pt

d. Explanation of solution: 1 pt

e. Correct answer: 1 pt

GLOSSARY TO GO

Today's Vocabulary *solid figures*

Have students complete an entry for today's vocabulary term in their Glossaries. Encourage students to use both words and drawings.

MATH JOURNAL

- *Explain what you have learned about elapsed time.* (Be sure students mention working with a start and an end time. The time elapsed can be minutes, hours, days, and so on.)

REACHING ALL LEARNERS

If students have difficulty with the problem, guide them through verbally. Find the elapsed time by counting forward by the hour or half hour from the start time to the end time.

© Great Source. Copying is prohibited.

NUMBER NAMES TODAY'S NUMBER $\frac{3}{4}$

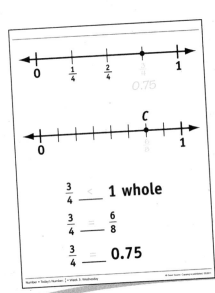

$\frac{3}{4}$ ___<___ 1 whole

$\frac{3}{4}$ ___=___ $\frac{6}{8}$

$\frac{3}{4}$ ___=___ 0.75

NUMBER **Equivalent fractions and decimals**

✎ *Halfway between 0 and $\frac{2}{4}$ is $\frac{1}{4}$. What is halfway between $\frac{2}{4}$ and 1 whole?* $(\frac{3}{4})$ Invite a volunteer to plot $\frac{3}{4}$ on the number line.

✎ *How do you write $\frac{3}{4}$ as a decimal?* (0.75)

✎ *The second number line is divided into 8 equal parts. How would you label Point C?* $(\frac{6}{8})$ Invite a volunteer to plot $\frac{6}{8}$ on the number line.

• *What can you tell about $\frac{3}{4}$, $\frac{6}{8}$, and 0.75?* (They are equal.) Complete the comparisons.

Math at Hand 031, 035

---

1 whole + $\frac{3}{4}$ = ____ $1\frac{3}{4}$

1 whole − $\frac{3}{4}$ = ____ $\frac{1}{4}$

____ $\frac{4}{4}$ − $\frac{3}{4}$ = $\frac{1}{4}$

Problem Solving:

sample answer:

• 4 out of 8 burgers equals $\frac{1}{2}$, and $\frac{3}{4}$ is greater than $\frac{1}{2}$

• $\frac{1}{4}$ of 8 is 2, so $\frac{3}{4}$ must be 2 + 2 + 2, or 6

OPERATIONS **Compute with $\frac{3}{4}$**

✎ *If you add 1 whole and $\frac{3}{4}$, will the sum be greater than or less than 2?* (less than) *What is the sum?* $(1\frac{3}{4})$

✎ *If you have 1 whole and you subtract $\frac{3}{4}$, will the difference be greater than or less than 1?* (less than) *What is the difference?* $(\frac{1}{4})$

✎ **Problem Solving** *There are 8 hamburgers. Suppose $\frac{3}{4}$ have cheese on them, is that 4 burgers?* (no) *How many burgers have cheese?* (6) *How do you know?* (see recording pad)

REACHING ALL LEARNERS Use counters to represent the 8 burgers and the fractional equivalents.

Math at Hand 157, 162

___$10\frac{3}{4}$___, $9\frac{3}{4}$, $8\frac{3}{4}$, ___$7\frac{3}{4}$___, $6\frac{3}{4}$,

$5\frac{3}{4}$, ___$4\frac{3}{4}$___

Rule: sample answer: Subtract 1 whole from the number that comes before.

PATTERNS AND ALGEBRA **Write a rule**

• *What do you see on the recording pad?* (whole numbers and fractions)

• *Starting from the left, would you say the numbers are getting bigger or smaller?* (smaller) *How can you tell?* (the whole numbers are going down from 9 to 5)

✎ *What are the missing terms?* $(10\frac{3}{4}, 7\frac{3}{4}, 4\frac{3}{4})$

✎ *Write a rule to describe the pattern.* (sample answer: subtract 1 whole from the number that comes before)

REACHING ALL LEARNERS Read the numbers aloud. Stress the whole number parts to help students recognize the pattern.

Math at Hand 401

KEY ✎ = record on pad

© Great Source. Copying is prohibited.

GEOMETRY Prisms

✎ *A prism is a solid with 2 sides at opposite ends called bases that are exactly the same and parallel to each other. Loop the prisms on the recording pad.*

✎ *To name a prism, we use the shape of the base. How would you name the prisms on the recording pad?* (see recording pad) Invite volunteers to name the prisms.

• **Problem Solving** *I am a rectangular prism. My faces are all the same size and shape. What am I?* (cube)

REACHING ALL LEARNERS Have cardstock solids available as models.

Math at Hand 382

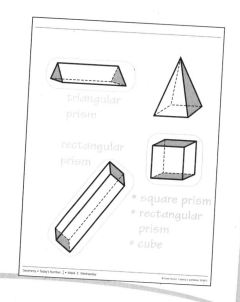

MEASUREMENT Customary capacity

• Capacity *measures how much a container can hold. In the customary system, familiar units are ounces, cups, pints, quarts, and gallons.*

✎ **Problem Solving** *Shawn bought $\frac{3}{4}$ gallon of kerosene for the portable heater. How many quarts is that?* (3)

✎ **Problem Solving** *Carrie mixes $\frac{3}{4}$ gallon of blue paint with yellow paint to make a special green color. How many pints of blue paint is that?* (6) *How many cups?* (12)

Math at Hand 313–314

1 gallon = 4 quarts

$\frac{3}{4}$ gallon = ___3___ quarts

1 gallon = 8 pints

$\frac{3}{4}$ gallon = ___6___ pints

1 gallon = 16 cups

$\frac{3}{4}$ gallon = ___12___ cups

VOCABULARY *prism*

• *What are some prisms we see in our world?* (cereal box, a number cube, a room)

• *What makes a 3 dimensional solid a prism?* (It has 2 identical parallel bases and parallelograms for its other faces.)

• *Why is a pyramid not a prism?* (It does not have 2 identical parallel bases)

Math at Hand 383, 531

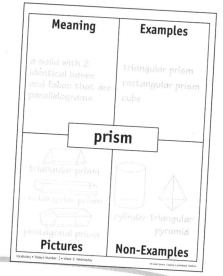

© Great Source. Copying is prohibited.

PRACTICE

Written Practice

CONCEPTS AND SKILLS

- Use pictorial fraction models
- Compute with $\frac{3}{4}$
- Numeric patterns and rules
- Review area of rectangle and triangle
- Problem Solving Strategies and Skills: *Make a Table, Make an Organized List, Write an Equation; Solve in More Than One Way*

PREVIEW THE PRACTICE

- **What would a drawing of $\frac{6}{8}$ look like?** (sample answers: it can be a rectangle with 8 equal sections, and 6 of them shaded; 8 circles, 6 shaded, 2 not shaded) Invite a volunteer to make the drawing.

SUPPORT THE PRACTICE

- Problems 1–3 model the fraction $\frac{3}{4}$. Revisit today's Number recording pad, if needed.
- Problems 4–7 compute with $\frac{3}{4}$. Use a number line to help students visualize the addition and subtraction.
- Problems 8–9 focus on number patterns. Help students articulate simple rules to describe the patterns.
- Problems 10–11 review area of rectangle and triangle. Remind students of the relationship between a triangle and a rectangle.

PRACTICE TODAY'S NUMBER $\frac{3}{4}$

Name _____

NUMBER AND OPERATIONS

Use the pictures to show your answers. ◄1–3. MAH 028–033

1. Draw a loop around $\frac{3}{4}$ of the triangles. Answer can show any 9 triangles looped.

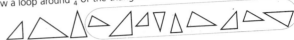

2. Loop the point that shows $\frac{3}{4}$ on the number line.

3. Shade $\frac{3}{4}$ of the clock.

Answer can show any 9 hours shaded.

Add or subtract. ◄4–7. MAH 157, 162

4. $1 + \frac{3}{4} =$ ___ $1\frac{3}{4}$

5. $\frac{4}{4} - \frac{3}{4} =$ ___ $\frac{1}{4}$

6. $\frac{1}{4} + \frac{3}{4} =$ ___ 1

7. $\frac{3}{4} - \frac{1}{4} =$ ___ $\frac{2}{4}$ or $\frac{1}{2}$

PATTERNS AND ALGEBRA

Fill in the blanks and write a rule. ◄8–9. MAH 401

8. $1\frac{3}{4}, 2\frac{3}{4}, 3\frac{3}{4},$ ___ $4\frac{3}{4}$, $5\frac{3}{4},$ ___ $6\frac{3}{4}$, $7\frac{3}{4}$

Rule: sample answer: add 1 whole to the number that comes before

9. $\frac{1}{4}, \frac{2}{4}, \frac{3}{4}, 1,$ ___ $1\frac{1}{4}$, $1\frac{2}{4}, 1\frac{3}{4},$ ___ 2, $2\frac{1}{4}$

Rule: sample answer: add $\frac{1}{4}$ to each fraction that comes before

REVIEW

Compute the area of the shaded figure. ◄10–11. MAH 299, 303

10.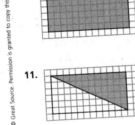

Units in one row: ___ 13 ___ square units

Number of rows: ___ 6 ___

Area of rectangle: ___ 13 ___ sq. units × ___ 6 ___ = ___ 78 ___ sq. units

11.

Units in one row: ___ 12 ___ square units

Number of rows: ___ 6 ___

Area of rectangle: ___ 12 ___ sq. units × ___ 6 ___ = ___ 72 ___ sq. units

Area of triangle: ___ 36 ___ sq. units

© Great Source. Permission is granted to copy this page.

SUMMER SUCCESS: MATH **59** MAH: *Math at Hand*

REACHING ALL LEARNERS

Help students recall that they can use the area of a rectangle to find the area of a triangle. This is because the triangle is half the area of the rectangle.

Math at Hand

If students need help, encourage them to refer to the MAH items shown on the student page.

© Great Source. Copying is prohibited.

Complete each step. ◄ 12. MAH 396

12. Alberta volunteered to label envelopes for a fundraiser. During the first hour she worked, Alberta labeled 38 envelopes. Each hour she worked, Alberta labeled 5 more envelopes than the previous hour. If she worked 4 more hours, what would be the range and mean number of envelopes Alberta labeled?

   a. Underline the question you need to answer.

   b. Loop the details about the envelopes Alberta labeled.

   c. Mark the strategy/strategies you will use.

   d. Solve the problem. Explain your thinking.

   _____

   _____

   _____

   _____

   _____

   _____

   _____

   _____

   _____

   _____

   e. Answer the question.

   The range of envelopes Alberta labeled is 20, and the mean number of envelopes she labeled is 48.

POSSIBLE STRATEGIES

- Make a Table

- Make an Organized List

- Write an Equation

sample strategies:
Make a Table
Write an Equation

Hour	Envelopes Labeled
1	38
2	43
3	48
4	53
5	58

range = 58 − 38 = 20
mean = 240 ÷ 5 = 48

© Great Source. Permission is granted to copy this page.

PROBLEM SOLVING

Work in small groups of 3 or 4 students.

- Encourage students to find ways to identify needed information to solve the problem.

- *What information do you need to answer the question?* (the number of envelopes Alberta labeled each hour that she volunteered)

- *How can you use the information?* (to write an equation, to make a table, to make an organized list)

SCORING

   a. Last sentence underlined: 1 pt

   b. Details about envelopes circled: 1 pt

   c. Choose and apply an appropriate strategy: 1 pt

   d. Explanation of solution: 1 pt

   e. Correct answer: 1 pt

GLOSSARY TO GO

Today's Vocabulary *prism*

Have students complete an entry for today's vocabulary term in their Glossaries. Encourage students to use both words and drawings.

MATH JOURNAL

- *Draw a table to display the ages of the members of your family. How would you figure the mean (average) age of your household?* (Be sure students add the individual ages, and then divide by the number of people.)

REACHING ALL LEARNERS

If students have difficulty with the problem, draw a table on the board with column headings "Hours" and "Envelopes." Encourage students to look up the definitions for *range* and *mean*.

© Great Source. Copying is prohibited.

Active Practice

CONCEPTS AND SKILLS

- Review factors and products
- Review multiplication and division facts

MATH TALK

Model the correct use of these words and encourage students to use them as they work.

- **factor** a whole number that divides evenly into another
- **product** the result of multiplication

MATERIALS

For each pair: One 1–6 number cube, One 4–9 number cube, paper, pencil

Factor Frenzy

Object: To collect as many factor pairs as possible in seven rounds of play.

MATERIALS

One 1–6 number cube, one 4–9 number cube, paper, pencil

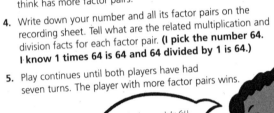

Factor Frenzy			
Name _____			
	Number	Factors	Total Factors
Example:	64	1, 64	
		2, 32	
		4, 16	
		8	7
Round 1			

DIRECTIONS

1. Make a recording sheet like this one.
2. In this game for two players, the object is to collect as many factor pairs as possible in seven rounds of play.
3. Take turns tossing the number cubes and arranging them to make the 2-digit number with more factors. For example, if you roll 4 and 6, you can make 46 or 64. Choose the number you think has more factor pairs.
4. Write down your number and all its factor pairs on the recording sheet. Tell what are the related multiplication and division facts for each factor pair. **(I pick the number 64. I know 1 times 64 is 64 and 64 divided by 1 is 64.)**
5. Play continues until both players have had seven turns. The player with more factor pairs wins.

I pick the number 64. I know 1 times 64 is 64 and 64 divided by 1 is 64.

© Great Source. Permission is granted to copy this page.

REACHING ALL LEARNERS

Simplify Play the game using one cube only. For example, play with the 1–6 cube until students are comfortable with the game. Then, add in the 4–9 cube.

Variation If a student fails to name all of the factors of the number that he or she formed, the opponent may, at the beginning of his or her turn, name the factors that were overlooked. The opponent scores the factors on his or her recording sheet.

Math at Hand

- Factors, 050–051
- Multiplication, 136

© Great Source. Copying is prohibited.

Day 1

- Review the idea that multiplication is repeated addition of equal groups.
- Write the number 8 on the chalkboard. Draw an array that is one row by eight columns. Draw another array that is 2 rows by 4 columns. Explain that these arrays represent the creation of equal groups using eight objects. Therefore, the factors of 8 are 1, 2, 4, and 8.

MODEL THE GAME

Invite a volunteer to help demonstrate how to play the game and how to keep score.

Day 2

PLAY THE GAME

- Review the directions for playing the game.
- Assign partners to play the game.

REFLECT ON THE MATH

Encourage students to ask themselves:

- *Did I remember to include 1 and the number itself as factors?*
- *How do I know when I've found all the factors?*
- *Will an even number always have more factors than and odd number?*
- *What's the best roll I can possible get?*
- *How can I find factors for large numbers?*

MODEL THE GAME

Teacher: I just rolled a 5 and a 6. What two numbers can I make?

Student: How about 56 or 65?

T: Which one has more factor pairs?

S: Maybe 65. It's a bigger number.

T: So, what do we know about 65?

S: 1 and 65 are factors of 65.

T: What else?

S: The 5 in the ones place tells me that 5 is a factor. Since 5 times 13 equals 65, I know 5 and 13 is another factor pair.

T: How many factors so far?

S: Four. 1 and 65, 5 and 13.

T: Let's check out 56. What are the factors besides 1 and 56?

S: 56 is an even number, so 2 is a factor. Since 2 times 28 is 56, another factor pair is 2 and 28.

T: Any more?

S: How about 7 and 8?

T: Good! 7 times 8 is 56. More?

S: Oh, I know. 4 times 14 equals 56.

T: How many factors now?

S: Eight. The factors of 56 are 1, 2, 4, 7, 8, 14, 28, and 56.

T: What does this tell you about choosing a number to factor?

S: The larger number doesn't always have more factors.

ONGOING ASSESSMENT

If students need more help, use the hints below, or refer to the *Math at Hand* items shown to the left.

- **Are students having trouble working with 2-digit numbers?** Simplify the game. See the suggestion in *Reaching All Learners*.

- **Do students recognize that each number has 1 and itself as a factor?** Use smaller numbers to demonstrate.

© Great Source. Copying is prohibited.

TODAY'S FOCUS

CONCEPT BUILDER
MAKE & TAKE

Additional Support

CONCEPTS AND SKILLS

- Use metric units to measure
- State the relationship of a centimeter to a meter in decimal form
- State the relationship of a centimeter to a meter in fraction form

MATH TALK

Model the correct use of these words and encourage students to use them as they work.

- **centimeter** a unit of measure that is a fraction of a meter
- **linear** straight line
- **meter** a unit of length in the metric system
- **metric system** a method of measuring that is based in groups of 10s and 100s

MATERIALS FOR DAY 1

Centimeter strips (SE page 63), scissors, tape or glue, crayons or markers, adding machine tape

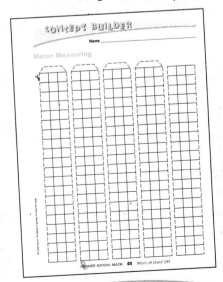

Meter Measuring **Day 1**

GET READY

Follow the instruction below to prepare a sample centimeter ruler to use for demonstration.

BUILD THE METER RULER

1. Have students cut out the centimeter strips on page 63 of their books. They will have five columns that are each 20 centimeters long and 3 centimeters wide.

2. Have students glue or tape the five columns together at the tabs. The result is a ruler 100 centimeters long and 3 centimeters wide.

3. Have students mark the ruler with two alternating colors to show lengths 10 centimeters long.

4. The ruler can be glued to the adding machine tape to make it sturdier. The edge of the adding machine tape and the ruler should be aligned to make it easier to use during the activity.

FOCUS ON THE MATH

- *How might a bendable ruler, like the one you just built, be better than a stiff one?* (You can measure things that aren't straight, like the circumference of a globe.) *What other measuring tool is similar to the ruler you have built?* (a measuring tape)

- *How many centimeter units are in a meter stick?* (100) *What fraction or decimal can you use to represent 1 centimeter?* ($\frac{1}{100}$, 0.01) *) How are pennies and centimeters similar?* (It takes 100 of each to make 1 whole. One hundred pennies make 1 dollar and 100 centimeters make 1 meter.)

- *What types of objects can be measured with a meter stick?* (Things that are not too large or too small.) *Give an example of something that might be too large or too small to measure with a meter stick.* (sample answer: the size of a molecule; the distance to the end of the galaxy.)

© Great Source. Copying is prohibited.

Meter Measuring **Day 2**

1. Have students find objects in the classroom that they estimate to be about 10 cm, 100 cm, 500 cm, and 1 meter long. For example, ask students to estimate the width of their desks.

2. Students then measure the item with the Meter Ruler.

3. On the Recording Sheet, students should write the names of the items and the actual length of the items expressed as a whole number of centimeters and in decimal form to represent the relationship of the length to 1 whole meter. Then they should calculate and record the difference between the estimated length and the actual length of the item.

4. As students record their measures, ask them to say it. For example, if the width of their desk is 0.80 m, they should say *eighty hundredths of a meter.*

MODEL THE ACTIVITY

To prepare students to work on their own, ask volunteers to explain how estimation is used in real life. For example, students might estimate if they have enough money to buy more than one item while shopping. Or, the time it will take to walk from home to a friend's house.

Demonstrate how to find an actual measurement. Emphasize that the 0 end of the ruler should be aligned with the starting point of the object being measured.

Explain how to find the difference between an estimate and an actual measurement. Review the meaning of the word *difference,* and if necessary, the process of subtracting. Demonstrate how to find the difference on the meter stick itself. Mark both the estimate and the actual length. Count either forward or backward between the two values to find the difference.

REFLECT ON THE MATH

Encourage students to ask themselves:

- *How would I know if I did not measure correctly?*
- *What should I do if the estimate and the actual measurements are really far apart?*

REACHING ALL LEARNERS

Have students discuss their estimates before measuring.

Math at Hand

Measurement, Length, 294
Computing with Measures, 327

© Great Source. Copying is prohibited.

MATERIALS FOR DAY 2

Centimeter strip assembled previously, Recording Sheet (SE p. 63A)

Note: Send these materials home with the Newsletter at the end of the week.

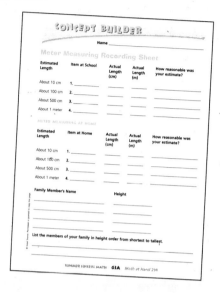

ONGOING ASSESSMENT

If students need more help, use the hints below, or refer to the *Math at Hand* items shown to the left.

- **Are students able to estimate reasonably?** Suggest to a student experiencing difficulty with estimating reasonably to use body references (width of a finger, width of a hand) when making estimates.

- **Are students able to measure accurately?** Assign students to work in pairs. One student is responsible for holding the 0 end of the meter ruler in its proper place; the other student is responsible for finding and "reading" the length of the object being measured. The partners should switch roles before each object is measured.

- **Are students able to express measurements in whole number and decimal forms?** Relate each centimeter to 1 of the 100 pennies that make a dollar.

NUMBER NAMES

TODAY'S NUMBER $\frac{1}{3}$

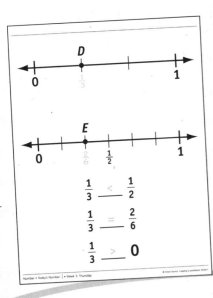

$\frac{1}{3}$ ___<___ $\frac{1}{2}$

$\frac{1}{3}$ ___=___ $\frac{2}{6}$

$\frac{1}{3}$ ___>___ 0

NUMBER Equivalent fractions

✎ *The top number line has 3 equal parts between 0 and 1. How would you use a fraction to label Point D?* $\left(\frac{1}{3}\right)$

✎ *The second number line has 6 equal parts between 0 and 1. How would you label Point E?* $\left(\frac{2}{6}\right)$ *What is special about* $\frac{1}{3}$ *and* $\frac{2}{6}$? (They're equal.)

✎ *How do you know* $\frac{1}{3}$ *is less than* $\frac{1}{2}$? (sample answer: If you cut something into 3 equal parts, each part is smaller than if you cut it into 2 equal parts.) Complete the comparisons.

Math at Hand 031, 035

---

1 whole + $\frac{1}{3}$ = ___ $1\frac{1}{3}$

5 wholes + $\frac{1}{3}$ = ___ $5\frac{1}{3}$

10 wholes + $\frac{1}{3}$ = ___ $10\frac{1}{3}$

Problem Solving:

sample drawing:

OPERATIONS Compute with $\frac{1}{3}$

✎ *When you add* $\frac{1}{3}$ *to 1 whole, what is the sum?* $\left(1\frac{1}{3}\right)$ *What is the sum of 5 wholes plus* $\frac{1}{3}$? $\left(5\frac{1}{3}\right)$ *10 wholes plus* $\frac{1}{3}$? $\left(10\frac{1}{3}\right)$

✎ **Problem Solving** *If Padre pours out* $\frac{1}{3}$ *of 1 whole bottle of water, how much is left?* $\left(\frac{2}{3} \text{ bottle}\right)$ Invite a volunteer to draw a diagram to show how s/he got the answer.

REACHING ALL LEARNERS Illustrate the word problem. Fold a strip of paper into thirds. Tear off one part. Show students the 2 parts remaining.

Math at Hand 159, 164

$\frac{1}{3}$ × 1 = $\frac{1}{3}$

10 × 1 = 10

0.25 × 1 = 0.25

365 × ___1___ = 365

Rule: sample answer: Any number times 1 is that number.

PATTERNS AND ALGEBRA Write a rule

• *What is the same about the first 3 number sentences?* (sample answers: 1 is one of the factors; the product is the same as a factor in the sentence)

✎ *What is the missing factor in the last number sentence?* (1) *How do you know?* (sample answer: the product is the same as one of the factors)

✎ *Write a rule to describe multiplication by 1.* (sample answer: any number times 1 is that number)

REACHING ALL LEARNERS Some students might recall that the number 1 is called *The Identity Element for Multiplication.*

Math at Hand 227

© Great Source. Copying is prohibited.

KEY ✎ = record on pad

Geometric nets

- *A flat figure that can be folded into a 3-dimensional figure is called a* net *of that solid figure. Which column shows nets of the solids?* (left side) *On the right side?* (solids)

- *How can you tell what the net will become when folded?* (sample answer: the faces of the solid are on the net)

✎ Invite volunteers to match each net with its solid. *Tell how you know which net folds into which solid?* (sample answer: the net of the cube has 6 square faces)

REACHING ALL LEARNERS Fold and unfold the cardstock solids in the kit for students to get hands-on experience.

Math at Hand 384–391

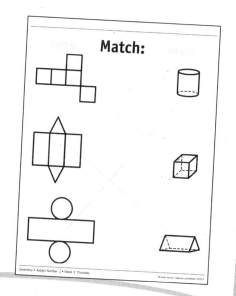

Match:

Circumference

- *The distance around a circle is called the* circumference. *To find the circumference, you multiply the diameter by the value of* pi, *which is about 3.*

- ✎ **Problem Solving** *Can you estimate the circumference of Circle A?* (about 6 inches) *Tell how you found the answer.* (see recording pad)

REACHING ALL LEARNERS Help students recall that the center of a circle is always shown with a dot. So, any line that goes through the center and stops on the edge of the circle at both ends is the diameter.

Math at Hand 367

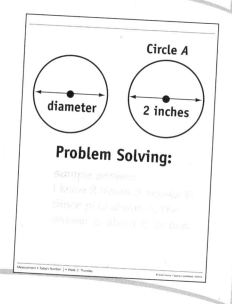

Circle A

diameter   2 inches

Problem Solving:

---

net

- *Suppose you open up both ends of a cereal box and cut along one edge of the box. What happens?* (sample answers: you flatten the box; the box is no longer 3-dimensional)

- *Can you cut along a different edge?* (yes) *Tell what happens?* (sample answer: you end up with a different shape for the net)

- *Why do you think the cut-out is called a* net? (sample answer: because the faces look like a fishing net) *What is special about a net?* (It shows all the faces of a solid.)

Math at Hand 384–391

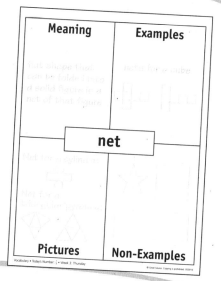

Meaning	Examples
net	
Pictures	Non-Examples

© Great Source. Copying is prohibited.

PRACTICE

Written Practice

CONCEPTS AND SKILLS

- Locate fractions on a number line
- Compute with $\frac{1}{3}$
- Match geometric nets with its solid figure
- Review modeling fractions
- Problem Solving Strategies and Skills: *Make a Model, Make a Diagram, Write an Equation; Use Logical Reasoning*

PREVIEW THE PRACTICE

- *Does $\frac{1}{3}$ come before or after $\frac{1}{2}$ on the number line?* (before) *Tell how you know.* (sample answer: 1 of 3 equal pieces is smaller than 1 of 2 equal pieces)

SUPPORT THE PRACTICE

- Problems 1–2 ask students to locate a fraction given a choice of 2 points. Help students recognize the number of equal parts between 0 and 1 on each number line.
- Problems 3–5 compute with $\frac{1}{3}$. Use a number line to help students visualize the addition and subtraction.
- Problems 6–9 allow students to role play. Revisit today's Geometry recording pad, if needed.
- Problems 10–12 review drawing diagrams to model fractions. Use counters for students who need tactile manipulation.

Name _____

NUMBER AND OPERATIONS

Loop the point on the number line that shows the fraction. ◄1–2. MAH 031

1. $\frac{1}{3}$

2. $\frac{2}{6}$

Add or subtract. ◄3–5. MAH 159, 164

3. $76 + \frac{1}{3} =$ _____ $76\frac{1}{3}$

4. $10 + \frac{1}{3} =$ _____ $10\frac{1}{3}$

5. $1 - \frac{1}{3} =$ _____ $\frac{2}{3}$

GEOMETRY

Match the solid with its net. ◄6–9. MAH 384

6.   **7.** 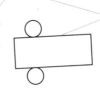   **8.**   **9.**

REVIEW

Draw a diagram for each fraction. Use shading to show the numerator. ◄10–12. MAH 028

10. $\frac{1}{2}$

11. $\frac{1}{4}$

12. $\frac{3}{4}$

Sample drawings. Check to be sure the drawings show equal parts of the whole.

SUMMER SUCCESS: MATH **65** MAH: *Math at Hand*

© Great Source. Permission is granted to copy this page.

REACHING ALL LEARNERS

Use the cardstock solids to help students associate each solid with its net.

Math at Hand

If students need help, encourage them to refer to the MAH items shown on the student page.

© Great Source. Copying is prohibited.

Complete each step. ◀ 13. MAH 396

13. Mr. Parker is building a round fishpond in the middle of his garden. The pond is (8 feet in diameter.) Mr. Parker will put a temporary fence around the pond. The fence will be (12) (inches) from the edge of the pond. Will (20 feet) of fencing be enough for Mr. Parker to surround his pond?

Remember: the value of *pi* is about 3

a. Underline the question you need to answer.

b. Loop the details about the pond and the fence.

c. Mark the strategy/strategies you will use.

d. Solve the problem. Explain your thinking.

_____

_____

_____

_____

_____

_____

_____

_____

_____

e. Answer the question.

No. 20 feet won't be enough fencing to surround the pond.

_____

_____

POSSIBLE STRATEGIES

• Make a Model

• Make a Diagram

• Write an Equation

Sample strategies:
Make a Diagram
Write an Equation
8 feet + 2 feet = 10 feet
10 feet × 3 = 30 feet

12 inches, or 1 foot

8 feet

© Great Source. Permission is granted to copy this page.

PROBLEM SOLVING

Work in small groups of 3 or 4 students.

• Encourage students to find ways to identify needed information to solve the problem.

• *What information do you need to answer the question?* (the diameter of the pond and extra width for the fence)

• *How can you use the information?* (to write an equation, to draw a diagram, to make a model)

SCORING

a. Last sentence underlined: 1 pt

b. Details of the pond and fence circled: 1 pt

c. Choose and apply an appropriate strategy: 1 pt

d. Explanation of solution: 1 pt

e. Correct answer: 1 pt

GLOSSARY TO GO

Today's Vocabulary *net*

Have students complete an entry for today's vocabulary term in their Glossaries. Encourage students to use both words and drawings.

MATH JOURNAL

• *Is it possible to make a net of a sphere? Use a ball to explain why.* (Students should recognize that it is not possible to cut a ball to make a flat image of it.)

REACHING ALL LEARNERS

Help students see that the 12 inches apply to the entire outer circle. So, the full diameter is 8 feet + 2 feet.

© Great Source. Copying is prohibited.

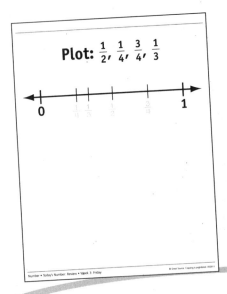

Plot: $\frac{1}{2}$, $\frac{1}{4}$, $\frac{3}{4}$, $\frac{1}{3}$

0 $\frac{1}{4}$ $\frac{1}{3}$ $\frac{1}{2}$ $\frac{3}{4}$ 1

NUMBER Order fractions

✎ *If you have to plot these fractions, which one might be most helpful to do first?* $\left(\frac{1}{2}\right)$ *Tell why you think so.* (sample answer: because it is in the middle between 0 and 1) Invite students to plot the fractions on the number line.

✎ *Each mark on the number line represents one of the four fractions. Explain where you would plot each fraction.* Encourage students to share their strategies.

REACHING ALL LEARNERS Trace the number line and fold to show $\frac{1}{2}$. Then fold again to show $\frac{1}{4}$ and $\frac{3}{4}$. Repeat with another number line to show $\frac{1}{3}$.

Math at Hand 031, 038

Problem Solving:

$1 \text{ whole} - \frac{2}{3} = \underline{\ \frac{1}{3}\ }$

$1 \text{ whole} + \frac{2}{3} = \underline{\ \ \ \ }$

sample answer: The orange is cut into 3 equal parts, Mia eats 2 parts, so only 1 part is left.

OPERATIONS Compute with fractions

✎ **Problem Solving** *Mia has 1 whole orange. She eats $\frac{2}{3}$ of it. How much is left?*

✎ *Loop the number sentence that describes the problem. How much is left?* $\left(\frac{1}{3}\right)$

• *Tell how you got the answer.* (sample answer: the orange is cut into 3 equal parts, Mia eats 2 parts, so only 1 part is left)

REACHING ALL LEARNERS Help students recognize that, for this problem, another way to write 1 is $\frac{3}{3}$.

Math at Hand 164

Order of Operations:

$\times \div + -$

$3 + (3 \times 6) \div 9 - 1 = \underline{\ 4\ }$

$3 + (18 \div 9) - 1$

$(3 + 2) - 1$

$5 - 1$

$(3 + 3) \times 6 \div 9 - 1 = \underline{\ 3\ }$

$(6 \times 6) \div 9 - 1$

$(36 \div 9) - 1$

$4 - 1$

PATTERNS AND ALGEBRA Order of Operations

✎ *The* Order of Operations *tells exactly which operations to do first when there is more than one operation in an equation. Starting from the left, the order is—multiply, divide, add, subtract.* Invite a volunteer to list the operation symbols on the recording pad.

✎ *Let's try this equation using the order of operations. What do we do first?* (multiply 3×6) *Second?* (divide $18 \div 9$) *Next?* (add $3 + 2$) *Finally?* ($5 - 1$) *Answer?* (4)

• *What happens if you start at the left and work across?* ($3 + 3 = 6$, $6 \times 6 = 36$, $36 \div 9 = 4$, $4 - 1 = 3$) *Answer?* (3)

Math at Hand 212

© Great Source. Copying is prohibited.

KEY ✎ = record on pad

GEOMETRY Solids and nets

✎ **Problem Solving** *My net has 2 circles and 1 rectangle. Which solid am I?* (cylinder) Invite a volunteer to draw the net next to the cylinder.

✎ **Problem Solving** *My net has 4 triangles and 1 square. Which solid am I?* (pyramid) Invite a volunteer to draw the net next to the pyramid.

✎ **Problem Solving** *My net has 6 faces, 4 identical ones and 2 squares. Which solid am I?* (prism) Invite a volunteer to draw the net next to the prism.

REACHING ALL LEARNERS Use cardstock solids, if needed.

Math at Hand 384, 387, 389

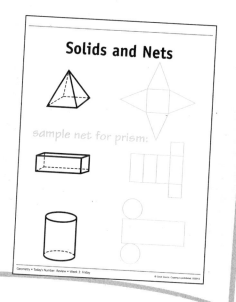

MEASUREMENT Customary length

✎ **Problem Solving** *To cover the living room walls, would you buy 3 gallons or 3 cups of paint?* (3 gallons) *Tell why.* (sample answer: 3 cups is too small an amount)

✎ **Problem Solving** *Do you think the time it takes to bake muffins is about 20 minutes or 20 hours?* (20 minutes) *Tell why.* (sample answer: 20 hours is almost one whole day, that's too long)

✎ **Problem Solving** *Is the diameter of a round table about 60 inches or 60 yards?* (60 inches) *Tell why.* (sample answer: 60 yards is almost the length of a football field)

Math at Hand 313–314, 322

Problem Solving:

Living room wall:

3 _____ gallons

Bake muffins:

20 _____ minutes

Diameter of table:

60 _____ inches

VOCABULARY Review

Let's work together to do today's matching exercise.

- *Algebra is the study of numerical relationships. What is the study of shapes, figures, position, and direction?* (geometry)
- *Remember what we just did with nets. Which do you think is the best match for the word?* (D)
- *Which is the better match for Solid figures, choice A or choice C?* (C) *Tell why.* (sample answer: choice A shows one type of solid, but choice C applies to all solid figures)

Math at Hand 333, 382–391, 528

Match

A, B,
C, D geometry | A. ▭

___ D net

B. shapes, figures, position, direction

___ A prism

C. 3-dimensional figures

___ C solid figures

D. ▱

© Great Source. Copying is prohibited.

PRACTICE

Written Practice

CONCEPTS AND SKILLS

- Order fractions from least to greatest
- Plot fractions on a number line
- Compute with fractions
- Draw solids and nets
- Review quarter hour
- Problem Solving Strategies and Skills: *Look for a Pattern, Make a Diagram, Write an Equation; Take Notes*

PREVIEW THE PRACTICE

- *What does the top number in a fraction mean?* (the number of equal parts you are looking at) *What does the bottom number represent?* (the full amount, all the equal parts)

SUPPORT THE PRACTICE

- Problems 1–2 order from least to greatest. Draw a number line to help students gauge the position of each number.
- Problems 3–5 asks students to use fractions to name points on a number line. Refer students to $\frac{1}{2}$ to help them position the other fractions.
- Problems 6–9 allow students to role play as the teacher. Help students articulate a comment for Problem 9.
- Problems 10–13 ask students to draw a solid and its net. Refer to the cardstock solids, if needed.
- Problems 14–16 review elapsed time in $\frac{1}{4}$-hour increment. Students should use the clock face, if needed.

PRACTICE TODAY'S NUMBER Review

Name _____

NUMBER AND OPERATIONS

Order from least to greatest. ◄1–2. MAH 038

1. $\frac{1}{2}, \frac{1}{3}, \frac{1}{4}, 1$ _____ $\frac{1}{4}, \frac{1}{3}, \frac{1}{2}, 1$

2. $\frac{2}{6}, \frac{2}{8}, 0, \frac{3}{4}$ _____ $0, \frac{2}{8}, \frac{2}{6}, \frac{3}{4}$

Write the fraction that identifies the point on the number line. ◄3–5. MAH 031

A B C
0 $\frac{1}{2}$ 1

3. Point A __$\frac{1}{4}$__   **4.** Point B __$\frac{1}{3}$__   **5.** Point C __$\frac{3}{4}$__

Help the teacher correct this paper. Write a note to the student.

Fill in the blank. ◄6–9. MAH 157, 164, 227

6. __1__ $+ \frac{3}{4} = 1\frac{3}{4}$ ✓   **7.** $\frac{1}{2} +$ __$\frac{1}{2}$__ $= 1$ ✓   **8.** $\frac{1}{4} +$ __+__ $1 = \frac{1}{4}$ ✗

9. Comment: ___The symbol for #8 is ✗, because any number times 1 equals that number.___

Sample drawings. Check student's work.

GEOMETRY

Draw the solid and its net. ◄10–13. MAH 382 Sample drawing. Check student's work.

10. cube   **11.** cylinder

12. any prism   **13.** any pyramid

SUMMER SUCCESS: MATH **67** MAH: *Math at Hand*

© Great Source. Permission is granted to copy this page.

REACHING ALL LEARNERS

Provide the cardstock solids for students to manipulate.

Math at Hand

If students need help, encourage them to refer to the MAH items shown on the student page.

© Great Source. Copying is prohibited.

What is $\frac{1}{4}$ hour from the Start time? Use the clock face, if needed. ◄14–16. MAH 322

14. Start: 8:00

End: _____8:15_____

15. Start: 3:30

End: _____3:45_____

16. Start: 6:00

End: _____6:45_____

PROBLEM SOLVING · **UNDERSTAND · PLAN · TRY · LOOK BACK**

Complete each step. ◄17. MAH 396

17. Mr. Ewell always cooks at the Pancake Breakfast. He stacked 15 pancakes on the first platter, 20 on the second platter, and 18 on the third platter. The next three platters had 23, 21, and 26 pancakes each. If the stacks of pancakes are served in a pattern, how many pancakes will be served on the next three platters?

POSSIBLE STRATEGIES

- Look for a Pattern
- Make a Diagram
- Write an Equation

Sample strategy:
Look for a Pattern

a. Underline the question you need to answer.

b. Loop the numbers of pancakes that have been served.

c. Mark the strategy/strategies you will use.

d. Solve the problem. Explain your thinking.

numbers: 15, 20, 18, 23, 21, 26

pattern: + 5, – 2, + 5, – 2, + 5

next three: 24, 29, 27

_____

_____

e. Answer the question.

Mr. Ewell will serve 24, then 29, and finally 27 pancakes.

_____

© Great Source. Permission is granted to copy this page.

PROBLEM SOLVING

Work in small groups of 3 or 4 students.

- Encourage students to find ways to identify needed information to solve the problem.
- *What information do you need to answer the question?* (the numbers of pancakes in the last three batches)
- *How can you use the information?* (to look for a pattern, to draw a picture, to write an equation)

SCORING

a. Question underlined: 1 pt

b. The numbers of pancakes circled: 1 pt

c. Choose and apply an appropriate strategy: 1 pt

d. Explanation of solution: 1 pt

e. Correct answer: 1 pt

GLOSSARY TO GO

Today's Vocabulary Review

Have students review and share the entries they made for this week's vocabulary words, *geometry*, *solid figures*, *prism*, and *net*. Ask students to add more words and/or drawings to the maps if they can.

MATH JOURNAL

- *Why do you think it is a good idea to have an* Order of Operations? (sample answer: so that we can all get the same answer when computing a string of operations)

REACHING ALL LEARNERS

If students have difficulty with the problem, use tokens or other appropriate manipulative to represent the pancakes. Students can create the stacks to visualize the stacks.

© Great Source. Copying is prohibited.

READ AND REASON

Additional Support

CONCEPTS AND SKILLS

- Multiplication
- Concept of finding volume

MATH TALK

Model the correct use of these terms and encourage students to use them as they work.

- **dimensions** the lengths of sides of a geometric figure
- **solid figure** a geometric shape with 3 dimensions
- **volume** the number of cubic units it takes to fill a solid

SUPPORT PROBLEM 1

Read the story aloud, then have a volunteer read the problem again.

- *What is the story about?* (putting boxes on a platform)
- *What is the math about?* (how many boxes and books the platform can hold)
- *Where do you think we should start?* (Answers will vary.)
- *Are there any answers you can rule out?* (0 and 8,400) *Why?* (0 because the product would be zero, and 8,400 because it is too big of a number)

READ AND REASON

Name _____

Fill in each blank with the choice that makes the *most* sense. Do not use any choice more than once.

1. Jon is placing boxes of books on a platform to ship. The platform can hold a total of ____36____ boxes. Jon can put ___3 or 4___ boxes across, 3 deep and ___3 or 4___ high as he unloads the boxes. If there are 6 books in each box, the platform holds ____216____ books.

ANSWER CHOICES

- 0
- 8,400
- 216
- 3
- 4
- 36

Explain your thinking.

a. How did you begin?
   Example: I made a picture in my mind.

b. Which choice(s) did you rule out?
   Example: 0, because the product would be zero; and 8,400, because it is too big of a number.

c. How are you sure that your answers make sense in the story?
   Example: I multiplied 3 × 3 × 4 and got 36, and then multiplied that by 6 to get 216.

© Great Source. Permission is granted to copy this page.

SUMMER SUCCESS: MATH   **69**

REACHING ALL LEARNERS

- Provide cubes for students to stack so that they can visualize the problem in three dimensions.
- Invite students to show the different configurations of a solid that measures 3 by 3 by 4.

Math at Hand

- Multiplication, 136
- Volume of Rectangular Prisms, 310

© Great Source. Copying is prohibited.

Fill in each blank with the choice that makes the *most* sense. Do not use any choice more than once.

2. Sarah is helping out in the Afterschool program. She is keeping track of how long each task takes. On ___Monday___, she works in the art room for just less than an hour, or ___55___ minutes. Then she is in the tutoring center for ___half___ an hour, or 30 minutes. Sarah also helps to shelve books in the library for a quarter of an hour. If Sarah gets to Afterschool at 2:30 P.M., she is finished ___after 4:10 P.M.___

ANSWER CHOICES

- 25
- after 4:10 P.M.
- at 1:30 A.M.
- 55
- Monday
- half

Explain your thinking.

a. How did you begin?

Example: I added up all the times.

b. Which choice(s) did you rule out?

Example: 1:30 A.M. because that is nighttime and 25 because that is way less than an hour.

c. How are you sure that your answers make sense in the story?

Example: I added up the times, double checked my totals, and read the story again to make sure that it made sense.

SUMMER SUCCESS: MATH **70**

© Great Source. Permission is granted to copy this page.

CONCEPTS AND SKILLS

- Elapsed time
- Add minutes and hours

MATH TALK

Model the correct use of these terms and encourage students to use them as they work.

- **A.M.** the hours from midnight until noon
- **P.M.** the hours from noon until midnight
- **elapsed time** the hours and minutes between a start time and an end time

SUPPORT PROBLEM 2

Read the story aloud, then have a volunteer read the problem again.

- *What is the story about?* (Sarah keeping track of her tasks at Afterschool)
- *What is the math about?* (adding minutes and finding elapsed time)
- *Where do you think we should start?* (Answers will vary.)
- *Are there any answers you can rule out?* (1:30 A.M. and 25) *Why?* (1:30 A.M. because that is nighttime and 25 because that is way less than an hour)

REACHING ALL LEARNERS

- Discuss adding units of time.
- Help students convert time greater than 60 minutes into hours and minutes.

Math at Hand

- Time, 322
- Elapsed Time, 324

© Great Source. Copying is prohibited.

GRADE 5 • WEEK 3 **70**

NEWSLETTER

This Newsletter is designed to be sent home with students at the end of the week along with the completed *Meter Measuring* Concept Builder materials.

The first page suggests a simple way for students to share with their parent or guardian basic math skills they have been practicing in class.

NEWSLETTER

Summer Success: Math

What a great week of learning in summer school! Your child has explored a lot of math topics.

Earlier in the week, your child learned about nets of solid figures. He/she learned that a net is a flat image of a solid, one that can be folded into the solid.

Here is an activity to encourage your child to share with you what he/she learned.

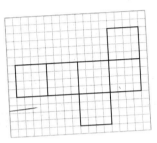

- Ask your child to take a guess at what solid this net makes. (Hint: it has 6 square faces)

- Cut out the net and fold it to make the solid.

- Are there other nets that also fold to make the same solid? (Hint: Yes. At least 3 more!)

On the back of this page are directions for using the project called *Meter Measuring* that your child built this week. Invite your child to share this fun activity with you.

 Enjoy the time with your child, and thank you for helping to strengthen the mathematical tie between home and school.

© Great Source. Permission is granted to copy this page.

© Great Source. Copying is prohibited.

NEWSLETTER

Sharpen Measuring Skills with Meter Measuring

Your student made a meter ruler in summer school. Work with your child to complete the recording sheet.

1. Have your child identify objects that he or she estimates to be about 10 cm, 100 cm, 500 cm, and 1 meter long. On the *Meter Measuring* recording sheet, write the names of four objects.

2. Then have your child measure each item with the meter ruler and write the actual lengths of the items on the recording sheet.

3. Compare the estimates and the actual measurements. Were the estimates reasonable?

You can add more things to the list just for fun.

Next, ask your child to measure the height of each family member. Record the information. Who is the tallest? The shortest?

The back side of this week's Newsletter includes instructions for the parent or guardian to help their student demonstrate the *Meter Measuring* Concept Builder activity at home.

CONCEPT BUILDER

Name _____

Meter Measuring Recording Sheet

Estimated Length	Item at School	Actual Length (cm)	Actual Length (m)	How reasonable was your estimate?
About 10 cm	1.			
About 100 cm	2.			
About 500 cm	3.			
About 1 meter	4.			

METER MEASURING AT HOME

Estimated Length	Item at Home	Actual Length (cm)	Actual Length (m)	How reasonable was your estimate?
About 10 cm	1.			
About 100 cm	2.			
About 500 cm	3.			
About 1 meter	4.			

Family Member's Name	Height

List the members of your family in height order from shortest to tallest.

_____

SUMMER SUCCESS: MATH **63A** *Math at Hand* 294

© Great Source. Permission is granted to copy this page.

Enjoy exploring metric measurement with your child using *Meter Measuring*. Remember, using math in the real world helps your child understand that math is important in school.

72

© Great Source. Copying is prohibited.

WEEKLY OVERVIEW	MONDAY	TUESDAY
Materials Read across to find materials needed for this week's daily activities. *Optional material	**Game** Build a Net Spinner, Build a Net Polygon Cards, large paper clip, counters **Data Study** Measuring tapes*, 2-foot pieces of string, scissors; rulers	**Game** Build a Net Spinner, Build a Net Polygon Cards, large paper clip, counters **Data Study** Measuring tapes*, 2-foot pieces of string, scissors; rulers
NUMBER NAMES *Instruction: 20–30 min* **Number** Fractions, Decimals, Percents **Operations** Compute with fractions **Patterns and Algebra** Fraction pattern, Expressions/Equations, Use a pattern **Geometry** Transformations, Ordered pairs, Coordinate grid **Measurement** Volume, Explore area, Customary weight, Metric length **Vocabulary** Measurement terms	**Number Names** p. 72C **Today's Numbers:** $\frac{1}{5}$ Equivalent fractions Compute with fractions Fraction pattern Translation Volume of prisms *measure*	**Number Names** p. 78A **Today's Numbers:** $\frac{1}{6}$ Equivalent fractions Compute with fractions Write expressions Reflection Explore surface area of a cube *area*
PRACTICE *Written Practice: 20–30 min* **Number and Operations** Equivalent fractions, decimals, percents, Model, compare, and compute with fractions **Patterns and Algebra** Table of values, Rules **Geometry** Rotation, Cube **Measurement** Volume, Area **Review** Coordinate grid, Order of Operations, Ordering numbers, Fractional measures, Math vocabulary **Problem Solving** Strategies and skills	**Practice** p. 73 Equivalent fractions, decimals, and percents Compute with fractions Volume of prisms Points on the coordinate grid Make a Diagram Make an Organized List Make a Table Use Logical Reasoning	**Practice** p. 79 Compare fractions Model and compute with fractions Area of a cube Order of Operations Make a Table Look for a Pattern Make an Organized List Solve in More Than One Way
GAME *Active Practice: 20–30 min* Geometric solid (faces, nets) Equivalent fractions and decimals Order fractions and decimals Models for decimals and fractions	**Game** p. 75 **Build a Net** Geometric solid faces Geometric nets	**Game** p. 75 **Build a Net** Geometric solid faces Geometric nets
FOCUS *Additional Support: 20–30 min* Gather data, Line plot, Compare and summarize data, Find range, mode, median Fractions, Multiplication and division, Logical reasoning, Data, Understand average/mean, range	**Data Study** p. 77 **Making a Line Plot** Gather data Make a line plot Find range, mode, and median Compare and summarize data	**Data Study** p. 77 **Making a Line Plot** Gather data Make a line plot Find range, mode, and median Compare and summarize data

© Great Source. Copying is prohibited.

PLANNER

Game Fraction/Decimals Cards I, II, counters
Concept Builder Fraction Kit pieces, scissors, crayons, storage bags

Game Fraction/Decimals Cards I, II, counters
Concept Builder materials previously prepared

Game See Tuesday and Thursday.
Newsletter SE p. 93 (Send home with the Concept Builder materials at the end of the week.)

Number Names p. 80A

Today's Numbers: $\frac{1}{8}$
Fractions greater than 1
Compute with fractions
Use a pattern
Rotation
Customary weight
volume

Number Names p. 86A

Today's Numbers: $\frac{1}{100}$
Fractions, decimals, and percents
Compute with fractions
Write an equation
Ordered pairs
Metric length
capacity

Number Names p. 88A

Today's Number: Review
Fractions, decimals, and percents
Compute with fractions
Write a rule
Transformations on a coordinate grid
Volume and area
Vocabulary review

Practice p. 81

Compare fractions
Model and compute with fractions
Work with rotation
Ordering numbers
Make a Table
Guess, Check, and Revise
Make an Organized List
Take Notes

Practice p. 87

Write equivalent fractions, decimals, and percents
Compute with fractions
Complete table of values and write equations
Fractional measures
Make a Model
Make a Diagram
Make a Table
Use Logical Reasoning

Practice p. 89

Model fraction, decimal, percents
Compute fractions
Area and volume
Math vocabulary
Act It Out
Make a Diagram
Make an Organized List
Use Logical Reasoning

Game p. 83

Ordering Fractions and Decimals
Equivalent fractions and decimals
Order fractions and decimals
Models for decimals and fractions

Game p. 83

Ordering Fractions and Decimals
Equivalent fractions and decimals
Order fractions and decimals
Models for decimals and fractions

Game pp. 75 and 83

Choice
Build a Net or variation
Ordering Fractions and Decimals or variation

Concept Builder p. 85

**Make & Take:
Decimal Kit**
Understand fractions
Equivalent fractions
Add fractions

Concept Builder p. 85

**Make & Take:
Decimal Kit**
Understand fractions
Equivalent fractions
Add fractions

Read and Reason p. 91

Multiplication
Multiplication and division
Logical reasoning
Use data words in context
Understand average/mean, range

© Great Source. Copying is prohibited.

NUMBER NAMES TODAY'S NUMBER $\frac{1}{5}$

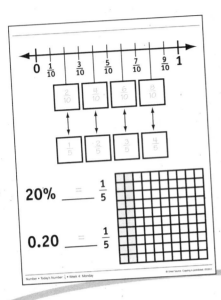

20% ___ = $\frac{1}{5}$

0.20 ___ = $\frac{1}{5}$

NUMBER Equivalent fractions and percents

✎ *What fractions are missing on the number line?* ($\frac{2}{10}$, $\frac{4}{10}$, $\frac{6}{10}$, $\frac{8}{10}$) Fill in the first row of boxes.

✎ *Suppose the number line had been divided into only 5 equal parts. How would you write the fractions for fifths?* ($\frac{1}{5}$, $\frac{2}{5}$, $\frac{3}{5}$, $\frac{4}{5}$) Fill in the second row of boxes.

✎ *Percent means how many of 100 equal parts. How many squares would you shade to show 10%?* (10) *20%?* (20) *What fractions can you write to describe 20 out 100?* ($\frac{20}{100}$, $\frac{2}{10}$, $\frac{1}{5}$) *Decimals?* (0.20, 0.2) *Tell what you know about $\frac{1}{5}$, $\frac{2}{10}$, $\frac{20}{100}$, 0.20, 0.2, and 20%.* (They are equal.)

Math at Hand 020, 035, 044

OPERATIONS Explore dividing by a fraction

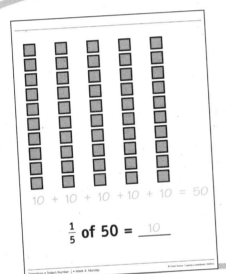

10 + 10 + 10 + 10 + 10 = 50

$\frac{1}{5}$ of 50 = ___ 10

• **Problem Solving** *There are 50 seats in the front row of the auditorium. Suppose $\frac{1}{5}$ of the seats are reserved for your class. How many seats is that?*

✎ *How can you use the diagram to find the answer:* (make 5 equal sections) *How many sections would you shade to show $\frac{1}{5}$ of the seats?* (1)

✎ *What number repeated 5 times equals 50?* (10) *So, what can you tell about $\frac{1}{5}$ of 50?* (It is equal to 10.)

✎ *How many seats are reserved for your class?* (10 seats)

Math at Hand 168

PATTERNS AND ALGEBRA Fraction pattern

10, 10$\frac{1}{5}$, 11, 11$\frac{1}{5}$, 12, 12$\frac{1}{5}$, ___ 13 , ___ 13$\frac{1}{5}$, ___ 14

Rule: Add $\frac{1}{5}$ to the whole number before, then add $\frac{4}{5}$ to get to the next whole number.

• *What pattern do you see?* (sample answer: whole number, mixed number, whole number, mixed number)

• *Can you tell how the numbers change starting with 10?* (sample answer: add $\frac{1}{5}$, add $\frac{4}{5}$, add $\frac{1}{5}$, add $\frac{4}{5}$, and so on)

✎ *What are the next three terms in the pattern?* (13, 13$\frac{1}{5}$, 14)

✎ *How would you write a rule that describes the pattern?* (sample answer: add $\frac{1}{5}$ to the whole number before, then add $\frac{4}{5}$ to get to the next whole number)

Math at Hand 034, 401

© Great Source. Copying is prohibited.

KEY ✎ = record on pad

GEOMETRY Translation

- *How can you describe the way this house moved?* (It slid from left to right.) *This movement is called a* translation, *or* slide.

✎ Every point in a slide moves the same distance in the same direction. *Cross out the diagram that does not show a translation.*

✎ Invite volunteers to draw sample translations.

REACHING ALL LEARNERS Make cutouts of simple shapes for students to trace the translation.

Math at Hand 376

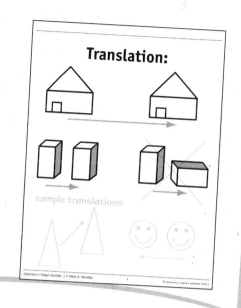

MEASUREMENT Volume of prisms

- Volume *is the number of cubic units it takes to fill a solid. Volume is found using 3 measurements: length, width, and height.*

- *How can you find the number of cubic units it takes to fill the prism?* (sample answers: count the cubes; count the cubes in one layer, then multiply by the number of layers; multiply length × width × height)

✎ *What is the total number of cubes?* (30) *What is the volume?* (30 cubic units)

REACHING ALL LEARNERS Use the number cubes from the kit to give students hands-on experience with volume.

Math at Hand 309–312

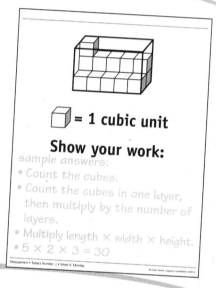

VOCABULARY *measure*

- *What are some things you measure?* (sample answers: someone's height, weight of a watermelon, temperature, time, and so on)

- *What are two familiar systems of measure?* (customary and metric)

- *What are some tools used to find the measure of items?* (sample answers: rulers, tape measures, balance scales)

Math at Hand 293

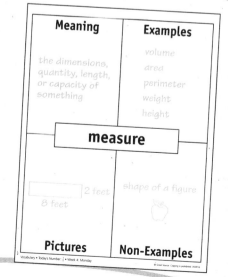

© Great Source. Copying is prohibited.

PRACTICE

Written Practice

CONCEPTS AND SKILLS

- Equivalent fractions, decimals, and percents
- Compute with fractions
- Volume of prisms
- Review points on the coordinate grid
- Problem Solving Strategies and Skills: *Make a Diagram, Make an Organized List, Make a Table; Use Logical Reasoning*

PREVIEW THE PRACTICE

- *What does* percent *mean?* (100 equal parts) *What is the symbol for percent?* (%)
- *How can you write* $\frac{1}{2}$ *as a percent?* (50%) *Decimal?* (0.5, 0.50)

SUPPORT THE PRACTICE

- Problems 1–4 work with write equivalent decimal, percents, and fractions. Students can use the number line to relate the equivalents.
- Problems 5–7 model computing with fractions. Careful counting helps with finding the correct answer.
- Problems 8–9 model volume. Students show how they find the answer. Remind students that units hidden from sight still count.
- Problems 10–14 review points on a coordinate grid. Go over how to read the axes, the origin.

Name _____

NUMBER AND OPERATIONS

Use the number line to help you write an equivalent decimal and percent for the fraction. ◄1–4. MAH 020, 035, 044

1. $\frac{1}{5}$ _____ 0.2; 20%
2. $\frac{5}{10}$ _____ 0.5; 50%
3. $\frac{1}{10}$ _____ 0.1; 10%
4. $\frac{1}{4}$ _____ 0.25; 25%

Fill in the blank. Use the diagram to check your answer. ◄5–7. MAH 168

5. $\frac{1}{5}$ of 10 = ___2___

6. $\frac{1}{5}$ of 20 = ___4___

7. $\frac{1}{5}$ of 15 = ___3___

MEASUREMENT

What is the volume of the prism? ◄8–9. MAH 309–312

8.

□ = 1 cubic unit

Volume: ___54___ cubic units
Show your work.
sample work:
$6 \times 3 \times 3 = 18 \times 3 = 54$

9.

Volume: ___42___ cubic units
Show your work.
sample work:
$7 \times 3 \times 2 = 21 \times 2 = 42$

© Great Source. Permission is granted to copy this page.

REACHING ALL LEARNERS

Refer to the number line on today's Number recording pad for the equivalent fractions. You can write in the decimal units for each mark across the top of the number line.

Math at Hand

If students need help, encourage them to refer to the MAH items shown on the student page.

© Great Source. Copying is prohibited.

Plot and label the point on the coordinate grid. ◀ 10–14. MAH 265–266

10. Point A (5, 1)

11. Point B (0, 4)

12. Point C (2, 3)

13. Point D (1, 6)

14. Point E (3, 5)

PROBLEM SOLVING · **UNDERSTAND** · **PLAN** · **TRY** · **LOOK BACK**

Complete each step. ◀ 15. MAH 396

15. At Langston Elementary "Buddy Fun Day" is the last Friday of each month. There are 7 girls and 9 boys in Paul's class. Paul's teacher randomly pairs students by drawing their names from a bowl. David and Wendy, Patrick and Ted, Lisa and Hilda, and Matthew and Helene have already been paired. Paul's name has been drawn. What is the chance Paul will be paired with another boy?

   a. Underline the question you need to answer.

   b. Loop the details about the students in Paul's class.

   c. Mark the strategy/strategies you will use.

   d. Solve the problem. Explain your thinking.

   _____

   _____

   _____

   _____

   _____

   e. Answer the question.

   Paul has a 4 out of 7 chance of being paired with another boy.

POSSIBLE STRATEGIES

- Make a Diagram
- Make an Organized List
- Make a Table

sample strategy:
Make an Organized List

9 boys	7 girls
David	Wendy
Patrick	Lisa
Ted	Hilda
Matthew	Helene
Paul	
(4 boys left)	(3 girls left)

total of 7 students left, of which 4 are boys

© Great Source. Permission is granted to copy this page.

SUMMER SUCCESS: MATH **74** MAH: *Math at Hand*

REACHING ALL LEARNERS

If students have difficulty with the problem, simulate the problem by role playing using the details and names of the students in the problem.

© Great Source. Copying is prohibited.

PROBLEM SOLVING

Work in small groups of 3 or 4 students.

- Encourage students to find ways to identify needed information to solve the problem.

- *What information do you need to answer the question?* (the number of boys' names still left in the bowl and the total number of names left in the bowl)

- *How can you use the information?* (to make an organized list)

SCORING

   a. Last sentence underlined: 1 pt

   b. Details about the people circled: 1 pt

   c. Choose and apply an appropriate strategy: 1 pt

   d. Explanation of solution: 1 pt

   e. Correct answer: 1 pt

GLOSSARY TO GO

Today's Vocabulary *measure*

Have students complete an entry for today's vocabulary term in their Glossaries. Encourage students to use both words and drawings.

MATH JOURNAL

- *Name 3 examples of how measures are a part of your everyday life.* (sample answers: time of day, distance of walk, weight of book bag)

GAME

Active Practice

CONCEPTS AND SKILLS

- Faces of geometric solids
- Nets of geometric solids

MATH TALK

Model the correct use of these words and encourage students to use them as they work.

- **base of a solid** a special face of a solid figure
- **face** a flat figure that is one side of a solid figure
- **net** a 2-dimensional shape that can be folded into a 3-dimensional shape
- **prism** a solid that has two identical parallel bases that are polygons and 4-sided faces for each side of its base
- **pyramid** a solid that has one base that is a polygon and triangular faces for each side of its base

MATERIALS

For each pair: 1 Spinner; 1 set each of Square and Triangle Cards, Rectangle Cards; 1 large paper clip; 5 counters

Cardstock solids from the kit for reference.*

*Optional materials

GAME

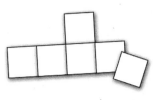

Build a Net

Object: Be the first to collect all the faces of any geometric solid to build its net.

MATERIALS

1 Spinner; 1 set each of Square and Triangle Cards, Rectangle Cards; 1 large paper clip; 5 counters

Cardstock solids from the kit for reference.*

*Optional material

DIRECTIONS

1. Display the polygons in separate piles faceup. Make one pile for squares, one for triangles, and one for rectangles.

2. Players take turns spinning the paper clip on the spinner to collect different polygon cards. If the spinner points to a polygon that is not available, take a shape from one of the other polygon piles.

3. The first player to collect all the faces of any geometric solid and build the net for the solid gets 1 counter. You must name your solid. **(Hey, look, I just got the sixth square to make the net for a cube!)**

4. Then collect all the shapes and put them back into the three separate piles of polygon. Start the next round.

5. After 5 rounds, the player with the most counters wins.

Hey, look, I just got the sixth square to make the net for a cube!

© Great Source. Permission is granted to copy this page.

REACHING ALL LEARNERS

Simplify Limit the game to only prisms or only pyramids.

Variation Before each round, players agree upon one geometric solid to build, for instance a triangular prism. At the end of 7 turns, players evaluate who needs the least number of pieces to complete the prism. The player who needs the least number of pieces takes a counter and another round begins. Players should change the targeted solid for each round of play.

Math at Hand

- Prisms, 383–384
- Pyramids, 385–387

© Great Source. Copying is prohibited.

Day 1

REVIEW THE MATH

- Review the vocabulary (face, base, prism, pyramid, and net) associated with models of geometric solids.
- Review the different types of prisms and pyramids.
- Draw or show a physical model of two different solids, such as a rectangular prism and a square pyramid. Ask students to draw different nets for those particular solids.
- Refer to the cardstock solids from the kit, as needed.

MODEL THE GAME

- Demonstrate with a volunteer how to play the game and how to keep score.
- Show students how to hold the pieces together to form a solid.

Day 2

PLAY THE GAME

- Review the directions for playing the game.
- Assign pairs of students to play the game.

REFLECT ON THE MATH

Encourage students to ask themselves:

- *Which solid requires the fewest pieces?*
- *Which solid am I on the way to building with the pieces I already have?*
- *What faces do I still need to complete the net?*
- *What is my strategy at this point?*

MODEL THE GAME

Teacher: The paper clip landed on a square. What solid can I build?

Student: Lots! You can build a rectangular prism, a cube, or a square pyramid.

T: Great! On my second spin, I land on a triangle. Can I still build the same solids?

S: Not really. You can't build a cube or a rectangular prism any more. But, you can still build a square pyramid.

T: On this spin, I land on "Take a polygon from another player." The player has a rectangle and a triangle. Which one should I take?

S: I'd take another triangle to build the pyramid.

T: If I take the triangle, what else do I need to finish the net?

S: 2 more triangles.

T: What are the different ways I can get those 2 triangles?

S: It depends on what you land on next time.

S: That's right. You might land on a shape or you might need to take a shape from the other players.

ONGOING ASSESSMENT

If students need more help, use the hints below, or refer to the *Math at Hand* items shown to the left.

- **Can students visualize the solids being built?** Have students make a sketch of the net. Refer to the cardstock solids from the kit, as needed.

- **Can students verbalize the steps needed to build their net?** Have students talk to you as they build their nets. Observe whether they are able to use the targeted vocabulary words appropriately.

© Great Source. Copying is prohibited.

DATA STUDY

Additional Support

CONCEPTS AND SKILLS

- Gather data
- Make a line plot
- Find range, mode, and median
- Compare and summarize data

MATH TALK

Model the correct use of these words and encourage students to use them as they talk about math.

- **circumference** the perimeter (distance around) of a circle
- **frequency** the number of times something occurs in a set of data
- **line plot** a diagram that shows the frequency of data on a number line
- **mode** the number that appears most frequently in a set of data; there may be one, more than one, or no mode

MATERIALS

For each pair of students: measuring tape; two pieces of string, 2 feet each; scissors; rulers; yardstick*

*Optional materials

GET STARTED

- Read and discuss the directions on page 77 with students.
- Assign partner pairs to work together.

DATA STUDY

Name _____

Making a Line Plot

How big is your head?

COLLECT THE DATA

Measure the circumference of your head and your partner's head, to the nearest quarter inch, and record them in the table. Then record the measurements of all your classmates.

Name	Circumference (Inches)

Name	Circumference (Inches)

DISPLAY THE DATA

- Draw a number line at the bottom of the grid paper. The numbers should start with the least value and end with the greatest value in the set of data. Write whole number inches and mark quarter-inch increments between them. Title your line plot.
- For each measurement, write an **x** above the corresponding numbers.

ANALYZE THE DATA

1. What are the least and the greatest measurements of the set of data? _____
   What is the range? _____ Answers will vary.

2. What is the mode? How do you know?
   Depending upon the data, there may be one, more than one, or no mode.

3. What is the median? How did you find it?
   Answers will vary. It's the middle number for an odd number of students.
   It's the average of the two middle numbers for an even number of students.

SUMMER SUCCESS: MATH **77** *Math at Hand* 282

© Great Source. Permission is granted to copy this page.

REACHING ALL LEARNERS

- Review how to measure the length of an object to the nearest quarter inch using a customary ruler with $\frac{1}{8}$-inch increments.
- Review how to make a number line with $\frac{1}{4}$-unit increments between whole numbers as well as not starting at 0.
- Review how to add and subtract mixed numbers.

Math at Hand

- Line Plots, 282
- Range, 257
- Mode, 262
- Median, 261
- Median, 263

© Great Source. Copying is prohibited.

Day 1

Before students begin to collect the data, ask them to estimate the circumference of their own head and explain their reasoning. Although a person's head is not perfectly round, it is quite circular. Write the estimates on the board so that students can compare them later to actual measurements.

Day 2

GRAPH THE DATA

Work with students to help them create their line plots. Be sure they think about what information they want someone else to see when the graph is completed.

ANALYZE THE DATA

Discuss with the class their answers to the questions at the bottom of student page 77. Then have them consider the following questions:

- *Is the range for the set of data very small or very great? Why do you think so?* (Since the sizes of students' heads are quite similar, the range is probably a very small number.)

- *Is the data on your graph bunched up or spread out? If it's bunched up, which body of measurements does this part of the line plot include?* (Answers depend on the data; however, measurements may cluster around the mode if there is one.)

- *Which types of statistics are easy to find using a line plot—range, mode, median?* (The range and mode can be seen immediately. Since the data is recorded on a line plot in order, you can simply count to find the middle number or middle pair or numbers.)

- **What if?** *Suppose you are a hat maker. How could you use this type of data to manufacture hats in three sizes for students—small, medium, and large?* (sample answer: I would separate the range of sizes into three groups. For example, head circumferences of 16–17 inches would be a small size, 18–19 inches would be an average size, and 20–21 inches would be a large size.)

COLLECT THE DATA

Teacher: Today we are going to use string to measure the circumference of our heads. How can we measure the length of the string to the nearest quarter inch?

Student: Use an inch ruler.

T: Okay. What if it's longer than a 12-inch ruler?

S: Use two rulers and place them end-to-end.

S: Or, we could mark 12 inches on the string. Then continue measuring from that point with the same ruler.

S: We could use a yardstick.

S: Or, we could just wrap a tape measure around our head.

T: Good ideas. Regardless of what you use, be sure you are as accurate as possible.

Sample Line Plot: Answers will vary. The number of x's should correspond to data collected in the table.

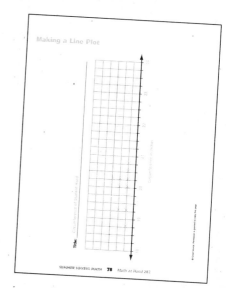

© Great Source. Copying is prohibited.

NUMBER NAMES

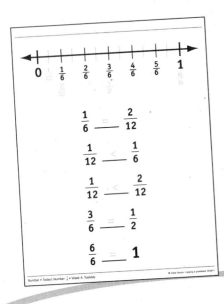

NUMBER Equivalent fractions

- *The number line is divided in to how many equal parts between 0 and 1?* (6) *Name the fractions.* ($\frac{1}{6}$, $\frac{2}{6}$, $\frac{3}{6}$, $\frac{4}{6}$, $\frac{5}{6}$) *What is another name for 1?* ($\frac{6}{6}$)

- ✎ *Invite a volunteer to divide the number line into 12 equal parts between 0 and 1.* **Which mark would you label $\frac{2}{12}$?** (second from zero, same as $\frac{1}{6}$) *Where is $\frac{1}{12}$?* (first from zero)

- *What can you tell about $\frac{1}{6}$ and $\frac{2}{12}$?* (they are the same, or equal) *$\frac{1}{6}$ and $\frac{1}{12}$?* ($\frac{1}{12}$ is halfway between 0 and $\frac{1}{6}$)

- ✎ Complete the comparisons.

Math at Hand 035

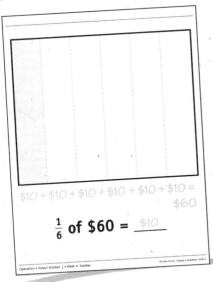

OPERATIONS Explore dividing by a fraction

- **Problem Solving** *You have $60. Suppose you want to save $\frac{1}{6}$ of the money towards birthday gifts for your family. How much money is that?*

- ✎ *How can you use the diagram to find the answer?* (make 6 equal sections) *How many sections would you shade to show $\frac{1}{6}$ of the money?* (1)

- ✎ *What number repeated 6 times equals 60?* (10) *So, what can you tell about $\frac{1}{6}$ of 60?* (It is equal to 10.)

- ✎ *How much money will you set aside for birthday gifts?* ($10)

Math at Hand 168

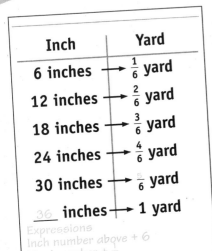

PATTERNS AND ALGEBRA Write expressions

- *What do you see?* (sample answer: Inch, Yard; whole numbers, fractions; equal symbol)

- ✎ *What can you tell about the numbers in the Inch column?* (increasing by 6 each time) *What is an expression to find the next number in this column?* (sample answer: Inch number above + 6)

- ✎ *How are the fractions in the Yard column changing?* (increasing by $\frac{1}{6}$ each time) *What is an expression to find the next number in this column?* (sample answer: Yard number above + $\frac{1}{6}$)

Math at Hand 237–238

© Great Source. Copying is prohibited.

KEY ✎ = record on pad

GEOMETRY Reflection

- *Describe the way the figure "L" changed from left to right.* (sample answers: you can see its mirror image; or, it flipped across the line) *This change is called a* reflection.

- *Did the size or the shape of the figure change?* (no) *Is the figure on the right side closer to the line of reflection, farther away, or the same distance?* (sample answer: everything is the same except the image is flipped over)

- ✎ *What should you watch out for when you draw the reflection?* (sample answers: check the distance; be sure it is a mirror image; use cut outs to check the reflection)

Math at Hand 379

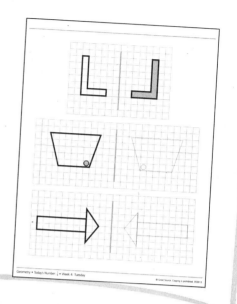

MEASUREMENT Explore surface area of a cube

- *What is the area of any shape?* (the space covered by the shape)

- ✎ *Tell what happens if you cut along the edge of the cube.* (sample answer: you get a flat image made up of 6 squares) *The flat image is called a* net. *Invite a volunteer to draw a net of the cube.* (see recording pad)

- ✎ *The square is 2 inches on each side.* *What is the area of one square?* (4 inches squared) *What is the area of the 6 squares?* (24 inches squared) *Show your work.* (see recording pad)

- ✎ *The sum of the areas is called the* surface area *of the cube. The area of one face is what fraction of the total surface?* ($\frac{1}{6}$)

Math at Hand 306–307

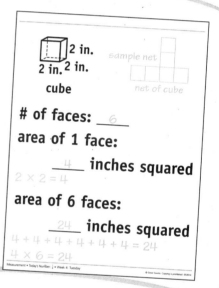

VOCABULARY *area*

- *What does it mean when you are looking for the area of a shape?* (sample answer: find the space covered by the shape)

- *When might you need to find the area of something in real life?* (sample answer: if you need to paint a wall)

- *How is area different from perimeter?* (sample answer: perimeter is the distance around the edge of a shape)

REACHING ALL LEARNERS Encourage students to brainstorm examples of the word *area* used in everday language. For example, *grassy area*, *shady area*, and *area rug*.

Math at Hand 299

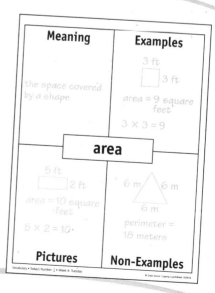

© Great Source. Copying is prohibited.

PRACTICE

Written Practice

CONCEPTS AND SKILLS

- Compare fractions
- Model and compute with fractions
- Surface area of a cube
- Review order of operations
- Problem Solving Strategies and Skills: *Make a Table, Look for a Pattern, Make an Organized List; Solve in More than One Way*

PREVIEW THE PRACTICE

- Divide a circle into 6 equal sections. Shade one section. *What fraction describes the shaded part of the circle?* ($\frac{1}{6}$)
- Divide each sixth into 2 equal sections. *What fraction describes the shaded parts of the circle?* ($\frac{2}{12}$) *Describe $\frac{1}{6}$ and $\frac{2}{12}$.* (They are equal.)

SUPPORT THE PRACTICE

- Problems 1–3 compare fractions. Review how to read the number line.
- Problems 4–6 compute with fractions. Help students connect the shaded part with the answer.
- Problems 7–10 work with area. Help students recall the attributes of a cube.
- Problems 11–13 revisit order of operations. Remind students to work inside the parentheses first.

Name _____

NUMBER AND OPERATIONS

Use the number line to help you compare. Write <, >, or =. ◄1–3. MAH 035

1. $\frac{1}{6}$ __<__ $\frac{3}{6}$ 2. $\frac{1}{2}$ __>__ $\frac{1}{6}$ 3. $\frac{1}{2}$ __=__ $\frac{3}{6}$

Fill in the blank. Use the diagram to check your answer. ◄4–6. MAH 168

4. $\frac{1}{6}$ of 12 = __2__   5. $\frac{1}{6}$ of 24 = __4__   6. $\frac{1}{6}$ of 18 = __3__

GEOMETRY AND MEASUREMENT

Use the diagram of the cube to answer the question. ◄7–10. MAH 306–307

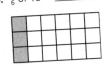

7. A cube has how many faces? __6__

8. What is special about the faces on a cube?

   all squares

9. What is the area of one square face with 4-inch sides?

   16 inches squared

10. What is the area of all 6 faces of the cube?

    96 inches squared

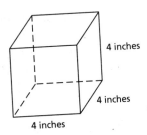

4 inches
4 inches
4 inches

© Great Source. Permission is granted to copy this page.

SUMMER SUCCESS: MATH   **79**   MAH: *Math at Hand*

REACHING ALL LEARNERS

You might ask students to fold sheets of paper to visualize the fractional parts in Problems 4–6.

Math at Hand

If students need help, encourage them to refer to the MAH items shown on the student page.

© Great Source. Copying is prohibited.

Follow the order of operations to compute. ◀11–13. MAH 212-213

11. $(2 \times 3 + 10) \div 8 - 1 =$ ___1___

12. $10 \times 5 + 24 \div 6 =$ ___54___

13. $9 \times 2 - 7 + (21 \div 3) =$ ___18___

ORDER OF OPERATIONS
From left to right:
$\times, \div, +, -$

PROBLEM SOLVING · **UNDERSTAND** · **PLAN** · **TRY** · **LOOK BACK**

Complete each step. ◀14. MAH 396

14. A local grocery store wants to know whether shoppers can tell the difference between beef hot dogs and turkey hot dogs. Of the 6 people surveyed in the morning, 1 shopper could tell the difference. In the afternoon, 5 shoppers out of 30 could tell the difference. And, in the evening 6 out 36 shoppers could tell the difference. At this rate, predict how many people out of 24 shoppers can tell the difference.

a. Underline the question you need to answer.

b. Loop the details about the people surveyed.

c. Mark the strategy/strategies you will use.

d. Solve the problem. Explain your thinking.

POSSIBLE STRATEGIES

- Make a Table
- Look for a Pattern
- Make an Organized List

sample strategies:
Look for a Pattern,
Make an Organized List

can tell	people surveyed	fraction
1	6	$\frac{1}{6}$
5	30	$\frac{5}{30} = \frac{1}{6}$
6	36	$\frac{6}{36} = \frac{1}{6}$
4	24	$\frac{4}{24} = \frac{1}{6}$

e. Answer the question.

4 out 24 can tell the difference.

© Great Source. Permission is granted to copy this page.

SUMMER SUCCESS: MATH **80** MAH: *Math at Hand*

REACHING ALL LEARNERS

If students have difficulty with the problem use two-colored counters to represent the data. Help students see that in each group, $\frac{1}{6}$ of the total could tell the difference.

© Great Source. Copying is prohibited.

PROBLEM SOLVING

Work in small groups of 3 or 4 students.

- Encourage students to find ways to identify needed information to solve the problem.
- *What information do you need to answer the question?* (the number of people who could tell the difference; the total number of people surveyed in each group)
- *How can you use the information?* (to look for a pattern, to make an organized list)

SCORING

a. Last sentence underlined: 1 pt

b. Details about people surveyed circled: 1 pt

c. Choose and apply an appropriate strategy: 1 pt

d. Explanation of solution: 1 pt

e. Correct answer: 1 pt

GLOSSARY TO GO

Today's Vocabulary *area*

Have students complete an entry for today's vocabulary term in their Glossaries. Encourage students to use both words and drawings.

MATH JOURNAL

- *Write about a real life example of when you needed to use area.* (sample answer: I needed to see whether the tablecloth was big enough for the card table.)

NUMBER NAMES TODAY'S NUMBER $\frac{1}{8}$

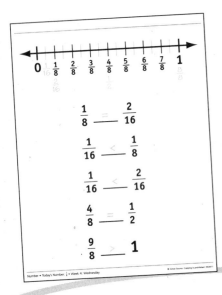

$$\frac{1}{8} = \frac{2}{16}$$

$$\frac{1}{16} < \frac{1}{8}$$

$$\frac{1}{16} < \frac{2}{16}$$

$$\frac{4}{8} = \frac{1}{2}$$

$$\frac{9}{8} > 1$$

NUMBER Fractions greater than 1

- *How many equal parts are shown between 0 and 1?* (8) *Let's count by eighths from 0 to 1.* $\left(\frac{1}{8}, \frac{2}{8}, \frac{3}{8}, \ldots, \frac{7}{8}\right)$

- *What is another name for 1?* $\left(\frac{8}{8}\right)$ $\frac{1}{8}$ *more than 1?* $\left(\frac{9}{8}\right)$ *What can you tell about fractions greater than 1?* (the numerator is bigger than the denominator)

- ✎ *Suppose the number line is divided into 16 equal parts. Which mark would you label* $\frac{2}{16}$? (second from 0, same as $\frac{1}{8}$) $\frac{1}{16}$? (first from 0) *What can you tell about* $\frac{1}{8}$ *and* $\frac{2}{16}$? (They are equal.) $\frac{1}{8}$ *and* $\frac{1}{16}$? ($\frac{1}{16}$ is halfway between 0 and $\frac{1}{8}$)

- ✎ Use the number line to complete the comparisons.

Math at Hand 034–035

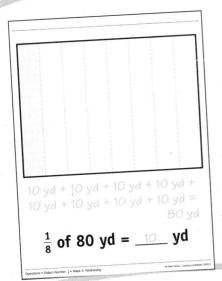

10 yd + 10 yd + 10 yd + 10 yd +
10 yd + 10 yd + 10 yd + 10 yd =
80 yd

$$\frac{1}{8} \text{ of } 80 \text{ yd} = \underline{10} \text{ yd}$$

OPERATIONS Explore dividing by a fraction

- **Problem Solving** *You have 80 yards of fabric. Suppose you want to use* $\frac{1}{8}$ *of it to make a tablecloth. How many yards is that?*

- ✎ *How can you use the diagram to find the answer?* (make 8 equal sections) *How many sections would you shade to show* $\frac{1}{8}$ *of the fabric?* (1)

- ✎ *What number repeated 8 times equals 80?* (10) *So, what can you tell about* $\frac{1}{8}$ *of 80?* (It is equal to 10.)

- ✎ *How much fabric will you have to make the tablecloth?* (10 yards)

Math at Hand 168

Day	Resurfacing
1	→ $\frac{1}{8}$ mile
2	→ $\frac{2}{8}$ mile
3	→ $\frac{3}{8}$ mile
4	→ $\frac{4}{8}$ mile
5	→ $\frac{5}{8}$ mile
6	→ $\frac{6}{8}$ mile
7	→ $\frac{7}{8}$ mile

PATTERNS AND ALGEBRA Using a pattern

- **Problem Solving** *Every day the construction crew resurfaces about* $\frac{1}{8}$ *mile of the road. On what day will* $\frac{3}{4}$ *of a mile of the road be completed?*

- ✎ *How can you write* $\frac{3}{4}$ *as an equivalent fraction using eighths?* (sample answer: think: 2 out of 8 is 1 fourth; to get 3 fourths you'd need 6 eighths) *What is the equivalent fraction?* $\left(\frac{6}{8}\right)$

- ✎ *On what day will* $\frac{3}{4}$ *of a mile of the road be completed?* (Day 6)

REACHING ALL LEARNERS Some students might find it easier to visualize the equivalent fractions using a number line.

Math at Hand 401

© Great Source. Copying is prohibited.

KEY ✎ = record on pad

GEOMETRY Rotation

- *How has the position of the figure T changed?* (sample answer: it turned) This change is called a *rotation*.

- ✎ *Describe how the figure made the rotation.* (sample answer: it turned around the point) Another name for the point is the *turn center. Why would that point be called a turn center?* (sample answer: if you turn the shape all the way around, the point would be in the center; it doesn't move.)

- ✎ **Problem Solving** *The figure T shown made a $\frac{1}{4}$-turn to the right. Draw a diagram to show a $\frac{1}{2}$-turn, then a $\frac{3}{4}$-turn to the right.* (see recording pad)

REACHING ALL LEARNERS Use cutouts to model the turns.

Math at Hand 377

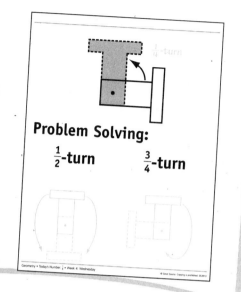

MEASUREMENT Customary weight

- *What are some familiar customary units of weight?* (ounces, pounds, tons) *Which unit usually describes lighter things?* (ounces) *Very heavy things?* (tons) *And, most everything else?* (pounds)

- ✎ There are 16 ounces in 1 pound. *What fraction of a pound is 1 ounce?* ($\frac{1}{16}$)

- ✎ *Is 1 ounce, 1 pound, or 1 ton a more reasonable estimate for the weight of a slice of bread?* (1 ounce) *A loaf of bread?* (1 pound) *A small car?* (1 ton)

Math at Hand 317

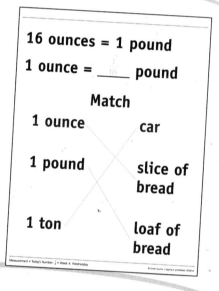

VOCABULARY *volume*

- *What does the volume of a container tell you?* (sample answer: the amount of space inside the container)

- *Suppose you fill a box, or prism, with cubes. How can you use that information?* (sample answer: the number of cubes equals the volume of the box)

- *How can you find the volume of a rectangular prism?* (sample answer: find the area of the base, then multiply by the height of the prism)

REACHING ALL LEARNERS Fit 27 wooden number cubes into the cardstock solid cube to demonstrate measuring volume.

Math at Hand 309

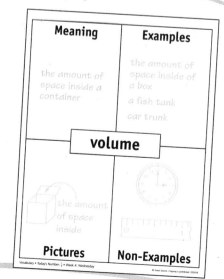

© Great Source. Copying is prohibited.

PRACTICE

Written Practice

CONCEPTS AND SKILLS

- Compare fractions
- Model and compute with fractions
- Work with rotation
- Review ordering numbers
- Problem Solving Strategies and Skills: *Make a Table, Guess, Check, and Revise, Make an Organized List; Take Notes*

PREVIEW THE PRACTICE

- Draw a large rectangle on the board, and then divide it into 4 equal parts. *How many parts will there be if each of the 4 parts is divided in half?* (8) *And, in half again?* (16) *What is the result of each division?* (the number of parts gets greater, but each individual part gets smaller)

SUPPORT THE PRACTICE

- Problems 1–3 compare fractions. Review how to read the number line.
- Problems 4–6 compute with fractions. Help students connect the shaded part with the answer.
- Problems 7–9 look at rotation. Help students see that a $\frac{1}{4}$-turn to the right is the same as a $\frac{3}{4}$-turn to the left.
- Problems 10–11 review ordering from least to greatest. Help students identify the greatest place value of each number before they begin to order the numbers.

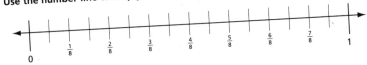

PRACTICE TODAY'S NUMBER $\frac{1}{8}$

Name _____

NUMBER AND OPERATIONS

Use the number line to help you compare. Write <, >, or =. ◄1–3. MAH 034–035

(number line from 0 to 1 marked in eighths: $\frac{1}{8}, \frac{2}{8}, \frac{3}{8}, \frac{4}{8}, \frac{5}{8}, \frac{6}{8}, \frac{7}{8}, 1$)

1. $\frac{1}{8}$ __<__ $\frac{4}{8}$

2. $\frac{1}{2}$ __>__ $\frac{1}{16}$

3. $\frac{9}{8}$ __=__ $1\frac{1}{8}$

Fill in the blank. Use the diagram to check your answer. ◄4–6. MAH 168

4. $\frac{1}{8}$ of 16 = __2__

5. $\frac{1}{8}$ of 32 = __4__

6. $\frac{1}{8}$ of 24 = __3__

GEOMETRY

Show the rotation. ◄7–9. MAH 377

7. $\frac{1}{4}$-turn to the right

8. $\frac{1}{2}$-turn

9. $\frac{3}{4}$-turn to the left

REVIEW

Order from least to greatest. ◄10–11. MAH 010

10. 120, 306, 603, 411 __120, 306, 411, 603__

11. 4.0, 0.04, 40, 0.40 __0.04, 0.40, 4.0, 40__

SUMMER SUCCESS: MATH **81** MAH: *Math at Hand*

REACHING ALL LEARNERS

Use cutouts to help students visualize the turns.

Math at Hand

If students need help, encourage them to refer to the MAH items shown on the student page.

© Great Source. Permission is granted to copy this page.

© Great Source. Copying is prohibited.

Complete each step. ◀12. MAH 396

12. Blake wrote the clues below to solve a number riddle for a 5-digit number.

   - The digits in the 1s and 100s place is neither prime nor composite.

   - Only 2 of the digits in the entire mystery number are odd numbers.

   - The digit in the 10s place is 3 times greater than the digit in the 1,000s place.

   - The sum of the digits equals 16.

   What is Blake's 5-digit mystery number?

   a. Underline the question you need to answer.

   b. Loop the number of digits in the mystery number.

   c. Mark the strategy/strategies you will use.

   d. Solve the problem. Explain your thinking.

POSSIBLE STRATEGIES

- Make a Model
- Guess, Check, and Revise
- Make an Organized List

Sample strategies:
Make an Organized List
Guess, Check, and Revise

5-digit number:

Clue 1: ___ , 1 ___ 1

Clue 2: ___ . 1 ___ 1

Clue 3: ___ 2, 1 6 1

Clue 4: 6 2, 1 6 1

6 + 2 + 1 + 6 + 1 = 16

e. Answer the question.

Blake's 5-digit mystery number is 62,161.

© Great Source. Permission is granted to copy this page.

Work in small groups of 3 or 4 students.

- Encourage students to find ways to identify needed information to solve the problem.

- *What information do you need to answer the question?* (the number of digits in the mystery number, and the clues for the numbers)

- *How can you use the information?* (to make an organized list, to guess, check, and revise)

SCORING

   a. Question underlined: 1 pt

   b. Number of digits in the mystery number circled: 1 pt

   c. Choose and apply an appropriate strategy: 1 pt

   d. Explanation of solution: 1 pt

   e. Correct answer: 1 pt

GLOSSARY TO GO

Today's Vocabulary *volume*

Have students complete an entry for today's vocabulary term in their Glossaries. Encourage students to use both words and drawings.

MATH JOURNAL

- *What are the 3 transformations? Use an arrow to draw an example of each.* (translation, reflection, and rotation; sample drawing at left)

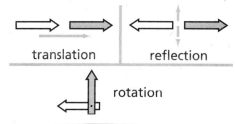

REACHING ALL STUDENTS

- If students have difficulty with the problem, revisit the meaning for the words *prime, composite, odd, place, sum*.

- Help students start solving the problem. Organize the clues, as shown in the answer, with blanks for students to fill in.

© Great Source. Copying is prohibited.

GAME

Active Practice

CONCEPTS AND SKILLS

- Equivalent fractions and decimals
- Order fractions and decimals
- Use models for decimals and fractions

MATH TALK

Model the correct use of these words and encourage students to use them as they work.

- **decimal number** a number containing a decimal point
- **equivalent** having the same value
- **fraction** a number that tells the number of equal parts
- **sequence** a set of numbers arranged in a special order or pattern

MATERIALS

For each pair: 1 set each of Fraction/Decimal Cards I and II; 5 counters

GAME

Ordering Fractions and Decimals

Object: Be the first to order fractions and decimals from least to greatest.

MATERIALS

1 set each of Fraction/Decimal Cards I and II; 5 counters

DIRECTIONS

1. A dealer shuffles the Fraction/Decimal cards, then passes 5 cards, facedown in a row, to each player. The left-over cards, placed facedown, form a draw pile.

2. Players turn their cards faceup, without changing the order of the cards.

3. Taking turns, each player draws a card from the pile. Players must decide whether the new card can be used to replace one of his/her 5 existing cards. *Remember*, the order of the 5 cards can't be changed!

4. The new card can replace an existing card, or be rejected. Either way, a card is placed faceup in the discard pile.

5. The next player can choose to pick up a rejected card, or to pick one from the draw pile. The rejected card can only be picked up by the next immediate player.

6. If a rejected card is picked up, the player must explain why. **(I want the 0.1 card to replace the 0.60 card.)**

7. The first player to have all 5 cards ordered from least to greatest wins the round and takes one counter.

8. Shuffle the cards before beginning each new round. After 5 rounds, the player with the most counters wins.

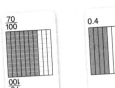

© Great Source. Permission is granted to copy this page.

REACHING ALL LEARNERS

Simplify Reduce the number of cards from 5 to 3 or 2, depending on ability levels.

Variation Players have a one-time option to switch one card with a card from an opponents' hand. This becomes the player's turn, so the player doesn't get to draw a card.

Math at Hand

- Equivalent Decimals, 015
- Ordering Decimals, 018
- Relating Decimals to Fractions, 019
- Comparing and Ordering Fractions, 038–039

© Great Source. Copying is prohibited.

Day 1

- Review relating fractions with denominators of 10 and 100 to decimal numbers.
- Review how to write decimal numbers as fractions.
- Have students order a sequence of number from least to greatest: $\frac{4}{10}$, 0.10, 0.3, $\frac{25}{100}$ *What do I do first?* (Sample response: Write all the numbers as decimals—0.4, 0.10, 0.3, 0.25." *What should I do next?* (Sample response: Write all the decimals in hundredths: 0.40, 0.10, 0.30, and 0.25.) *Are the decimals in order?* (no)

MODEL THE GAME

- Demonstrate with 2 volunteers how to play the game and how to keep score. To model the game, use only 4 cards per player.
- Show students how to identify equivalent decimals and fractions. Also, decide when it would be good to draw from the discard pile or from the draw pile.

Day 2

PLAY THE GAME

- Review the directions for playing the game.
- Assign pairs of students to play the game.

REFLECT ON THE MATH

Encourage students to ask themselves:

- *What value do I want next and why?*
- *Is the left-most card the one with the smallest value?*
- *What is my strategy at this point?*
- *Am I reading the shaded parts of the cards correctly?*
- *Can I use the shaded parts of each card to compare the values?*

MODEL THE GAME

Teacher: I have $\frac{10}{100}$, 0.10, $\frac{90}{100}$, and $\frac{50}{100}$. What do you think I should do?

Student: The first two are the same.

S: Ten hundredths is the smallest value in the deck so the first card is in position, but the rest are not.

T: On my first draw, I get a 0.50 card. What should I do?

S: You can trade it for the second or third card. Fifty hundredths will give you more room to work with later.

T: Let's use it to replace $\frac{90}{100}$, because $\frac{90}{100}$ is the highest number in the deck. It has to go.

S: Too bad it isn't in the last spot.

T: Okay, now my cards are $\frac{10}{100}$, 0.10, 0.50, and $\frac{50}{100}$. The next card I draw is 0.30. What to do?

S: It needs to be the second card. Trade it with the 0.10 card.

T: What do I need to order my cards from least to greatest?

S: Any card greater than 0.50.

T: The player before me just threw out 0.20. Can I use 0.20?

S: Not really. I'd draw one instead.

T: Say I draw 0.9. How can I use it?

S: Trade it with $\frac{50}{100}$. Now the cards are in order from least to greatest: $\frac{10}{100}$, 0.30, 0.50, and 0.9. You win the round!

ONGOING ASSESSMENT

If students need more help, use the hints below, or refer to the *Math at Hand* items shown to the left.

- **Can students handle 5 cards?** Reduce the number of cards so that the game is more manageable.
- **Can students order fractions and decimals?** Go through the deck of cards. Ask students to match equivalent cards. Talk about what they see and how their matching strategies.

© Great Source. Copying is prohibited.

CONCEPT BUILDER
MAKE & TAKE

Additional Support

CONCEPTS AND SKILLS

- Understand fractions as ways to name parts of 1 whole
- Find equivalent fractions
- Add fractions

MATH TALK

Model the correct use of these words and encourage students to use them as they talk about math.

- **denominator** the number of equal parts into which a whole is divided
- **equivalent** of the same amount or value
- **numerator** the equal parts of a whole

MATERIALS FOR DAY 1

Fraction Kit Pieces (SE pp. 85, 85A); scissors; crayons; storage bags

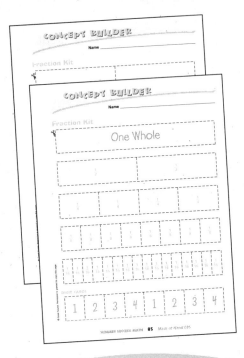

Fraction Kit **Day 1**

GET READY

Follow the instruction below to prepare a sample Fraction Kit to use for demonstration.

BUILD THE FRACTION KIT

1. Have students tear out pp. 85 and 85A of their books. The Fraction Kit pieces should not be cut out yet.

2. Identify the "One Whole" strips as game boards. Have students label the rows representing halves, quarters, eighths, and sixteenths with the appropriate fraction. Each row should be shaded in a different color. Repeat the labeling and coloring with the Fraction Kit pieces on p. 85A.

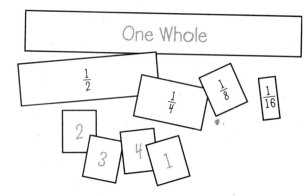

3. Review the relationships between the fraction bars.

4. When the concepts are clear, the rows have been colored, and the fractions written on each piece, have students cut out all the pieces on both pages. Explain that the digit cards 1–4 at the bottom of pp. 85 and 85A are also part of this activity.

5. Students should write their names or initials on their storage bags and on every piece of the cutouts. Store everything until tomorrow.

FOCUS ON THE MATH

- *How are the fraction pieces similar to a ruler?* (Rulers mark off half, quarter, eighth, and sixteenth inches.) *On what other measuring tools might you see halves, quarters, eighths, and sixteenths?* (measuring cups, measuring spoons, measuring tapes)

- *How many halves equal 1 whole?* (2) *Is that always true?* (yes) *How many fourths, or quarters?* (4) *Eighths?* (8) *Sixteenths?* (16)

- *How is looking at patterns of halves, fourths, eighths, and sixteenths different than looking at the pattern of the whole numbers 2, 4, 8, and 16?* (The whole numbers get larger in size; the fractions actually get smaller in size as the denominator increases.)

© Great Source. Copying is prohibited.

Fraction Kit **Day 2**

1. Each player uses a "One Whole" strip as a game board and plays with the fraction pieces. The digit cards are shuffled and placed facedown. The fraction pieces are spread out face up near the player.

2. Partner pairs alternate turns drawing one digit card at a time. Players place that many sixteenth pieces on the game board. Whenever possible, sixteenths are traded for eighths, eighths for fourths, and fourths for halves. Put the digit card back into the facedown stack. Reshuffle often.

3. The winner is the first player to completely fill the game board with two $\frac{1}{2}$ fraction pieces.

MODEL THE ACTIVITY

To prepare students to work on their own, ask them to manipulate their fraction pieces to show equivalent fractions. Ask students to find different ways to make $\frac{1}{2}$ with their fraction pieces. Possible solutions: 2 fourths, 4 eighths, 8 sixteenths, 1 fourth and 2 eighths, 1 fourth and 4 sixteenths, and so on.

Ask questions that focus on specific equivalencies, such as:

- *How many sixteenths equal an eighth?* (2) *two eighths?* (4)

- *How many eighths equal a fourth?* (2) *two fourths?* (4)

REFLECT ON THE MATH

Encourage students to ask themselves.

- *How is the numerator related to the denominator?*
- *Much many more pieces do I need before I can trade for an equivalent fraction?*
- *How can I use whole numbers to double check my work?*

Math at Hand

Equivalent Fractions, 035

REACHING ALL LEARNERS

Have pairs of students follow the rules and work together to build one whole before playing against each other.

Fraction Kits assembled yesterday.

Note: Send these materials home with the Newsletter at the end of the week.

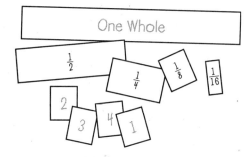

If students need more help, use the hints below, or refer to the *Math at Hand* items shown to the left.

- **Are students able to name fractional quantities correctly?** Have students construct all the "one wholes" that can be made with like denominator fraction pieces.

- **Are students able to exchange equivalent fractional quantities?** Compare the exchange process to trading equivalent values of money. One quarter is the same as 5 nickels or 2 dimes and 1 nickel.

- **Are students able to halve or double a fractional quantity to make an exchange?** Practice halving and doubling the whole numbers 2, 4, 8, and 16 to make a connection to the fractional quantities.

© Great Source. Copying is prohibited.

NUMBER NAMES TODAY'S NUMBER $\frac{1}{100}$

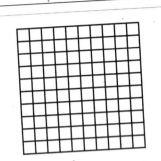

1 hundreth

as a fraction: $\frac{1}{100}$

as a decimal: 0.01

as a percent: 1%

NUMBER Decimals, fractions, and percents

✎ *There are 100 small squares in the large one. How would you show 1 hundredth?* (shade 1 small square) Invite a volunteer to shade 1 square. It can be any square.

✎ *Tell what 1 hundredth means.* (1 out of 100 equal parts)

✎ There are many different ways to write 1 hundredth. *How do you write it as a fraction?* $(\frac{1}{100})$ *A decimal?* (0.01) *A percent?* (1%)

REACHING ALL LEARNERS Use the Blank Hundred Chart to help students visualize the 100 squares within the large square.

Math at Hand 043–044

Problem Solving:

Ways to find the total:

• add 100 ten times

• skip count by 100s ten times

• multiply 100 by 10

• 10 × 100 = 1,000

Answer: $\frac{1}{1,000}$

OPERATIONS Compute with fractions

• **Problem Solving** *Suppose you have a huge sheet of paper with 10 blank Hundred Charts. You shade 1 little square. Let's figure out what fraction of the total that is.*

✎ First find how many little squares altogether. *How many squares are on 1 chart?* (100) *How many charts are there?* (10) *What is one way to find the total number of squares for the whole sheet?* (see recording pad) *Write a multiplication number sentence to find the answer.* (10 × 100 = 1,000)

✎ *What fraction of the total is 1 little square?* $(\frac{1}{1,000})$

Math at Hand 168

In	Out
1	$\frac{1}{100}$
2	$\frac{2}{100}$
3	$\frac{3}{100}$
4	$\frac{4}{100}$
5	$\frac{5}{100}$
6	$\frac{6}{100}$

Equation: In × $\frac{1}{100}$ = Out

PATTERNS AND ALGEBRA Write an equation

• *What pattern do you see in the table?* (sample answer: whole numbers and fractions)

• *How would you describe the Out column fractions?* (sample answers: they have 3-digit denominators; all the denominators are 100; the numerator is the same as the In number)

• *Use the fraction $\frac{1}{100}$ to write an equation that describes the fractions in the table.* (In × $\frac{1}{100}$ = Out)

Math at Hand 401

KEY ✎ = record on pad

© Great Source. Copying is prohibited.

GEOMETRY Ordered pairs

- We use ordered pairs to plot points on a coordinate grid. *How do you locate the ordered pair (9, 3)?* (from 0 go 9 spaces to the right on the *x*-axis, then 3 spaces up the *y*-axis)

✎ *Name the other ordered pairs in the arrow diagram.* (see recording pad)

✎ **Problem Solving** *Draw a figure using straight line segments in the coordinate grid. Use ordered pairs to name the corners, or vertices, in your diagram.* (Check student's work.)

REACHING ALL LEARNERS Some students may need to count aloud as they move along each axis.

Math at Hand 265–266

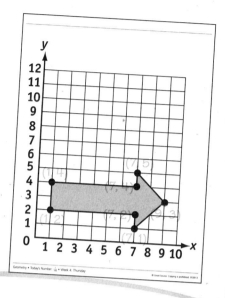

MEASUREMENT Metric length

✎ In the metric system, the prefix *centi* means $\frac{1}{100}$. *What fraction of a meter (m) is 1 centimeter?* ($\frac{1}{100}$) *3 centimeters?* ($\frac{3}{100}$)

✎ *How many centimeters are in 1 meter?* (100)

✎ **Problem Solving** *The polygon on the recording pad is labeled in centimeters (cm). Show how you would find its perimeter in meters.* (see recording pad)

Math at Hand 294–295

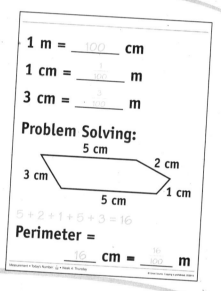

VOCABULARY *capacity*

- *What does the capacity tell you?* (sample answer: the maximum amount that can be held by a container)

- *What are some units of capacity?* (sample answers: teaspoon, fluid ounce, cup, quart, liter)

- *Let's name some non-standard ways to describe capacity.* (a bucket-full, a handful, a scoop, a suitcase full, tub full, sink full)

Math at Hand 313

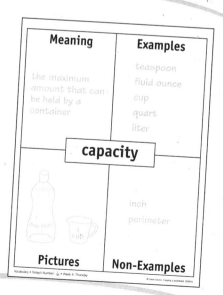

© Great Source. Copying is prohibited.

PRACTICE

Written Practice

CONCEPTS AND SKILLS

- Write equivalent fractions, decimals, and percents
- Compute with fractions
- Complete table of values and write equations
- Review fractional measures
- Problem Solving Strategies and Skills: *Make a Model, Make a Diagram, Make a Table; Use Logical Reasoning*

PREVIEW THE PRACTICE

- Refer to the Blank Hundred Chart. *How many little squares are in the chart?* (100) *What fraction of the chart is 1 little square?* ($\frac{1}{100}$)

SUPPORT THE PRACTICE

- Problems 1–4 ask students to write equivalent fraction, decimal, and percent values. Use the Hundred Chart to help students visualize the parts compared to the whole.
- Problems 5–7 allow students to role play as the teacher. Help students articulate a comment for Problem 7.
- Problems 8–9 work with patterns, and writing an equation to describe the pattern. Remind students to examine the terms in each row from left to right.
- Problems 10–12 review fractional amounts of familiar units of measure.

Name _____

NUMBER AND OPERATIONS

Use the hundred chart to help you complete the table. ◄1–4. MAH 043–044

	Fraction	Decimal	Percent
1.	$\frac{1}{100}$	0.01	1%
2.	$\frac{1}{1,000}$	0.001	0.1%
3.	$\frac{5}{100}$	0.05	5%
4.	$\frac{20}{100}$	0.20	20%

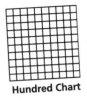

Hundred Chart

Help the teacher correct this paper. Write a note to the student.

Loop the best answer for the product. ◄5–7. MAH 168

5. $\frac{1}{10} \times 10 =$ a. 10   (b. $\frac{10}{10}$)   c. $\frac{10}{100}$ d. $\frac{1}{100}$ ✓

6. $\frac{1}{100} \times 5 =$ a. 5   b. $\frac{5}{10}$ c. $\frac{5}{100}$ (d. $\frac{1}{500}$) ✗

7. Comment: _Multiply the numerator by 5, not the denominator._

PATTERNS AND ALGEBRA

Complete the table of values. Write an equation to describe the pattern. ◄8–9. MAH 401

8.

In	Out
7 →	$\frac{7}{100}$
8 →	$\frac{8}{100}$
9 →	$\frac{9}{100}$
10 →	$\frac{10}{100}$
11 →	$\frac{11}{100}$
12 →	$\frac{12}{100}$

Equation: ___ $In \times \frac{1}{100} = Out$

9.

In	Out
1 →	$\frac{1}{1,000}$
2 →	$\frac{2}{1,000}$
3 →	$\frac{3}{1,000}$
4 →	$\frac{4}{1,000}$
5 →	$\frac{5}{1,000}$
6 →	$\frac{6}{1,000}$

Equation: ___ $In \times \frac{1}{1,000} = Out$

© Great Source. Permission is granted to copy this page.

SUMMER SUCCESS: MATH   **87**   MAH: *Math at Hand*

REACHING ALL LEARNERS

The Blank Hundred Chart is a useful tool. Ask students to point to each square as they count aloud.

Math at Hand

If students need help, encourage them to refer to the MAH items shown on the student page.

© Great Source. Copying is prohibited.

Complete the comparison. ◄10–12. MAH 023, 322

10. $\frac{1}{4}$-hour = ___15___ minutes   11. 6 months = $\frac{1}{2}$ ___year___   12. 1 penny = ___$\frac{1}{100}$___ dollar

PROBLEM SOLVING · **UNDERSTAND** · **PLAN** · **TRY** · **LOOK BACK**

Complete each step. ◄13. MAH 396

13. Yusef has (12 photographs) to display at the art fair. To get ready, Yusef wants to know all the different ways he can display his photographs in (equal rows.) What are all the different combinations possible?

  a. Underline the question you need to answer.

  b. Loop the details about the photographs.

  c. Mark the strategy/strategies you will use.

  d. Solve the problem. Explain your thinking.

POSSIBLE STRATEGIES

- Make a Model
- Make a Diagram
- Make a Table

sample strategy:
Make a Diagram

1 row of 12

2 rows of 6

3 rows of 4

  e. Answer the question.

The photographs can be displayed in 1 row of 12 or 12 rows of 1; 2 rows of 6 or 6 rows of 2; 3 rows of 4 or 4 rows of 3.

© Great Source. Permission is granted to copy this page.

REACHING ALL LEARNERS

Instead of drawing the arrays, students may need to actually manipulate counters to create the arrays for 12.

© Great Source. Copying is prohibited.

PROBLEM SOLVING

Work in small groups of 3 or 4 students.

- Encourage students to find ways to identify needed information to solve the problem.

- *Which clue helps you to get started?* (There are 12 photographs, and they have to be in equal rows.)

- *How can you use the information?* (to make a diagram)

SCORING

  a. Last sentence underlined: 1 pt

  b. Information about the photographs circled: 1 pt

  c. Choose and apply an appropriate strategy: 1 pt

  d. Explanation of solution: 1 pt

  e. Correct answer: 1 pt

GLOSSARY TO GO

Today's Vocabulary *capacity*

Have students complete an entry for today's vocabulary term in their Glossaries. Encourage students to use both words and drawings.

MATH JOURNAL

- *Why do you think the name* ordered pair *is a perfect name to describe numbers such as (4, 7)?* (sample answer: because there is an established way to read (4, 7); each number in the pair refers to a particular direction on the coordinate grid)

NUMBER NAMES TODAY'S NUMBER Review

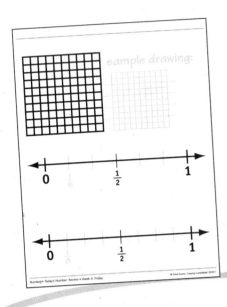

sample drawing:

0 $\frac{1}{6}$ $\frac{1}{2}$ 1

0 $\frac{1}{8}$ $\frac{1}{2}$ 1

NUMBER Fractions, decimals, and percents

✎ *Use the hundred chart to show $\frac{1}{5}$. What is the first step?* (divide the chart into 5 equal parts) *How would you show 1 out 5?* (shade any 1 section of the 5 parts) *What are some other names for $\frac{1}{5}$?* ($\frac{20}{100}$, 20%, or 0.20)

✎ *How would you use the number line to show $\frac{1}{6}$?* (mark 6 equal spaces between 0 and 1) *To show $\frac{1}{8}$?* (mark 8 equal spaces between 0 and 1)

✎ *What can you tell about $\frac{3}{6}$ and $\frac{4}{8}$?* (They are the same or equal.) *What is another name that describes both fractions?* ($\frac{1}{2}$)

Math at Hand 020, 031, 044

Problem Solving:

$\frac{1}{2}$ = $\frac{3}{6}$ sample fractions

= $\frac{4}{8}$

= $\frac{5}{10}$

$\frac{2}{6} + \frac{1}{6} = \frac{3}{6}$ or $\frac{1}{2}$

$\frac{2}{8} + \frac{2}{8} = \frac{4}{8}$ or $\frac{1}{2}$

$\frac{3}{10} + \frac{2}{10} = \frac{5}{10}$ or $\frac{1}{2}$

OPERATIONS Compute with fractions

• **Problem Solving** *Two fractions have a sum of $\frac{1}{2}$. What might they be?*

✎ *First let's think of a few fractions that equal $\frac{1}{2}$.* (sample answers: $\frac{3}{6}$, $\frac{4}{8}$, $\frac{5}{10}$, and so on)

✎ Let's work with $\frac{4}{8}$. *How would you write $\frac{4}{8}$ as the sum of two fractions?* (sample answers: $\frac{3}{8} + \frac{1}{8} = \frac{4}{8}$, $\frac{2}{8} + \frac{2}{8} = \frac{4}{8}$) *What other fraction sums could we use?* (see recording pad)

Math at Hand 159

In	Out
$\frac{1}{6}$	$\frac{1}{12}$
$\frac{1}{5}$	$\frac{1}{10}$
$\frac{1}{3}$	$\frac{1}{6}$
$\frac{1}{4}$	$\frac{1}{8}$
$\frac{1}{2}$	$\frac{1}{4}$
$\frac{1}{7}$	$\frac{1}{14}$

Rule: Each Out number is half as much as the In number.

PATTERNS AND ALGEBRA Write a rule

• *What pattern do you see in the table?* (sample answer: fractions)

• *How would you describe the Out column fractions?* (sample answers: all the denominators are the In denominators times 2; the numerator is the same as the In number)

✎ *Complete the pattern, then write a rule to describe the pattern.* (sample answer: each Out number is half as much as the In number)

Math at Hand 401

KEY ✎ = record on pad

© Great Source. Copying is prohibited.

GEOMETRY Transformations on a coordinate grid

✎ **Problem Solving** *Draw a figure using straight line segments in the coordinate grid.*

✎ *Use ordered pairs to name the corners, or vertices, in your diagram.* (Answers will vary.)

• *Select one of the 3 transformations — translation, reflection, or rotation — to move the diagram.* (Check student's work.)

Math at Hand 375–379

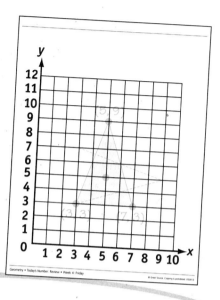

MEASUREMENT Volume and area

• *What is the same about volume and area?* (sample answer: they measure space) *Different?* (sample answer: area measures the space covered by a flat, 2-dimensional figure; volume measures the amount of space inside a 3-dimensional figure)

✎ Volume is measured in cubic units. *How do you write that?* (units^3) Area is measured in square units. *How do you write that?* (units^2)

✎ **Problem Solving** *What is the volume and the area of all the faces of the cube?* (see recording pad)

REACHING ALL LEARNERS Use the number cubes from the kit to give students hands-on experience with 3-dimensional figures.

Math at Hand 306–307, 309–312

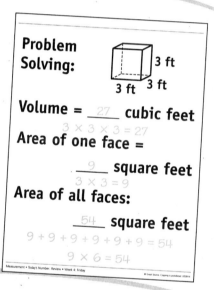

VOCABULARY Review

Let's work together to do today's matching exercise.

• *What units did we use to measure the volume of the cube on the Measurement recording pad?* (ft^3 or cubic feet)

• *We used square feet to measure area. Is that listed here?* (no) *What is listed that describes area?* (square inches and meters^2)

• *What is listed that could measure capacity?* (quart, teaspoon, liter)

• *Which of the choices are related to the word* measure? (all of them)

Math at Hand 293, 299, 309, 313

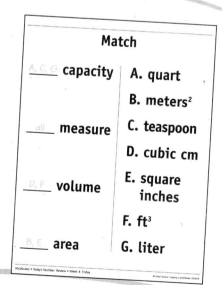

© Great Source. Copying is prohibited.

PRACTICE

Written Practice

CONCEPTS AND SKILLS

- Use a Hundred Chart and a number line to model percent, decimals, and fractions
- Compute fractions
- Surface area and volume
- Review math vocabulary
- Problem Solving Strategies and Skills: *Act It Out, Make a Diagram, Make an Organized List; Use Logical Reasoning*

PREVIEW THE PRACTICE

- *If you need to shade $\frac{5}{100}$ on a Hundred Chart, does it matter which 5 little squares you shade?* (no) *Why?* (as long as 5 little squares are shaded, it doesn't matter)

SUPPORT THE PRACTICE

- Problems 1–5 model percent, decimals, and fractions on a Hundred Chart or a number line. Revisit today's Number recording pad, if needed.
- Problems 6–7 add fractions. Students could use the number lines in problems 4–5, if needed.
- Problems 8–11 work with volume and area. Provide the cube from the kit to count the faces.
- Problems 12–14 revisit familiar vocabulary. Refer to the Glossary section of *Math at Hand*, or students' own glossaries, as needed.
- Problem 15 applies probability in a problem solving setting. Use play money to model, as needed.

PRACTICE TODAY'S NUMBER Review

Name _____

NUMBER AND OPERATIONS

Shade the Hundred Chart to show the number. ◄1–3. MAH 015, 020, 028

1. 20%

2. 0.50

3. $\frac{1}{100}$

Divide the number line into equal parts, then label the fraction. ◄4–5. MAH 031

4. $\frac{1}{8}$

5. $\frac{1}{6}$

Compute. ◄6–7. MAH 159

6. $\frac{1}{8} + \frac{3}{8} =$ ____ $\frac{4}{8}$ or ____ $\frac{1}{2}$

7. $\frac{1}{6} + \frac{2}{6} =$ ____ $\frac{3}{6}$ or ____ $\frac{1}{2}$

GEOMETRY AND MEASUREMENT

Use the diagram to answer questions 8–11. ◄8–11. MAH 301, 306, 311, 382

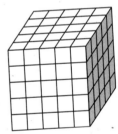

8. How many faces are on a cube? ___6___

9. What is the area of one face of the cube?
   25 square units or 25 units²

10. What is the total area of all the faces of the cube?
   150 square units or 150 units²

11. What is the volume of the cube?
   125 cubic units or 125 units³

© Great Source. Permission is granted to copy this page.

REACHING ALL LEARNERS

Provide a cube from the kit or use blank number cubes to focus on the 6 faces of a cube.

Math at Hand

If students need help, encourage them to refer to the MAH items shown on the student page.

© Great Source. Copying is prohibited.

REVIEW

Loop the word that does _not_ belong with the others. Explain your reasoning. ◄12–14. MAH 003, 012, 028, 294, 337

Answers may vary; a logical explanation may support an alternate answer.

12. numerator ⟨decimal⟩ denominator fraction

Reason: _Sample answer: Numerator and denominator are parts of a fraction._

13. ⟨ounce⟩ millimeter centimeter meter

Reason: _Sample answer: Ounce is not part of the metric system._

14. hundreds ones thousands ⟨tenths⟩

Reason: _tenths are not whole numbers._

PROBLEM SOLVING · **UNDERSTAND · PLAN · TRY · LOOK BACK**

Complete each step. ◄15. MAH 396

15. Marta has (three $1 bills,) (two $5 bills,) (four $10 bills,) and (two $20 bills in her purse.) If she reaches in her wallet without looking, what is the probability she will grab a $10 bill?

a. Underline the question you need to answer.

b. Loop the details about the bills.

c. Mark the strategy/strategies you will use.

d. Solve the problem. Explain your thinking.

_____

_____

_____

_____

_____

e. Answer the question.

The probability of Marta grabbing a $10 bill is $\frac{4}{11}$.

POSSIBLE STRATEGIES

- Act It Out
- Make a Diagram
- Make an Organized List

Sample strategy: Make a Diagram

$1	$5	$10	$20
$1	$5	$10	$20
$1		$10	
		$10	

© Great Source. Permission is granted to copy this page.

SUMMER SUCCESS: MATH **90** MAH: _Math at Hand_

REACHING ALL STUDENTS

For students having trouble, use play money to act out the word problem.

© Great Source. Copying is prohibited.

PROBLEM SOLVING

Work in small groups of 3 or 4 students.

- Encourage students to find ways to identify needed information to solve the problem.
- _What information do you need to answer the question?_ (how many of each type of bill in Marta's purse, total number of bills)
- _How can you use the information?_ (to make a diagram)

SCORING

a. Question underlined: 1 pt

b. Details about the bills circled: 1 pt

c. Choose and apply an appropriate strategy: 1 pt

d. Explanation of solution: 1 pt

e. Correct answer: 1 pt

GLOSSARY TO GO

Today's Vocabulary Review

Have students review and share the entries they made for this week's vocabulary words, _measure_, _area_, _volume_, and _capacity_. Ask students to add more words and/or drawings to the maps if they can.

MATH JOURNAL

- _This week's focus was on measurement topics. Which one did you like the best and why?_ (sample answer: I liked learning about volume because it is useful. Sometimes you need to know how much space is inside a container, especially if you putting things inside.)

READ AND REASON

Additional Support

CONCEPTS AND SKILLS

- Make sense of multiplication
- Relate multiplication and division
- Use logical reasoning

MATH TALK

Model the correct use of these terms and encourage students to use them as they work.

- **division** the operation of making equal groups
- **factor** a number that divides evenly into another
- **multiplication** a shortcut for repeated addition
- **product** the answer to a multiplication operation

SUPPORT PROBLEM 1

Read the problem aloud once, then have a volunteer read the problem again.

- *What is the story about?* (distributing pencils to students)
- *What is the math about?* (making sense of division and multiplication)
- *Where do you think we should start?* (Answers will vary.)
- *Are there any answers you can rule out?* (pound, year, and Monday.) *Why?* (sample answer: because they just don't fit the story)

READ AND REASON

Name _____

Fill in each blank with the choice that makes the *most* sense. Do not use any choice more than once.

1. Freddie is in charge of supplies for the class. He has a total of ___270___ pencils. There are ___27___ kids in the class. Each student gets the same number of pencils. So, Freddie will give you ___10___ pencils.

ANSWER CHOICES

- pound
- 10
- year
- 270
- Monday
- 27

Explain your thinking.

a. How did you begin?
   Example: I looked at the numbers to see which ones go together.

b. Which choice(s) did you rule out?
   Example: Pound, year, and Monday because they just don't fit the story.

c. How are you sure that your answers make sense in the story?
   Example: I tried to rule out the answers that do not make sense.

© Great Source. Permission is granted to copy this page.

SUMMER SUCCESS: MATH **91**

REACHING ALL LEARNERS

- Help students recognize that they could think in terms of factors and products as they make their answer choices.
- Provide counters for students to divide to see what numbers make sense.
- Reduce the difficulty level by using smaller numbers. For example, replace 10 and 27 with 2 and 3.

Math at Hand

- Multiplication, 136
- Relating Multiplication and Division, 145

© Great Source. Copying is prohibited.

Fill in each blank with the choice that makes the *most* sense. Do not use any choice more than once.

2. The average, or _____mean_____, grade in the class on the test was _____83_____. The _____range_____ between the highest score of _____100_____ and the lowest score of 34 was _____66_____ points.

ANSWER CHOICES

ANSWER CHOICES

- 83
- mean
- graph
- 100
- range
- 66
- 500

Explain your thinking.

a. How did you begin?

Example: I remembered the meaning for average and range.

_____

b. What choices did you rule out?

Example: I don't see a graph in the story and 500 seems too big.

c. How do you know your answers make sense in the story?

Example: I reread the story and it made sense.

_____

_____

© Great Source. Permission is granted to copy this page.

CONCEPTS AND SKILLS

- Use data words in context
- Understand average/mean
- Understand range

MATH TALK

Model the correct use of these terms and encourage students to use them as they work.

- **graph** a drawing that shows a relationship between sets of data
- **mean** another name for *average*; a number found by dividing the sum of two or more addends by the number of addends
- **range** the difference between the greatest and the least value in a set of data

SUPPORT PROBLEM 2

Read the problem aloud, then have a volunteer read the problem again.

- *What is the story about?* (a class test average)
- *What is the math about?* (understanding average and range)
- *Where do you think we should start?* (Answers will vary.)
- *Are there any answers you can rule out?* (graph and 500) *Why?* (sample answer: because I don't see a graph in the story and 500 seems too big)

REACHING ALL LEARNERS

- Review the meaning for *mean, range,* and *graph* to get students started.
- Use a small data set to model how to find the average and range.

Math at Hand

- Range, 257
- Types of Average, 259–260

© Great Source. Copying is prohibited.

This Newsletter is designed to be sent home with students at the end of the week along with the completed the *Fraction Kit* Concept Builder materials.

The first page suggests a simple way for students to share with their parent or guardian basic math skills they have been practicing in class.

NEWSLETTER

Summer Success: Math

This week in summer school, your child has worked hard learning all about fractions, decimals, and percents. In geometry, your child learned about the three types of transformations—translation (slide), rotation (turn), and reflection (flip).

Use the diagram to ask your child to demonstrate the three types of transformations.

- Translate the figure 3 spaces in any direction.
- Rotate the figure around the turn center.
- Reflect the figure across the line of reflection.

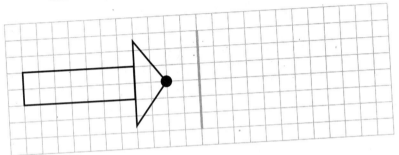

On the back of this page are directions for using the project called *Fraction Kit*. Your child made fraction strips to play a game that involves exchanging fractions with equal value. Invite your child to share this activity with you. Use it together to encourage your child to practice converting equivalent fractions.

 Enjoy the time with your child, and thank you for helping to strengthen the mathematical tie between home and school.

© Great Source. Permission is granted to copy this page.

© Great Source. Copying is prohibited.

Family Math with the Fraction Kit

This week, we have been studying fractions. Using the *Fraction Kit* with your child will help him/her remember what we have learned. You can use the *Fraction Kit* to show equivalent fractions. It can also be used to compare, order, add, and subtract fractions.

1. Have your child compare different fractional pieces. Encourage him or her to express comparisons, such as $\frac{1}{4}$ is greater than $\frac{1}{16}$ or $\frac{1}{8}$ is less than $\frac{1}{2}$.

2. Ask your child to place the fraction pieces in order from greatest to least or least to greatest.

3. Ask your child to show how many different ways fractions can be combined to make $\frac{1}{2}$.

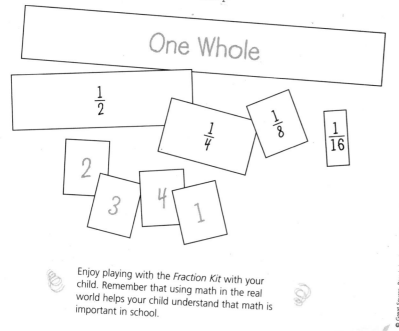

Enjoy playing with the *Fraction Kit* with your child. Remember that using math in the real world helps your child understand that math is important in school.

94

© Great Source. Permission is granted to copy this page.

The back side of this week's Newsletter includes instructions for the parent or guardian to help their student demonstrate the *Fraction Kit* Concept Builder activity at home.

© Great Source. Copying is prohibited.

WEEKLY

| WEEKLY OVERVIEW | MONDAY | TUESDAY |

Materials Read across to find materials needed for this week's daily activities.

*Optional material

Game 0–9 Digit Cards, paper, pencils
Data Study ruler*, calculator*

Game 0–9 Digit Cards, paper, pencils
Data Study ruler*, calculator*

NUMBER NAMES *Instruction: 20–30 min*

Number Place value, Large numbers
Operations Exponents, Compute with large numbers
Patterns and Algebra Table of values, Write equations and rules, Predictions
Geometry Polygons, Prisms, Interior angles
Measurement Area, Volume, Kilometers
Vocabulary Data and Problem Solving terms

Number Names p. 94C

Today's Number: 10
Place value
Exponents
Table of values
Polygons
Area of square
data

Number Names p. 100A

Today's Number: 1,000
One thousand
Compute with large numbers
Write an equation
Attributes of prisms
Volume of rectangular prism
graph

PRACTICE *Written Practice: 20–30 min*

Number and Operations Groups of 10s, Standard, expanded, exponential forms, Place value, Add, subtract, multiply 1,000, 100,000, 1,000,000, $\frac{1}{2}$, $\frac{1}{4}$
Patterns and Algebra Write an equation, Predictions
Geometry Interior angles
Measurement Area, Volume
Review Fractions, Number sense, Rounding, Interior angles, Place value
Problem Solving Strategies and skills

Practice p. 95

Find groups of 10s
Exponential forms
Area of regular polygons
Fractions on a number line
Make a Table
Make an Organized List
Write an Equation
Take Notes
Use Logical Reasoning

Practice p. 101

Place value
Add, subtract, multiply 1,000
Find a missing number in a table of values
Write an equation with variables
Number sense for 100
Draw a Diagram
Write an Equation
Make a Model
Find Needed Information

GAME *Active Practice: 20–30 min*

Read/write large numbers
Powers of 10 and exponents
Estimate product
Calculate exact product
Compare numbers

Game p. 97

Ten Times Ten
Read and write large numbers
Understand powers of 10
Apply exponents

Game p. 97

Ten Times Ten
Read and write large numbers
Understand powers of 10
Apply exponents

FOCUS *Additional Support: 20–30 min*

Data, Tables, Bar graphs, Range, mean, median, Rounding, Customary weight, Fractions, Decimals, Triangles

Data Study p. 99

Graphing Data
Data in tables and bar graphs
Range, mean, median
Rounding

Data Study p. 99

Graphing Data
Data in tables and bar graphs
Range, mean, median
Rounding

© Great Source. Copying is prohibited.

PLANNER

WEDNESDAY	THURSDAY	FRIDAY

Game 0–9 Digit Cards, counters, paper, pencils, calculator*
Concept Builder markers, scissors, tape, adding machine tape, bags

Game 0–9 Digit Cards, counters, paper, pencils, calculator*
Concept Builder materials prepared previously

Game See Tuesday and Thursday.
Newsletter SE p. 115 (Send home with the Concept Builder materials at the end of the week.)

Number Names p. 102A

Today's Number: 100,000
One hundred thousand
Compute with large numbers
Write an equation
Interior angles of rectangles
Kilometers
survey

Number Names p. 108A

Today's Number: 1,000,000
One million
Compute with large numbers
Write a rule
Interior angles of triangles
Area of prisms
strategy

Number Names p. 110A

Today's Number: Review
Large numbers
Compute with large numbers
Predictions
Interior angles of triangles
Big number measures
Vocabulary review

Practice p. 103

Write in exponential form
Add, subtract, multiply 100,000
Volume of prisms
Interior angles of rectangles
Draw a Diagram
Guess, Check, and Revise
Write an Equation
Find Needed Information

Practice p. 109

Write in exponential form
Multiply 1,000,000 by a fraction
Area
Rounding
Make a Model
Act It Out
Draw a Diagram
Use Logical Reasoning

Practice p. 111

Write large numbers in exponential and factored form
Compute with large numbers
Predict terms in a table of values
Place value
Make a Diagram
Look for a Pattern
Write an Equation
Solve in More Than One Way

Game p. 105

Eagle-Eye Estimation
Estimate product
Calculate exact product
Compare numbers

Game p. 105

Eagle-Eye Estimation
Estimate product
Calculate exact product
Compare numbers

Game pp. 97 and 105

Choice
Ten Times Ten or variation
Eagle-Eye Estimation or variation

Concept Builder p. 107

Make & Take:
Inch Ruler
Fractional amounts and equivalencies

Concept Builder p. 107

Make & Take:
Inch Ruler
Fractional amounts and equivalencies

Read and Reason p. 113

Customary weight
Decimals
Attributes of triangles

© Great Source. Copying is prohibited.

NUMBER NAMES TODAY'S NUMBER 10

$$120 = \underline{12} \text{ tens}$$

$$450 = \underline{45} \text{ tens}$$

$$990 = \underline{99} \text{ tens}$$

$$1{,}000 = \underline{100} \text{ tens}$$

NUMBER Place value

- *The number system we use is based on groups of 10s. How many ones are in 10?* (10 ones) *How many tens are in 100?* (10 tens) *How many hundreds are in 1,000?* (10 hundreds)
- ✎ *How many tens are in 120?* (12 tens) *In 450?* (45 tens) *In 990?* (99 tens) *In 1,000?* (100 tens)

REACHING ALL LEARNERS Cut equal lengths of the adding machine tape. Label each one *ten*. Use as many as needed to illustrate the number of tens in each number on the recording pad.

Math at Hand 002

$$10 \times 10 = 100 \text{ or } 10^2$$

$$10 \times 10 \times 10 = 10^3$$

$$10 \times 10 \times 10 \times 10 = 10^4$$

OPERATIONS Exponents

- *Repeated multiplication has a shortcut.*
- *Look at the equation 10 × 10 = 100. How many times is the factor repeated?* (2 times) *What do you think the raised digit 2 in the answer tells you?* (10 repeats 2 times) *The raised digit is called an exponent. How do you read 10 with a raised 2?* (10 to the second power, or 10 squared)
- ✎ *How many times is the factor 10 repeated in 10 × 10 × 10?* (3) *What is the exponent for this product?* (3) Invite a volunteer to fill in the blank for the last number sentence.

REACHING ALL LEARNERS Use the Blank Hundreds Chart to show that 10^2 means each column/row repeated 10 times.

Math at Hand 064–065

In	Out
10 →	10^1
100 →	10^2
1,000 →	10^3
10,000 →	10^4

Rule: Number of zeros equals the exponent.

PATTERNS AND ALGEBRA Table of values

- *Describe how the In numbers are related to the Out numbers.* (sample answers: the Out number is another way to write the In number; the exponent equals the number of zeros)
- ✎ *What do you think is the missing number?* (10^4) *Why?* (sample answers: it follows the pattern for the exponents; there are 4 zeros in 10,000)
- ✎ *Can you write a rule to describe what is happening to the numbers?* (number of zeros equals the exponent)

Math at Hand 401

© Great Source. Copying is prohibited.

KEY ✎ = record on pad

GEOMETRY Polygons

- *How are the three shapes alike?* (all are quadrilaterals)
- *Which shape is unlike the others?* (the trapezoid)
- *How are 2 of the 3 shapes alike?* (all sides have the same length and all angles the same measure) *Shapes with all sides congruent are described as* regular.
- ✎ *Which is the shape that is not regular?* (see recording pad)
- ✎ *Can you draw one more shape that is not regular?* (any closed shape with one or more different length sides)

Math at Hand 357

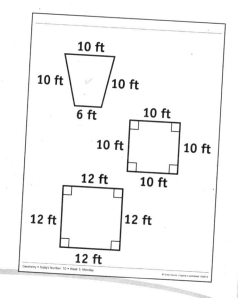

MEASUREMENT Area

- *What can you tell about this shape?* (It is a square with sides that are 10 units in length.)
- *How would you find the number of units inside the big square?* (sample answers: you can count them 1 by 1, you can skip count by 10s, you can multiply 10 by 10) *What do you call the space inside any shape?* (area)
- ✎ **Problem Solving** *How would you multiply to find the area of the square?* (see recording pad)

REACHING ALL LEARNERS Help students see that $10 \times 10 = 100$ and units $\times$ units $=$ units^2.

Math at Hand 299–301

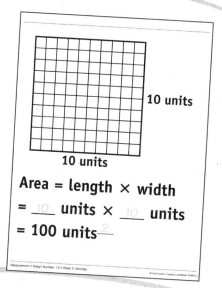

VOCABULARY *data*

- *What kind of data could you collect from your friends?* (sample answers: favorite color, number of pets, birth month, and so on)
- *What are ways to collect data?* (sample answers: take a survey, take a sample, do an experiment)
- *How do we show data?* (sample answers: in a graph, in an organized list, in a table, and so on)
- *What is another word that means the same as* data? (information)

Math at Hand 248

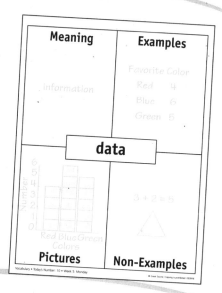

© Great Source. Copying is prohibited.

PRACTICE

Written Practice

CONCEPTS AND SKILLS

- Find groups of 10s
- Exponential forms
- Area of regular polygons
- Review fractions on a number line
- Problem Solving Strategies and Skills: *Make a Table, Make an Organized List, Guess, Check, and Revise; Use Logical Reasoning*

PREVIEW THE PRACTICE

- *Is 10^3 the same as 10×3 or $10 \times 10 \times 10$?* ($10 \times 10 \times 10$) *What does the raised digit 3 mean?* (tells the number of times 10 repeats in the multiplication)

SUPPORT THE PRACTICE

- Problems 1–3 ask students to find groups of 10s in a number.
- Problems 4–9 match multiplication expressions with equivalent exponential forms. Help students recall the connection between exponents and the number times a factor is repeated. Work on Problem 4 together, if needed.
- Problems 10–11 involve area of squares. Revisit today's Geometry and Measurement recording pads, if needed.
- Problems 12–16 review fractions on a number line. Help students recognize that Point C is halfway between 0 and 1.

Name _____

NUMBER AND OPERATIONS

Fill in the blank. ◄1–3. MAH 002

1. 150 = ___15___ tens   2. 620 = ___62___ tens   3. 930 = ___93___ tens

Complete the equation. ◄4–9. MAH 064–065

4. $10^3 = 10 \times$ ___10___ $\times$ ___10___   5. $9^3 =$ ___9___ $\times$ ___9___ $\times$ ___9___

6. $10^4 = 10 \times$ ___10___ $\times$ ___10___ $\times$ ___10___.

7. $3^4 =$ ___3___ $\times$ ___3___ $\times$ ___3___ $\times$ ___3___

8. $10 \times 10 \times 10 \times 10 \times 10 = 10$ ___5___   9. $3 \times 3 \times 3 \times 3 \times 3 \times 3 = 3$ ___6___

GEOMETRY AND MEASUREMENT

Select the regular polygon. What is its area? ◄10–11. MAH 299–301

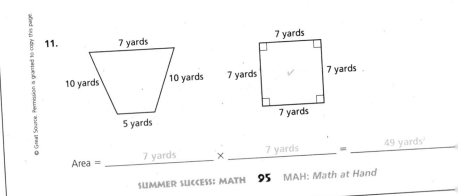

10.

Area = ___3___ miles $\times$ ___3___ miles = ___9___ miles²

11.

Area = ___7 yards___ $\times$ ___7 yards___ = ___49 yards²___

REACHING ALL LEARNERS

Provide students with calculators to demonstrate exponential power. For example, show that 5^3 means $5 \times 5 \times 5$ whose product is 125. Compare that product to $5 \times 3 = 15$ to illustrate the difference. Repeat with other numbers such 6^2 or 2^4.

Math at Hand

If students need help, encourage them to refer to the MAH items shown on the student page.

© Great Source. Permission is granted to copy this page.

© Great Source. Copying is prohibited.

Write a fraction in simplest form to name the point on the number line. ◀12–16. MAH 031

12. Point A = $\frac{2}{5}$

13. Point B = $\frac{1}{2}$

14. Point C = $\frac{7}{10}$

15. Point D = $\frac{4}{5}$

16. Point E = $\frac{9}{10}$

0    $\frac{1}{10}$ A   B   C   D   E   1

PROBLEM SOLVING · **UNDERSTAND · PLAN · TRY · LOOK BACK**

Complete each step. ◀17. MAH 396

17. Assignment: Make different 2-digit numbers using the digits 1, 5, 7, and 9. No digit can be repeated in the same number. How many different numbers can you make?

  a. Underline the question you need to answer.

  b. Loop the details about the type of number to be made.

  c. Mark the strategy/strategies you will use.

  d. Solve the problem. Explain your thinking.

  Possible list:

  15   17   19

  51   71   91

  57   59   79

  75   95   97

  e. Answer the question.

  There are twelve 2-digit numbers that can be made using 1, 5, 7, and 9.

POSSIBLE STRATEGIES

- Make a Table
- Make an Organized List
- Guess, Check, and Revise

Sample Strategy:
Make an Organized List

© Great Source. Permission is granted to copy this page.

PROBLEM SOLVING

Work in small groups of 3 or 4 students.

- Encourage students to find ways to identify needed information to solve the problem.

- *What information do you need to answer the question?* (the number of digits in each number, the digits to use, the do not repeat rule)

- *How can you use the information?* (to make an organized list)

SCORING

  a. Last sentence underlined: 1 pt

  b. Digits information circled: 1 pt

  c. Choose and apply an appropriate strategy: 1 pt

  d. Explanation of solution: 1 pt

  e. Correct answer: 1 pt

GLOSSARY TO GO

Today's Vocabulary *data*

Have students complete an entry for today's vocabulary term in their Glossaries. Encourage students to use both words and drawings.

REACHING ALL LEARNERS

If students have difficulty with the problem, begin an organized list or table using the first two digits, 1 and 5 to make the numbers 15 and 51. Explain why is it that 11 and 55 are not included. (The rule states no digits can be repeated in the same number.)

MATH JOURNAL

- *Suppose you have to create a survey to collect data about your classmates. What information would you want to gather?* (sample answers: person's age, birth date, birth year, birthplace, gender, and so on)

© Great Source. Copying is prohibited.

Active Practice

CONCEPTS AND SKILLS

- Read and write large numbers
- Understand powers of 10
- Apply exponents

MATH TALK

Model the correct use of these words and encourage students to use them as they work.

- **exponent** the number that tells how many times a number is repeated as a factor
- **factor** a whole number that divides evenly into another
- **power of 10** a number with 10 as a base and a whole-number exponent

MATERIALS

For each pair: 4 sets of 0–9 Digit Cards, paper, pencils

Ten Times Ten			
Round	Exponential Form	Factored Form	Standard Form
1.			
2.			
3.			
4.			
5.			
6.			

Round	Exponential Form	Factored Form	Standard Form
1.			
2.			
3.			
4.			
5.			
6.			

Round	Exponential Form	Factored Form	Standard Form
1.			
2.			
3.			
4.			
5.			
6.			

Ten Times Ten

Objective: To write powers of 10 using an exponent.

MATERIALS

4 sets of 0–9 Digit Cards, paper, pencil

DIRECTIONS

1. Use the recording sheet on p. 98.

Round	Exponential Form	Factored Form	Standard Form
1.	10^3	10 X 10 X 10	1,000
2.			
3.			
4.			

2. Each player takes and shuffles 2 sets of 0–9 digit cards. Place the pile facedown.

3. Turn over the top card from your pile.

4. The player with the greater digit plays the round. (If both players get the same digit card, repeat step 3.)

5. If your card is greater, begin by finding the difference between the two cards. Now build an expression using this difference as a power of 10. For example, if you draw an 8 and the other player draws a 5, the difference is 3. Write 10^3 on your recording sheet, the factored form, and the standard form. Announce the number of times 10 is used as a factor. **(In 10 to the third, the factor 10 is used 3 times.)** If you draw the same digit cards, shuffle well and draw again.

6. The standard form is your score for the round. The other player scores 0.

7. Discard your cards. Shuffle and play again.

8. Keep a running total of your scores. After six rounds, the player with the higher score wins.

In 10 to the third, the factor 10 is used 3 times.

© Great Source. Permission is granted to copy this page.

REACHING ALL LEARNERS

Simplify Each player gets 3 cards from the 0–9 Digit Card set. Shuffle and turn over his/her top card. Use that number as the exponent for the power of 10. Write the power of 10 in factored form.

Variation Instead of using the difference of the two cards to name the exponent, use the sum.

Math at Hand

- Reading and Writing Large Numbers, 005–006
- Powers of 10, 007

© Great Source. Copying is prohibited.

Day 1

- Review the terms *factor* and *exponent*.
- Have students find a few powers of 10, such as 10^2, 10^3, and 10^4.

MODEL THE GAME

- Demonstrate with a volunteer how to play the game and how to keep score.
- Emphasize the connection between the exponent and the number of times 10 is used as a factor.

Day 2

PLAY THE GAME

- Review the directions for playing the game.
- Assign partners pairs to play the game.

REFLECT ON THE MATH

Encourage students to ask themselves:

- *Did I find the correct difference?*
- *Do the numbers of factors equal the exponent?*
- *How far ahead (or behind) am I?*
- *Is it possible for me to win this game?*

MODEL THE GAME

Teacher: I have a 2 and my opponent has a 7. Who gets to play?

Student: Your opponent.

T: What happens first?

S: You find the difference between the two cards. It is 5.

T: How will my opponent use the number 5?

S: As an exponent by writing 10^5.

T: What is the factored form for 10^5?

S: $10 \times 10 \times 10 \times 10 \times 10$

T: Great. The factor 10 is repeated 5 times. What is the value of 10^5?

S: 100,000

T: How can you be sure?

S: Check if the number of zeros is equal to the exponent.

S: Yes. When you have 10 as a base, the exponent tells you how many zeros are in the answer.

ONGOING ASSESSMENT

If students need more help, use the hints below, or refer to the *Math at Hand* items shown to the left.

- **Can students show the different ways to express a power of 10?** Review with students how to write numbers in standard, word, factor, and exponential form.

- **Can students make the connection between the exponent and the factored form of a power of 10?** Write out the factored forms starting with 10^1 up to 10^{10}. Encourage students to describe the patterns they see between the exponent and the number of times 10 is repeated.

© Great Source. Copying is prohibited.

TODAY'S FOCUS

DATA STUDY

Additional Support

CONCEPTS AND SKILLS

- Read a table
- Make and interpret a bar graph
- Find range, mean, and median for a set of data
- Compare and summarize data
- Round large numbers

MATH TALK

Model the correct use of these terms and encourage students to use them as they work.

- **axis** the horizontal or vertical reference lines on a graph
- **bar graph** a display that uses bars to represent data
- **scale** marks at fixed intervals used in measurement or graphing

MATERIALS

For each pair: straightedge or ruler*, calculator*

*Optional materials

GET STARTED

- Read and discuss the directions on page 99 with students.
- Give students about 10 minutes to complete the rounding task at the top of the page.

DATA STUDY

Name _____

Graphing Data

How much might the governor make?

READ A TABLE

Read each amount. Round the numbers to complete the table.

Some U.S. Governors' Salaries

State	Salary (2002)	Round to Nearest Thousand	Round to Nearest Ten Thousand
Nebraska (NE)	$65,000	$65,000	$70,000
Nevada (NV)	$117,000	$117,000	$120,000
New Hampshire (NH)	$100,690	$101,000	$100,000
New Jersey (NJ)	$130,000	$130,000	$130,000
New York (NY)	$179,000	$179,000	$180,000
North Dakota (ND)	$83,013	$83,000	$80,000

Source: 2003 Encyclopedia Britannica Almanac

GRAPH THE DATA

- Decide whether you want to make a horizontal or vertical bar graph.
- Think of a title for your graph. Draw the axes. Choose a scale. Label the axes.
- Use data from either column of rounded numbers to draw the bars on your graph.

ANALYZE THE DATA

1. Look at the graph. Which governor has the highest salary? _____New York_____

   Lowest salary? _____Nebraska_____

2. Look at the graph to estimate the range. _____About $110,000_____

   Look at the salaries in the table to find the exact range. _$179,000 − $65,000 = $114,000_

3. Find the exact mean. _$674,703 ÷ 6 = $112,450.50_

4. What is the median salary for this group of governors?

   _($100,690 + $117,000) ÷ 2 = $108,845_

© Great Source. Permission is granted to copy this page.

SUMMER SUCCESS: MATH **99** *Math at Hand* 267–273

REACHING ALL LEARNERS

- Review how to read, write, and compare large numbers through the hundred thousands.
- Review how to round numbers to a specified place value.
- Review how to estimate sums and differences.

Math at Hand

© Great Source. Copying is prohibited.

Day 1

Before completing the table on page 99, discuss the topic of salaries and then have students take turns reading the names of the states with corresponding salary amounts. Reading the large numbers aloud may indicate their grasp or lack of understanding of whole numbers. Then, have students round the numbers to the nearest thousand and ten thousand to complete the table.

Work with students as needed to create an accurate graph of the data using the grid on the back page. Students may use straightedges or rulers to draw the axes and bars on their graphs. Discuss as a group how to choose an appropriate scale for the axis that is to be used to indicate the increments for the salary amounts.

Day 2

Invite students to share their graphs. Ask them to talk about the title, labels, and the scale used on their graphs and why they chose to make a vertical or horizontal bar graph.

Before completing the questions at the bottom of page 99, allow students to use calculators to find answers to questions 2 and 3 to avoid computational errors. Then work with students to consider the following:

- *How could you tell how many times more the governor of New York earned compared to the governor of Nebraska by just looking at your graph?* (The bar for the New York salary is about three times longer than the bar for the Nebraska salary.)

- **What if?** *Suppose you want to know the average salary of all the state governors. Could you use this set of data to make a reasonable estimate? Explain your reasoning.* (sample answer: Using the mean and median found for this set of data, the average salary for a state governor of about $110,000 is reasonable.)

Teacher: Look at the table of data. What is the greatest rounded number?

Student: It's $180,000.

T: Look at the grid. How many rows and columns are there?

S: I counted 20 of each.

T: How can we figure out a scale for the salary axis using such large numbers?

S: We could label the salary axis Number of Dollars and then put the words *in thousands* in parentheses. Then we could work with numbers up to 180.

T: How could we draw a bar for $85,000 on the graph?

S: I'd make a bar that ends halfway between 80 and 90 on the graph.

Sample graph:

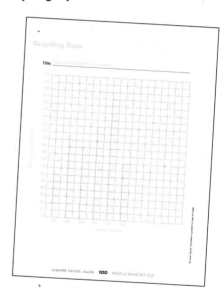

© Great Source. Copying is prohibited.

NUMBER NAMES TODAY'S NUMBER 1,000

_10_ hundreds = 1,000

_100_ tens = 1,000

How many 1,000?

8,000 _8_ thousands

12,000 _12_ thousands

300,000 _300_ thousands

Number • Today's Number: 1,000 • Week 5: Tuesday

NUMBER One thousand

✎ *How many groups of hundreds are in 1,000?* (10 groups) *How many groups of tens?* (100 groups)

• *Can you name something that could be measured in groups of thousands?* (sample answers: 1,000 years, 1,000 miles, 1,000 pounds)

✎ *How many thousands are in 8,000?* (8) *In 12,000?* (12) *In 300,000?* (300)

REACHING ALL LEARNERS Remind students that 2437 is the same as 2,437. The comma doesn't change the value of the number.

Math at Hand 004–005

1,000	1,000
+ 5,321	+ 9,000
6,321	10,000

1,000	1,000
× 3	× 20
3,000	20,000

$1,000 = 10^3$

$1,000 = 10 \times 10 \times 10$

$1,000 = 100 \times 10$

Operations • Today's Number: 1,000 • Week 5: Tuesday

OPERATIONS Compute with large numbers

✎ *When you add 1,000 to any whole number, how many digits will there be in the sum?* (4 or more) Invite a volunteer to write an example. (see recording pad)

✎ *When you multiply 1,000 by any whole number, how many digits will there be in the product?* (4 or more). Invite a volunteer to write an example. (see recording pad)

✎ *Tell how you know another way to write 1,000 is 10^3.* (sample answer: I know $10 \times 10 = 100$ and $100 \times 10 = 1,000$, so another way to write is 1,000 is 10^3.)

Math at Hand 007, 119, 136

---

x	y
25	→ 1,025
50	→ 1,050
10	→ 1,010
37	→ 1,037

Equation: x + 1,000 = y

Patterns and Algebra • Today's Number: 1,000 • Week 5: Tuesday

---

PATTERNS AND ALGEBRA Write an equation

• *How do the numbers change from the x-column to the y-column?* (getting bigger) *By how much?* (by 1,000)

✎ *What do you think is the missing number?* (1,037)

✎ **Problem Solving** *How would you write an addition equation to describe what you see?* (x + 1,000 = y)

REACHING ALL LEARNERS Tell students any letter, word, or symbol can replace x and y.

Math at Hand 236, 240–242, 244

© Great Source. Copying is prohibited.

100A SUMMER SUCCESS: MATH

KEY ✎ = record on pad

GEOMETRY Interior angles

✎ *Look at the rectangle. How many corners, or angles, do you see?* (4) *Since these angles are inside the shape, we call them* interior angles.

✎ *Remember that rectangles haves 90 degree angles. How would you find the total of the interior angles?* (multiply, 90° × 4; add, 90° + 90° + 90° + 90°)

✎ *What is the total?* (360 degrees, or 360°)

REACHING ALL LEARNERS Remind students that 90° angles are also called *right angles*.

Math at Hand 346–347

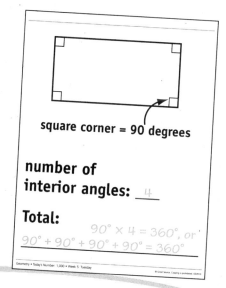

square corner = 90 degrees

number of interior angles: 4

Total:
90° × 4 = 360°, or
90° + 90° + 90° + 90° = 360°

Geometry • Today's Number: 1,000 • Week 5: Tuesday   © Great Source. Copying is prohibited. (5)3912

MEASUREMENT Metric measures

✎ In the metric system, the prefix *kilo* and *milli* mean 1,000. *How many grams are in 1 kilogram?* (1,000) *Meters in 1 kilometer?* (1,000) *Millimeters in 1 meter?* (1,000)

✎ *Name some things whose mass might be measured in kilograms.* (sample answers: animals, boulders, crates)

✎ *What lengths do you think might be measured in kilometers?* (sample answers: distance between cities; length of cable wires; large tracks of land) *In millimeters?* (sample answers: postage stamp length or width; caterpillar length; diameter of small circle)

Math at Hand 294

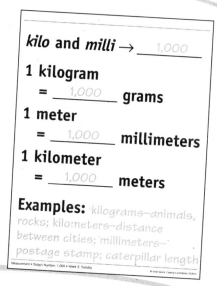

kilo and *milli* → 1,000

1 kilogram
= 1,000 grams

1 meter
= 1,000 millimeters

1 kilometer
= 1,000 meters

Examples: kilograms–animals, rocks; kilometers–distance between cities; millimeters– postage stamp; caterpillar length

Measurement • Today's Number: 1,000 • Week 5: Tuesday   © Great Source. Copying is prohibited. (5)3914

VOCABULARY *graph*

• *Why would you want to display data in a graph?* (sample answers: to help make predictions, comparisons, look for trends, and so on)

• *What are some different types of graphs?* (sample answers: bar graph, line graph, pictographs, circle graph, Venn diagram, time line, stem and leaf plot, line plot, and so on)

• *How would you define* graph? (A drawing that shows data.)

Math at Hand 269–284

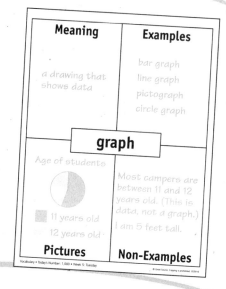

Meaning	Examples
a drawing that shows data	bar graph line graph pictograph circle graph

graph

Pictures	Non-Examples
Age of students 11 years old 12 years old	Most campers are between 11 and 12 years old. (This is data, not a graph.) I am 5 feet tall.

Vocabulary • Today's Number: 1,000 • Week 5: Tuesday   © Great Source. Copying is prohibited. (5)3916

© Great Source. Copying is prohibited.

PRACTICE

Written Practice

CONCEPTS AND SKILLS

- Place value
- Add, subtract, multiply 1,000
- Missing numbers in a table
- Write an equation with variables
- Review number sense for 100
- Problem Solving Strategies and Skills: *Draw a Diagram, Write an Equation, Make a Model; Find Needed Information*

PREVIEW THE PRACTICE

- Write the number 7,132 on the chalkboard. *Add 1,000 to this number. What is the sum?* (8,132) *Subtract 1,000. What is the difference?* (6,132)
- *What is 7,132 multiplied by 1,000?* (7,132,000)

SUPPORT THE PRACTICE

- Problems 1–3 work with the thousands place. If needed, draw a place value chart listing the periods.
- Problems 4–7 give students a chance to be the teacher. Help students articulate a comment to answer problem 7.
- Problems 8–9 ask students to name the missing number in a table of values. Then write an equation that describes the pattern. Revisit today's Patterns and Algebra recording pad, if needed.
- Problems 10–12 apply number sense for 100. Help students decide whether the 100 units mentioned are reasonable.

PRACTICE TODAY'S NUMBER **1,000**

Name _____

NUMBER AND OPERATIONS

How many thousands? Fill in the blank. ◀1–3. MAH 004

1. 11,050 → __11__ thousands   **2.** 6,020 → __6__ thousands   **3.** 9,300 → __9__ thousands

Help the teacher correct this paper. Write a note to the student.

> **Compute.** ◀4–7. MAH 119, 129, 136
>
> **4.** 8,930 + 1,000 = __9,930__ ✔   **5.** 8,930 × 1,000 = __89,300__ ✗
>
> **6.** 8,930 − 1,000 = __7,930__ ✔
>
> **7.** Comment: __#5 should have 4 zeros because 8,930 has 1 zero and then 3__ __more zeros from multiplying by 1,000.__

PATTERNS AND ALGEBRA

Find the missing number. Write an equation that describes the pattern. ◀8–9. MAH 236, 240–241, 244

8.

x	y
65 →	1,065
30 →	1,030
84 →	1,084
120 →	1,120

Equation: ___ x + 1,000 = y ___

9.

x	y
2,800 →	1,800
7,010 →	6,010
5,600 →	4,600
4,004 →	3,004

Equation: ___ x − 1,000 = y ___

© Great Source. Permission is granted to copy this page.

REACHING ALL LEARNERS

Provide students with calculators to explore repeatedly multiplying 10 by 10.

Math at Hand

If students need help, encourage them to refer to the MAH items shown on the student page.

© Great Source. Copying is prohibited.

Which choice is most reasonable? Explain why you think so. ◀10–12. MAH 413

10. Can 100 students sit at your desk?
    Why?   yes   (no)   maybe

    My desk is not large enough to sit 100 students.

11. Are there more than 100 days in one year?
    How do you know?   (yes)   no   maybe

    There are 365 days in one year.

12. Could a rock weigh 100 pounds?
    Why?   yes   no   (maybe)

    If it is a big rock. Small rocks will weigh less.

PROBLEM SOLVING • **UNDERSTAND** • **PLAN** • **TRY** • **LOOK BACK**

Complete each step. ◀13. MAH 396

13. Franklin's house has an unusual patio. It is a 5-sided shape. (Two sides) of the patio are each (3 meters) long. One side is (5 meters) long, and another side is (4 meters) long. The fifth side is only (2 meters) long. What is the perimeter of Franklin's patio?

    POSSIBLE STRATEGIES
    • Make a Model
    • Write an Equation
    • Draw a Diagram

    a. Underline the question you need to answer.

    b. Loop the lengths of the 5-sided patio.

    c. Mark the strategy/strategies you will use.

    d. Solve the problem. Explain your thinking.

    $3 + 5 + 3 + 2 + 4 = 17$

    Sample Strategies:
    Draw a Diagram, Write an Equation

    Sample drawing:

    3 meters   4 meters
                         2 meters
    5 meters   3 meters

    e. Answer the question.

    The perimeter is 17 meters.

© Great Source. Permission is granted to copy this page.

PROBLEM SOLVING

Work in small groups of 3 or 4 students.

• Encourage students to find ways to identify needed information to solve the problem.

• *What information do you need to answer the question?* (the length of each side of the patio)

• *Is this a regular 5-sided shape?* (no) *How do you know?* (not all lengths are the same for the 5 sides)

• *How can you use the information?* (to draw a diagram, write an equation)

SCORING

a. Last sentence underlined: 1 pt

b. Dimensions circled: 1 pt

c. Choose and apply an appropriate strategy: 1 pt

d. Explanation of solution: 1 pt

e. Correct answer: 1 pt

GLOSSARY TO GO

Today's Vocabulary *graph*

Have students complete an entry for today's vocabulary term in their Glossaries. Encourage students to use both words and drawings.

MATH JOURNAL

• *Write 3 questions similar to the ones in problems 10–12. Then answer them.* (Questions should ask for reasonableness in relation to a quantity of 100 units. Answers to *Why?* should support the answer choice of Yes, No, or Maybe.)

REACHING ALL LEARNERS

If students have difficulty with the problem, draw a 5-sided polygon for students to label. Check to be sure that the sides are proportional.

© Great Source. Copying is prohibited.

NUMBER NAMES   TODAY'S NUMBER 100,000

<table>
<tr><td>100,000</td><td>zeros: <u>5</u></td></tr>
<tr><td></td><td>exponent: <u>5</u></td></tr>
</table>

$10^5 = $ <u>10</u> × <u>10</u> × <u>10</u> × <u>10</u> × <u>10</u>

Examples:

sample answers: population of a medium-size city; long distances; acreage of a national park; weight of battleship; budgets; cost of a house

Number • Today's Number: 100,000 • Week 5: Wednesday   © Great Source. Copying is prohibited. 053911

NUMBER One hundred thousand

✎ *How many zeros are in 100,000?* (5) *What is another way to write the number using exponents?* (10^5) *How do you read the number in exponential form?* (10 to the fifth)

✎ *How do you write 100,000 in factored form?* (10 × 10 × 10 × 10 × 10)

✎ *Think of some examples of how the number 100,000 might be used.* (sample answers: to describe the population of a medium-size city; distances; acreage of a national park; weight of battleships; budgets; cost of a house)

Math at Hand 005–007

<table>
<tr><td>100,000
+ 2,871
102,871</td><td>100,000
× 5
500,000</td></tr>
<tr><td>100,000
+ 545
100,545</td><td>100,000
× 4
400,000</td></tr>
</table>

Operations • Today's Number: 100,000 • Week 5: Wednesday   © Great Source. Copying is prohibited. 053912

OPERATIONS Compute with large numbers

✎ *When you add 100,000 to any whole number, how many digits will there be in the sum?* (6 or more) Invite a volunteer to write an example. (see recording pad)

✎ *When you multiply a whole number by 100,000 how many digits will there be in the product?* (6 or more). Invite a volunteer to write an example. (see recording pad)

Math at Hand 007, 119, 136

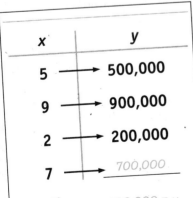

x	y
5	→ 500,000
9	→ 900,000
2	→ 200,000
7	→ 700,000

Equation: $x × 100,000 = y$

Patterns and Algebra • Today's Number: 100,000 • Week 5: Wednesday   © Great Source. Copying is prohibited. 053913

PATTERNS AND ALGEBRA Write an equation

• *How do the numbers change as you move from the x-column to the y-column?* (getting bigger) *How many times greater?* (100,000 times)

✎ *What do you think is the missing number?* (700,000)

✎ **Problem Solving** *How would you write a multiplication equation to describe what you see?* ($x × 100,000 = y$)

REACHING ALL LEARNERS Remind students any letter, word, or symbol can replace x and y.

Math at Hand 236, 240–241

KEY ✎ = record on pad

© Great Source. Copying is prohibited.

GEOMETRY Prisms

- *How are the 3 solids alike?* (sample answers: they have 3 dimensions; they have length, width, and depth; they are not flat; they have flat faces)

- ✎ *A prism is a solid with 2 parallel bases, and faces that are parallelograms. Select the solid that is a prism.* (see recording pad) *How do you know?* (it has faces that are parallelograms) *What is its name?* (cube or rectangular prism)

- ✎ *What are the geometric names of the other two solids?* (cylinder, pyramid or square pyramid)

Math at Hand 383

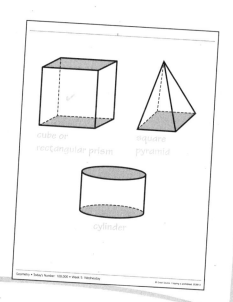

MEASUREMENT Volume of prisms

- *What does the volume of a prism tell you?* (How much space there is inside.) *How many cubes do you think can fit inside the rectangular prism?* (24 cubes) *How could you tell?* (sample answer: count the base, then triple it)

- ✎ *Is there a shortcut to find the volume?* (yes) *Can you explain?* (sample answers: multiply, $4 \times 2 \times 3 = 24$; find the area of the base, then multiply by the height)

- *What does the label* units³ *tell you?* (sample answers: It shows that the label *units* is multiplied three times; there are 3 dimensions.) *How do you read it?* (units cubed)

Math at Hand 309–310

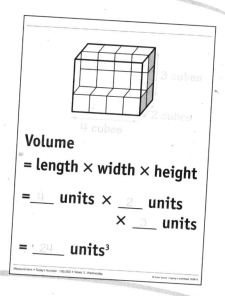

VOCABULARY survey

- *When you take a survey, what are you doing?* (asking a group a people one or more questions) *Why would you take a survey?* (to collect information or data)

- *Would you ask a different set of questions each time or the same set of questions?* (the same) *Why is that?* (so you can see the response from a large group)

- *How would you define survey?* (The process of collecting information by asking a question for people to answer.)

Math at Hand 248

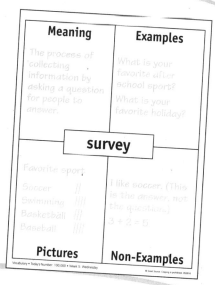

© Great Source. Copying is prohibited.

PRACTICE

Written Practice

CONCEPTS AND SKILLS

- Write in exponential form
- Add, subtract, multiply 100,000
- Volume of prisms
- Review interior angles
- Problem Solving Strategies and Skills: *Draw a Diagram, Guess, Check, and Revise, Write an Equation; Find Needed Information*

PREVIEW THE PRACTICE

- Review with students the powers of 10. *What is the connection between the number of zeros, the number of times 10 repeats, and the exponent?* (they are the same value)

SUPPORT THE PRACTICE

- Problems 1–4 ask students to write multiples of 100,000 in exponential form. Encourage students to think of each multiple as groups of 100,000.

- Problems 5–7 require students to show how a value is changed due to adding, subtracting, or multiplying by 100,000. Help students write the number, isolate the digit, show its new value, and then explain the computation.

- Problems 8–9 focus on volume of prisms. Help students identify the area of the base, then the height of the prism.

- Problems 10–12 review interior angles. Remind students the squares indicate 90-degree angles.

Name _____

NUMBER AND OPERATIONS

Fill in the blank. ◄1–4. MAH 005–007

1. $300,000 = 3 \times 100,000$
   $= \underline{} \times 10^5$

2. $500,000 = 5 \times \underline{100,000}$
   $= \underline{5} \times 10^5$

3. $700,000 = 7 \times \underline{100,000}$
   $= \underline{7} \times 10^5$

4. $900,000 = \underline{9} \times \underline{100,000}$
   $= \underline{9} \times 10^5$

Tell how the value is changed. ◄5–7. MAH 007, 119, 136

5. The digit 2 in <u>2</u>00,000 increases to 3. How is its value changed? ___ $+ 100,000$

6. The digit 6 in <u>6</u>00,000 decreases to 5. How is its value changed? ___ $- 100,000$

7. The number 3 changes to 300,000. How is the number changed? ___ $\times$ by 100,000

MEASUREMENT

What is the volume of the prism? ◄8–9. MAH 309–310

8. Volume = length × width × height
   $= \underline{5}$ units $\times \underline{3}$ units $\times \underline{2}$ units
   $= \underline{30}$ units³

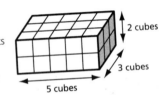

2 cubes
3 cubes
5 cubes

9. Volume = length × width × height
   $= \underline{3}$ units $\times \underline{3}$ units $\times \underline{3}$ units
   $= \underline{27}$ units³

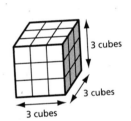

3 cubes
3 cubes
3 cubes

SUMMER SUCCESS: MATH **103**   MAH: *Math at Hand*

© Great Source. Permission is granted to copy this page.

REACHING ALL LEARNERS

For problems 5–7, you might wish to create simpler problems with smaller numbers. Increase or decrease the targeted place value by ones, then tens.

Math at Hand

If students need help, encourage them to refer to the MAH items shown on the student page.

© Great Source. Copying is prohibited.

REVIEW

Look at the rectangle to answer. ◄10–12. MAH 346–347

10. What do the squares inside the rectangle tell you?

sample answer: angles that measure 90 degrees

11. Which two operations can you use to find the total of the interior angles? multiply or add

12. How would you find the total of the interior angles? multiply, 90° × 4;

add, 90° + 90° + 90° + 90°

PROBLEM SOLVING · UNDERSTAND · PLAN · TRY · LOOK BACK

Complete each step. ◄13. MAH 396

13. Every month, Ava visits the retirement center. She always brings a treat. Last month, Ava and 3 friends had lunch with 5 of the residents. She brought 3 dozen treats that she divided equally for everyone to share. How many treats did each person have?

POSSIBLE STRATEGIES

• Guess, Check, and Revise

• Write an Equation

• Draw a Diagram

Sample Strategy: Write an Equation

a. Underline the question you need to answer.

b. Loop the details about the number of people and the treats.

c. Mark the strategy/strategies you will use.

d. Solve the problem. Explain your thinking.

how many treats: 3 × 12 = 36

how many people:

Ava + 3 friends + 5 residents = 9

36 ÷ 9 = 4

e. Answer the question.

Each person can have 4 treats.

REACHING ALL LEARNERS

If students have difficulty with the problem, encourage them to act out the situation. Provide counters to represent the 36 treats.

© Great Source. Copying is prohibited.

© Great Source. Permission is granted to copy this page.

PROBLEM SOLVING

Work in small groups of 3 or 4 students.

• Encourage students to find ways to identify needed information to solve the problem.

• *What information do you need to answer the question?* (the number of people and the number of fruit treats)

• *How can you use the information?* (to write an equation)

SCORING

a. Last sentence underlined: 1 pt

b. Details about the number of people and treats circled: 1 pt

c. Choose and apply an appropriate strategy: 1 pt

d. Explanation of solution: 1 pt

e. Correct answer: 1 pt

GLOSSARY TO GO

Today's Vocabulary *survey*

Have students complete an entry for today's vocabulary term in their Glossaries. Encourage students to use both words and drawings.

MATH JOURNAL

• *Write about a situation where knowing the volume of a container would be helpful.* (sample answers: putting beverages in a cooler for a picnic; boxing gifts to be mailed)

GAME

Active Practice

- Estimate product
- Calculate exact product
- Compare numbers

MATH TALK

Model the correct use of these words and encourage students to use them as they work.

- **difference** the result of subtraction
- **estimate** to find a number close to an exact amount
- **product** the result of multiplication

MATERIALS

For each pair: 2 sets of 0–9 Digits Cards, counters, paper, pencils, calculator*

*Optional materials

GAME

Eagle-Eye Estimation

Object: To create a multiplication problem with an answer as close as possible to a target number.

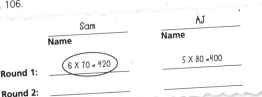

The difference between AJ's product and Target A is 50 and mine is only 30.

MATERIALS

4 sets of 0–9 Digit Cards, counters, paper, pencil, calculator*

*Optional material

DIRECTIONS

1. Use the recording sheet on p. 106.

	Sam	AJ
	Name	Name
Target A: Multiplication	Round 1: 6 X 70 = 420	5 X 80 = 400
Use 3 cards.	Round 2:	

2. Shuffle the 0–9 digit cards and place them facedown in a pile.

3. Begin with **Target A:** Multiplication. Each player draws 3 cards from the pile. Arrange your cards to make a multiplication problem with a product as close as possible to 450.

4. Figure out your exact product on scrap paper and then write it on the recording sheet. Compare the answers to find the one that is closer to Target A. The player with the closer answer states the comparison, and collects a counter. **(The difference between AJ's product and Target A is 50 and mine is only 30.)**

5. Play 3 rounds for each target. Reshuffle the cards to make a new pile before starting the next target.

6. After 6 rounds, the player with more counters wins.

© Great Source. Permission is granted to copy this page.

REACHING ALL LEARNERS

Simplify Use 2-digit numbers for the target. Students draw 3 digit cards. Select 2 cards to play the game.

Variation Change the operation from multiplication to division. Alert students they should use a fraction to write any quotient with a remainder.

Math at Hand

- Estimating Products, 106
- Multiplication, 136

© Great Source. Copying is prohibited.

Day 1

REVIEW THE MATH

- Review the terms *estimate, product,* and *difference.*
- Have students practice estimating a few products.

MODEL THE GAME

- Demonstrate with student volunteers how to play the game and how to keep score.
- Show students how to use the digit cards to set up multiplication problems.
- Explore with students how to estimate products that are close to the target number.

Day 2

PLAY THE GAME

- Review the directions for playing the game.
- Assign partners to play the game.

REFLECT ON THE MATH

Encourage students to ask themselves:

- *Which estimation strategy works best for me?*
- *What do I need to do in order to win this round?*
- *How are my opponents doing?*
- *Should I use a different estimation strategy?*

MODEL THE GAME

Teacher: I have drawn a 6, a 7, and a 2. What should I do?

Student: Try combining 7 and 6 to make 76.

T: Okay. So, how would you estimate the product for 76 times 2?

S: I know 76 is close to 80. And, 2 times that is 160.

S: I can round 76 to 80. And, 2 times 80 is 160.

S: I'm going to multiply 70 times 2, and get 140.

T: What do the estimates tell you?

S: Maybe we should try with a different number and see if we can get closer to 450.

T: What do you suggest?

S: I think you should take the two bigger numbers and multiply them together.

T: What happens when you do that?

S: Well, multiplying 6 and 7 will give the biggest product possible.

T: Terrific idea. So, let's estimate the product of 72 times 6. Anyone?

S: Sure. 7 times 6 is 42. So, 70 times 6 is 420.

ONGOING ASSESSMENT

If students need more help, use the hints below, or refer to the *Math at Hand* items shown to the left.

- **Do students estimate correctly and use the estimates as a strategy?** Use a number line to practice rounding numbers to the nearest 10. Refer to *Math at Hand*, 106 for additional suggestions.

- **Can students multiply correctly?** Refer to *Math at Hand*, 139 for alternative algorithms for multiplication.

© Great Source. Copying is prohibited.

CONCEPT BUILDER
MAKE & TAKE

Additional Support

CONCEPTS AND SKILLS

- Make and use a customary system measuring tool
- Understand equivalent fractions
- Verbalize and visualize fractional amounts

MATH TALK

Model the correct use of these terms and encourage students to use them as they work.

- **denominator** the number of equal parts into which a whole is divided
- **equivalent** of the same amount or value
- **numerator** the equal parts of a whole

MATERIALS FOR DAY 1

For each student: Inch Ruler (SE p. 107), markers, scissors, tape, adding machine tape, bags

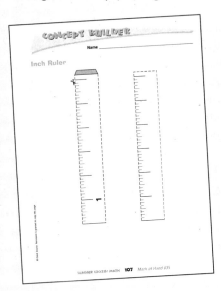

Inch Ruler **Day 1**

GET READY

Follow the instruction below to prepare a sample Inch Ruler to use for demonstration.

BUILD THE INCH RULER

1. Have students find the Inch Ruler on p. 107 of their books. Before cutting out the sections, direct students to label the inch increments. Note the first inch is already labeled on the cut out.

2. Have students cut out the two sections of the ruler and tape the tab-end of the first strip behind one end of the other strip. The inches need to be carefully aligned with the measurement marks on the same side.

3. The ruler can be made sturdier by taping it to a one-foot length of adding machine tape. Students should carefully place the edge of the ruler with the measuring marks on the edge of the adding machine tape before taping.

4. Have students write their names or initials on their rulers and on the storage bags. Store everything until tomorrow.

FOCUS ON THE MATH

- *Why is it helpful to label the ruler?* (sample answer: so that you can tell right away the length of what you are measuring)

- *How many inches are on a foot-long ruler?* (12) *What fractional part of a ruler is 1 inch?* ($\frac{1}{12}$)

- *One yard stick is equal to 3 foot-long rulers. What fractional part of a yardstick is 1 foot-long ruler?* ($\frac{1}{3}$)

© Great Source. Copying is prohibited.

Inch Ruler **Day 2**

1. Provide a list of five or six things in the classroom for the students to measure. Have them measure each object to the nearest inch, to the nearest half-inch, to the nearest quarter inch, and to the nearest eighth-inch. The measurements should be recorded on a piece of paper.

2. Have students look at their lists of measurements. Discuss the accuracy of measuring to each fractional unit of length. Discuss which is the most accurate unit of measure and why this is so.

3. Work together with the class to brainstorm a list of things that can be measured at home. Once the list is finalized, have students copy it and include it in the storage bag to take home at the end of the week.

MODEL THE ACTIVITY

Be sure students understand the words *numerator* and *denominator*. Use a rectangle to model $\frac{3}{4}$ on the chalkboard. Connect the model to the meaning and positioning of the numerator and the denominator.

Demonstrate how to interpret the lines on the ruler by isolating equivalent units. Draw or display on the chalkboard an enlarged scale model of a portion of the ruler. Begin by isolating the one-half and whole inch marks for students to identify. Next, help students identify the fourths on the ruler. Discuss the equivalent labels, such as $\frac{1}{2}$, $\frac{2}{4}$, and $\frac{4}{8}$, that name the same point.

To prepare students to work on their own, ask them to draw lines of predetermined lengths. Provide paper for students to draw lines with lengths such as $1\frac{3}{8}$ inches, $2\frac{3}{4}$ inches, $3\frac{1}{2}$ inches, and so on. Direct students to create a point of origin on the paper before each line is drawn.

REFLECT ON THE MATH

Encourage students to ask themselves:

- *Was it important for me to be careful when taping the two pieces together to make the inch ruler?*

- *What happens when I don't place the end of the rule exactly at the starting point?*

REACHING ALL LEARNERS

Help students recognize the start and end points of what they are measuring. Line up exactly at the start point. Press down on the ruler so that it remains straight all the way to the end.

Math at Hand

- Equivalent Fractions, 035

- Length, 294

© Great Source. Copying is prohibited.

MATERIALS FOR DAY 2

For each student: Inch Ruler assembled previously

Note: Send these materials home with the Newsletter at the end of the week.

ONGOING ASSESSMENT

If students need more help, use the hints below, or refer to the *Math at Hand* items shown to the left.

- **Are students able to express equivalent measurements?** Practice halving and doubling the whole numbers 2, 4, and 8 to make a connection to the fractional quantities.

- **Are students able to measure accurately?** Observe students as they measure to ensure they use the ruler correctly. Caution students about aligning the edge of the ruler with the edge of the item being measured or a point of origin.

- **Are students able to read the ruler correctly?** Have students isolate particular points on the ruler such as $1\frac{1}{2}$ inches, $4\frac{1}{8}$ inches, $\frac{3}{4}$ inch, and so on.

NUMBER NAMES   TODAY'S NUMBER 1,000,000

NUMBER One million

Examples: *distances in space, money for budgets, population*

$1,000,000 = 10^6$

2 groups of 10^6

→ _1,000,000 or 10^6_ + _1,000,000 or 10^6_

→ _2_ × 10^6

→ _2,000,000_

✎ *Name some examples of when the number 1,000,000 might be used in everyday life.* (distances in space, money for budgets, population count, and so on)

✎ *How do you write 1,000,000 as a power of 10?* (10^6) *How can you show that your answer is correct?* (sample answer: there are 6 zeros, so the exponent is 6)

✎ *Suppose you have 2 groups of 10^6. What are the different ways to write it as an addition expression?* (1,000,000 + 1,000,000) *As a multiplication expression?* ($2 × 10^6$) *In standard form?* (2,000,000)

Math at Hand 005–007

OPERATIONS Compute with large numbers

$\frac{1}{2}$ of 1,000,000 = _500,000_

$\frac{1}{4}$ of 1,000,000 = _250,000_

_100,000_ × 10 = 1,000,000

_10,000_ × 100 = 1,000,000

_1,000_ × 1,000 = 1,000,000

✎ *What is $\frac{1}{2}$ of 1,000?* (500) *How do you know?* (500 + 500 = 1,000) *Of 100,000?* (50,000) *Of 1,000,000?* (500,000)

✎ *What is $\frac{1}{4}$ of 1,000,000?* (250,000) *How do you know?* (add 250,000 four times)

✎ *What number times 10 has a product of 1,000,000?* (100,000) *Times 100?* (10,000) *Times 1,000?* (1,000)

REACHING ALL LEARNERS Remind students that when finding half of something, you are looking for 2 equal parts of a whole. And, $\frac{1}{4}$ is half of a half.

Math at Hand 007, 168

PATTERNS AND ALGEBRA Write a rule

x	y
5,000,000 →	5 × 10^6
9,000,000 →	9 × 10^6
2,000,000 →	2 × 10^6
3,000,000 →	_3 × 10^6_

sample answer:

Rule: *Multiply how many millions you have by 10^6.*

• *When you read across the columns, does the value of each number change?* (no) *Show how you know.* (sample answer: 10^6 = 1 million, so 5 × 10^6 is the same as 5 million)

✎ *What do you think is the missing term in the y-column?* ($3 × 10^6$) *Why?* (sample answer: in the y-column 1 million is written as 10^6, so 3 million is $3 × 10^6$)

✎ **Problem Solving** *How would you write a rule to describe what you see?* (sample answer: multiply how many millions you have by 10^6)

Math at Hand 236, 240–241

© Great Source. Copying is prohibited.

GEOMETRY Interior angles

✎ *Look at the triangle. How many corners, or angles, do you see?* (3) *Remember, since these angles are inside the shape, we call them* interior angles.

✎ *You know that square corners have 90-degree angles. How do you write 90 degrees?* (90°) *How would you find the total of the interior angles?* (add 90° + 60° + 30°)

✎ *What is the total?* (90° + 60° + 30° = 180°)

Math at Hand 354

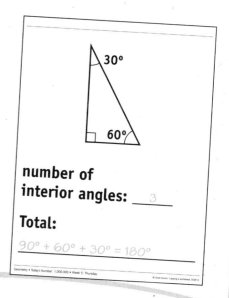

number of
interior angles: ___3___

Total:

90° + 60° + 30° = 180°

Geometry • Today's Number: 1,000,000 • Week 5: Thursday   © Great Source. Copying is prohibited. (05261)

MEASUREMENT Area of prisms

• *The amount of space covered by a flat shape is called* area.

✎ *How many faces does a cube have?* (sample answers: 6: front, back, top, bottom, left side, right side) *How can you describe them?* (sample answers: all squares; all the same size, all have 9 little squares inside them)

✎ *Tell how you would find the area of all the surfaces of this cube.* (multiply the area of 1 face by 6) *What is the total?*
3 cm × 3 cm = 9 cm², 9 cm² × 6 = 54 cm²)

Math at Hand 306–307

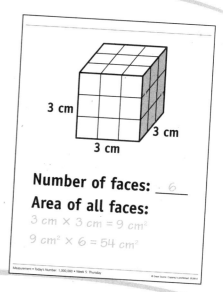

3 cm

3 cm

3 cm

Number of faces: ___6___
Area of all faces:

3 cm × 3 cm = 9 cm²
9 cm² × 6 = 54 cm²

Measurement • Today's Number: 1,000,000 • Week 5: Thursday   © Great Source. Copying is prohibited. (05261)

VOCABULARY *strategy*

• *Act It Out is one useful math strategy. Can you name some other strategies?* (sample answers: Make a Diagram, Make a Table, Guess, Check, and Revise, Make an Organized List, and so on)

• *Give a real life example of when a good strategy comes in handy?* (sample answer: when playing a board game, a competitive sport)

• *How would you define* strategy? (A plan for getting to an answer when solving a math problem.)

Math at Hand 396

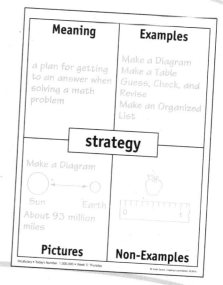

Meaning	Examples
a plan for getting to an answer when solving a math problem	Make a Diagram Make a Table Guess, Check, and Revise Make an Organized List

strategy

Make a Diagram

Sun ———→ Earth
About 93 million miles

Pictures	Non-Examples

Vocabulary • Today's Number: 1,000,000 • Week 5: Thursday   © Great Source. Copying is prohibited. (05261)

© Great Source. Copying is prohibited.

PRACTICE

Written Practice

CONCEPTS AND SKILLS

- Write in exponential form
- Multiply 1,000,000 by a fraction
- Area
- Review rounding
- Problem Solving Strategies and Skills: *Make a Model, Act It Out, Draw a Diagram; Use Logical Reasoning*

PREVIEW THE PRACTICE

- Write on the board, 3,000,000. *What is the greatest place value of this number?* (million) *How do you read the number?* (three million)

SUPPORT THE PRACTICE

- Problems 1–4 ask students to write multiples of 1,000,000 in exponential form. Encourage students to think of each multiple as groups of 1,000,000.
- Problems 5–10 work with benchmark fractions $\frac{1}{2}$ and $\frac{1}{4}$ of 1,000,000. Model with a smaller number such as 1,000 or 100 to establish a pattern, if needed.
- Problems 11–12 focus on area. Help students visualize the backsides of the cubes.
- Problems 13–16 review rounding to a given place value. Help students see that they should look at the number to the right of the underscored digit.

PRACTICE TODAY'S NUMBER **1,000,000**

Name _____

NUMBER AND OPERATIONS

Fill in the blank. ◄1–4. MAH 005–007

1. $6,000,000 = 6 \times 1,000,000$

    $= \underline{\quad 6 \quad} \times 10^6$

2. $5,000,000 = 5 \times \underline{\quad 1,000,000 \quad}$

    $= \underline{\quad 5 \quad} \times 10^6$

3. $8,000,000 = 8 \times \underline{\quad 1,000,000 \quad}$

    $= \underline{\quad 8 \quad} \times 10^6$

4. $7,000,000 = \underline{\quad 7 \quad} \times \underline{\quad 1,000,000 \quad}$

    $= \underline{\quad 7 \quad} \times \underline{\quad 10^6 \quad}$

Compute. ◄5–10. MAH 168

5. $\underline{\quad \frac{1}{2} \quad}$ of $1,000,000 = 500,000$

6. $\frac{1}{4}$ of $\underline{\quad 1,000,000 \quad} = 250,000$

7. $\underline{\quad \frac{1}{4} \quad}$ of $1,000,000 = 250,000$

8. $\frac{1}{2}$ of $\underline{\quad 1,000,000 \quad} = 500,000$

9. $\frac{1}{2}$ of $1,000,000 = \underline{\quad 500,000 \quad}$

10. $\frac{1}{4}$ of $1,000,000 = \underline{\quad 250,000 \quad}$

GEOMETRY AND MEASUREMENT

Find the area. ◄11–12. MAH 299

11.

2 cm

Number of faces: $\underline{\quad 6 \quad}$

Area of 1 face:

2 cm $\times \underline{\quad 2 \quad}$ cm $= \underline{\quad 4 \quad}$ cm²

Area of 6 faces:

$\underline{\quad 4 \quad}$ cm² $\times 6 = \underline{\quad 24 \quad}$ cm²

12.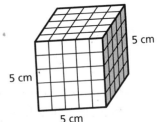

5 cm

Number of faces: $\underline{\quad 6 \quad}$

Area of 1 face:

$\underline{\quad 5 \quad}$ cm $\times \underline{\quad 5 \quad}$ cm $= \underline{\quad 25 \quad}$ cm²

Area of 6 faces:

$\underline{\quad 25 \quad}$ cm² $\times 6 = \underline{\quad 150 \quad}$ cm²

© Great Source. Permission is granted to copy this page.

SUMMER SUCCESS: MATH **109**   MAH: *Math at Hand*

REACHING ALL LEARNERS

Create a place value chart to help students read the numbers in the millions period.

Math at Hand

If students need help, encourage them to refer to the MAH items shown on the student page.

© Great Source. Copying is prohibited.

Round to the given place. ◀ 13–16. MAH 094–095

13. 8<u>6</u>1   hundreds place: _____ 900

14. 7<u>5</u>,821   thousands place: _____ 76,000

15. 498,8<u>7</u>4   tens place: _____ 498,870

16. 112,<u>9</u>65   hundreds place: _____ 113,000

PROBLEM SOLVING · **UNDERSTAND · PLAN · TRY · LOOK BACK**

Complete each step. ◀ 17. MAH 396

17. Kiya is learning a new dance step. From START she takes (2 steps to the right,) followed by (3 steps back.) Next she (turns 90° to the left,) followed by (2 steps forward.) What must Kiya do to return to start?

   a. Underline the question you need to answer.

   b. Loop the details about the dance steps.

   c. Mark the strategy/strategies you will use.

   d. Solve the problem. Explain your thinking.

POSSIBLE STRATEGIES
- Make a Model
- Act it Out
- Make a Diagram

Sample Strategies:
Make a Diagram, Act it Out

3 steps forward, back to START

3 steps back, but still facing forward

90° turn to the right

90° turn to the left

2 steps forward

© Great Source. Permission is granted to copy this page.

   e. Answer the question.

Kiya must turn 90° to the right and take three steps forward. Or, take 3 steps to the right, but still facing forward.

PROBLEM SOLVING

Work in small groups of 3 or 4 students.

- Encourage students to find ways to identify needed information to solve the problem.

- *What information do you need to answer the question?* (the direction and number of steps the dancer takes)

- *How can you use the information?* (to act it out, to draw a diagram)

SCORING

   a. Last sentence underlined: 1 pt

   b. Details about the dance steps circled: 1 pt

   c. Choose and apply an appropriate strategy: 1 pt

   d. Explanation of solution: 1 pt

   e. Correct answer: 1 pt

GLOSSARY TO GO

Today's Vocabulary *strategy*

Have students complete an entry for today's vocabulary term in their Glossaries. Encourage students to use both words and drawings.

REACHING ALL LEARNERS

- If students have difficulty with the problem, prompt them to act out the dance steps.

- Point out to students that moving backwards in a dance step doesn't require turning around.

MATH JOURNAL

- *How do you decide whether a strategy is good?* (sample answers: if it helps you find an answer, win a game, be successful, and so on)

© Great Source. Copying is prohibited.

NUMBER NAMES TODAY'S NUMBER Review

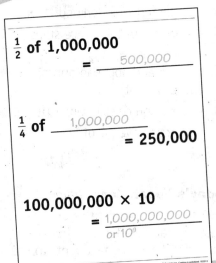

$$1,000,000 = 10^6$$
$$100,000 = 10^5$$
$$1,000 = 10^3$$

3 groups of 10^3

sample answers:
- 3,000
- 1,000 + 1,000 + 1,000
- $10^3 + 10^3 + 10^3$
- 3×10^3

Number • Today's Number: Review • Week 5: Friday   © Great Source. Copying is prohibited. 053911

NUMBER Big numbers

- *Let's revisit some of the big numbers from this week.* Point to 1,000,000 on the pad. *How do you read this number?* (one million) Point to 1,000. *This number?* (one thousand)

- ✎ *How do you write 1,000,000 as a power of 10?* (10^6) *100,000?* (10^5) *1,000?* (10^3) *How did you know what the exponent is?* (sample answer: count the number of zeros)

- ✎ *What is another way to write 3 groups of 10^3?* (see recording pad)

Math at Hand 006–007

$\frac{1}{2}$ of 1,000,000

= _____ 500,000

$\frac{1}{4}$ of _____ 1,000,000

= 250,000

100,000,000 × 10

= 1,000,000,000
or 10^9

Operations • Today's Number: Review • Week 5: Friday   © Great Source. Copying is prohibited. 053912

OPERATIONS Compute with large numbers

- ✎ **Problem Solving** *There must be half a million ants in the colony. What is that number in standard form?* (500,000)

- ✎ **Problem Solving** *Planners estimate that a quarter million people will watch the parade. Is that 250,000 or 250,000,000 people?* (250,000) *How do you know?* (sample answer: 250,000 four times is 1,000,000)

- ✎ **Problem Solving** *The distance from Earth to the Sun is roughly 100,000,000 miles. Suppose a star is 10 times that distance from Earth. About how many miles away is the star?* (about 1,000,000,000 miles)

Math at Hand 002, 136,168

---

x	y
1,000,000	→ 1×10^6
2,000,000	→ 2×10^6
3,000,000	→ 3×10^6
4,000,000	→ 4×10^6

8th term: 8,000,000; 8×10^6

15th term: 15,000,000; 15×10^6

Patterns and Algebra • Today's Number: Review • Week 5: Friday   © Great Source. Copying is prohibited. 053913

PATTERNS AND ALGEBRA Prediction

- *When you read across the columns, does the value of each number change?* (no) *Show how you know.* (sample answer: $10^6 = 1$ million, so 1×10^6 is still 1 million)

- *What do you notice about the first digit in the x-column and the first factor in the y-column?* (they are the same) Help student see that they can use this information to predict terms not shown in the chart.

- ✎ *What do you think the 8th term would be?* (8,000,000; 8×10^6) *The 15th term?* (15,000,000; 15×10^6)

Math at Hand 401

© Great Source. Copying is prohibited.

GEOMETRY Interior angles

- *What do you see?* (a triangle with a square angle, 30° angle measure, and an angle with *x* degrees)
- ✎ **Problem Solving** *Suppose you want to find the measure for the third angle. How would you go about it? Explain your method.* (see sample answers on recording pad)

REACHING ALL LEARNERS Help students recall that the sum of the measures of the interior angles of any triangle is 180°.

Math at Hand 354

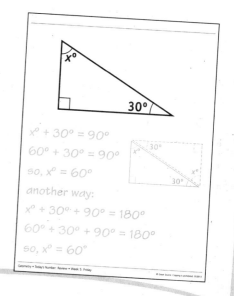

MEASUREMENT Big number measures

- ✎ **Problem Solving** *What is the value of 1,000,000 pennies in dollars?* ($10,000) *How do you know?* (sample answer: I know that there are 100 pennies in $1. So, I took off 2 zeros from 1,000,000 pennies to get $10,000.)
- ✎ **Problem Solving** *The circumference of Earth at the equator is about 40,000 kilometers. About how many meters is that?* (see recording pad)

Math at Hand 294

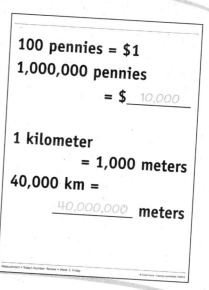

VOCABULARY Review

Let's work together to do today's matching exercise.

- *Which example is most different?* (the graph)
- *What is it called when you ask the same question to a lot of different people?* (taking a survey)
- *What is another word for information?* (data)
- *There are many ways to solve a problem.* Draw a Diagram is one method. *What is another word for method?* (strategy)

Math at Hand 248, 269–284, 396

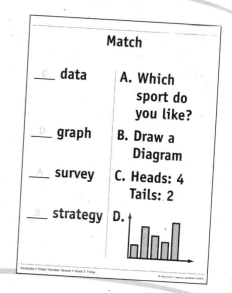

© Great Source. Copying is prohibited.

PRACTICE

Written Practice

CONCEPTS AND SKILLS

- Write large numbers in exponential and factored form
- Compute with large numbers
- Predict terms in a table of values
- Review place value
- Problem Solving Strategies and Skills: *Make a Diagram, Look for a Pattern, Write an Equation; Solve in More Than One Way*

PREVIEW THE PRACTICE

- Write 10^5 on the chalkboard. **Which number is the exponent?** (5) **What does it tell you?** (the number of times 10 repeats as a factor) **How do you write 10^5 in factored form?** ($10 \times 10 \times 10 \times 10 \times 10$)

SUPPORT THE PRACTICE

- Problems 1–3 ask for different ways to write large numbers. Help students see that Problem 3 works with a multiple of 1,000.
- Problems 4–7 work with unit fractions $\frac{1}{2}$ and $\frac{1}{4}$. Some students might want to use addition to check their answers.
- Problems 8–9 ask students to predict terms in a table of values. Review strategies for reading the table and for finding patterns.
- Problems 10–13 review adding and subtracting big numbers. Provide a place value chart for students having difficulty.

PRACTICE TODAY'S NUMBER Review

Name _____

NUMBER AND OPERATIONS

Show 2 different ways to write the number. ◄1–3. MAH 006–007

1. 100,000   Exponential Form: 10^5 Factored Form: $10 \times 10 \times 10 \times 10 \times 10$
2. 1,000,000   Exponential Form: 10^6 Factored Form: $10 \times 10 \times 10 \times 10 \times 10 \times 10$
3. 4,000   Exponential Form: 4×10^3 Factored Form: $4 \times 10 \times 10 \times 10$

Write the answer. ◄4–7. MAH 002, 168

4. $\frac{1}{2}$ of 100,000 ___ 500,000
5. $\frac{1}{4}$ of 1,000,000 ___ 250,000
6. $\frac{1}{4}$ of 100,000 ___ 25,000
7. $\frac{1}{2}$ of 1,000 ___ 500

PATTERNS AND ALGEBRA

Predict. ◄8–9. MAH 401

8.

	x		y
1st term:	10,000	→	1×10^4
2nd term:	20,000	→	2×10^4
3rd term:	30,000	→	3×10^4
4th term:	40,000	→	4×10^4
8th term:	80,000	→	8×10^4

9.

	x		y
1st term:	200,000	→	2×10^5
2nd term:	250,000	→	2.5×10^5
3rd term:	300,000	→	3×10^5
4th term:	350,000	→	3.5×10^5
8th term:	550,000	→	5.5×10^5

REVIEW

Answer the question. ◄10–13. MAH 119, 129

10. What is 10,000 less than 1,493,657? ___ 1,483,657
11. What is 100,000 more than 1,493,657? ___ 1,593,657
12. What is 1,000 less than 1,493,657? ___ 1,492,647
13. What is 1,000,000 more than 1,493,657? ___ 2,493,657

© Great Source. Permission is granted to copy this page.

SUMMER SUCCESS: MATH   **111**   MAH: *Math at Hand*

REACHING ALL LEARNERS

Provide a place value chart or have students draw a place value chart before they begin the Practice.

Math at Hand

If students need help, encourage them to refer to the MAH items shown on the student page.

© Great Source. Copying is prohibited.

Complete each step. ◀MAH 14. MAH 396

14. Eleven boys and 16 girls sign up for the field trip. Drivers can take up to 4 students in each car. What is the number of cars needed?

a. Underline the question you need to answer.

b. Loop the details about the students.

c. Mark the strategy/strategies you will use.

d. Solve the problem. Explain your thinking.

11 + 16 = 27

27 ÷ 4 = 6 R3

6 cars with 4 students

1 car with 3 students

7 cars in all

e. Answer the question.

7 cars are needed.

POSSIBLE STRATEGIES

- Look for a Pattern
- Make a Diagram
- Write an Equation

Sample Strategy:
Make a Diagram

Number of cars needed

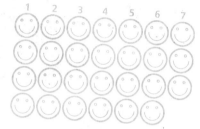

© Great Source. Permission is granted to copy this page.

PROBLEM SOLVING

Work in small groups of 3 or 4 students.

- Encourage students to find ways to identify needed information to solve the problem.
- *What information do you need to answer the question?* (the number of students in each car, the total number of students)
- *How can you use the information?* (to make a diagram)

SCORING

a. Last sentence underlined: 1 pt

b. Number of students circled: 1 pt

c. Choose and apply an appropriate strategy: 1 pt

d. Explanation of solution: 1 pt

e. Correct answer: 1 pt

GLOSSARY TO GO

Today's Vocabulary Review

Have students review and share the entries they made for this week's vocabulary words, *data*, *graph*, *survey*, and *strategy*. Ask students to add more words and/or drawings to the maps if they can.

MATH JOURNAL

- *Think back over what you learned this week. What is one topic you will want to remember?* (sample answers: how to write exponents for powers of 10; compute with big numbers.)

REACHING ALL LEARNERS

If students have difficulty with the problem, use counters to help them group the 27 students.

© Great Source. Copying is prohibited.

READ AND REASON

Additional Support

CONCEPTS AND SKILLS

- Work with customary measures of weight
- Compare and order decimals

MATH TALK

Model the correct use of these terms and encourage students to use them as they work.

- **customary units** system of measurement
- **pound** a unit of weight in the customary system
- **weight** a measure of how heavy an object is

SUPPORT PROBLEM 1

Read the story aloud, then have a volunteer read the problem again.

- *What is the story about?* (weighed packages)
- *What is the math about?* (customary units of weight, pounds)
- *Where do you think we should start?* (Answers will vary.)
- *Are there any answers you can rule out?* (liters, 5 ounces, and 16) *Why?* (because they did not fit with the story)

READ AND REASON

Name _____

Fill in each blank with the choice that makes the *most* sense. Do not use any choice more than once.

1. Maria works in the grocery store. She is putting packages of chicken pieces in the cold case by weight. The heaviest one weighs ___2.12 pounds___, then the next package weighs ___2.02 pounds___. The lightest package weighs less than 2 pounds but greater than ___1.5 pounds___. It weighs ___1.73 pounds___.

ANSWER CHOICES

- 2.12 pounds
- liters
- 2.02 pounds
- 1.73 pounds
- 5 ounces
- 16
- 1.5 pounds

Explain your thinking.

a. How did you begin?
   Example: I drew a picture and filled in the weights in order.
   _____

b. What choice(s) did you rule out?
   Example: liters, 5 ounces, and 16 because they did not fit with the story.
   _____

c. How are you sure that your answers make sense in the story?
   Example: I tried to rule out the answers that did not make sense.
   _____

© Great Source. Permission is granted to copy this page.

SUMMER SUCCESS: MATH   **113**

REACHING ALL LEARNERS

Use a decimal number line between 0 and 3 to help students visualize the numbers used in the story.

Math at Hand

- Weight, 317
- Comparing Decimals, 016–017
- Ordering Decimals, 018

© Great Source. Copying is prohibited.

Fill in each blank with the choice that makes the *most* sense. Do not use any choice more than once.

2. Alberto is drawing a 3-sided figure, called a(n) _____triangle_____. He wants it to have _____2_____ sides the same, which makes this a(n) _____isosceles_____ triangle.

ANSWER CHOICES

- triangle
- scalene
- isosceles
- 2
- 5
- equilateral
- quadrilateral

Explain your thinking.

a. How did you begin?

Example: I drew different kinds of triangles just to see what's possible.

_____

b. What choice(s) did you rule out?

Example: 5 and quadrilateral because I know that we're working with a 3-sided figure.

_____

c. How do you know your answers make sense in the story?

Example: I reread the story and it made sense.

_____
_____

© Great Source. Permission is granted to copy this page.

CONCEPTS AND SKILLS

- Work with triangles
- Apply attributes of triangles

MATH TALK

Model the correct use of these terms and encourage students to use them as they work.

- **equilateral** triangle where 3 sides have the same length
- **isosceles** triangle where 2 sides have the same length
- **scalene** triangle where no side is the same as any other
- **triangle** a 3-sided flat figure

SUPPORT PROBLEM 2

Read the story aloud, then have a volunteer read the problem again.

- *What is the story about?* (drawing a 3-sided figure)
- *What is the math about?* (attributes of triangles)
- *Where do you think we should start?* (Answers will vary.)
- *Are there any answers you can rule out?* (5 and quadrilateral) *Why?* (because I know that we're working with a 3-sided figure)

REACHING ALL LEARNERS

Sketch out the 3 types of triangles—scalene, isosceles, and equilateral. Review with students the attributes of each type of triangle.

Math at Hand

- Triangles, 358
- Using Side Length to Classify Triangles, 362

© Great Source. Copying is prohibited.

NEWSLETTER

This Newsletter is sent home with students at the end of the week, along with the completed *Inch Ruler* Concept Builder materials.

The first page suggests a simple way for students to share with their parent or guardian basic math skills they have been practicing in class.

NEWSLETTER

Summer Success: Math

Another week of summer school has gone by. Your child has worked hard and has a lot to share with you.

Use the number line below to ask your child to demonstrate how to label and read it.

- How many equal parts are there between 0 and 1 on the number line?
- Where do you think 0.50 belongs? How about $\frac{1}{2}$?
- Is it possible to use whole numbers, decimals, and fractions on the ruler?

On the back of this page are directions for using the project called *Inch Ruler*. Your child made an inch ruler to measure objects in the classroom and at home. The inch ruler can be used to measure things to the nearest eighth-inch. Invite your child to share this activity with you. Use it together to encourage your child to practice measuring.

Enjoy the time with your child, and thank you for helping to strengthen the mathematical tie between home and school.

© Great Source. Permission is granted to copy this page.

© Great Source. Copying is prohibited.

NEWSLETTER

Family Math with the Inch Ruler

We have been studying measurement and fractions in school this week. Your child made an inch ruler and used it to measure objects in the classroom. Our inch ruler can be used to measure things to the nearest eighth inch.

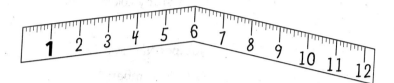

We worked together as a class to create a list of things for your child to measure at home. Ask your child to show you the list. Have your child measure some of the items on the list while you watch. Observe how your child handles and uses the ruler to be sure that he or she is measuring objects correctly. Then your child can measure the remaining items on the list.

You may think of other things around the house that can be measured. Don't forget to look outside for more ways to use the inch ruler. Using the ruler to practice measuring things will help strengthen your child's understanding of the role of fractions in measurement.

 Enjoy this activity with your child. Remember that using math in the real world helps your child understand that math is important in and out of school.

The back side of this week's Newsletter includes instructions for the parent or guardian to help their student demonstrate the *Inch Ruler* Concept Builder activity at home.

© Great Source. Permission is granted to copy this page.

© Great Source. Copying is prohibited.

WEEKLY OVERVIEW	MONDAY	TUESDAY
Materials Read across to find materials needed for this week's daily activities. *Optional material	**Game** 0–9 Digit Cards, paper, pencil **Data Study** colored paper*	**Game** 0–9 Digit Cards, paper, pencil **Data Study** colored paper*
NUMBER NAMES *Instruction: 20–30 min* **Number** Place value, Even and odd numbers, Prime and composite numbers **Operations** Compute with 0, Divisibility by 2, 3, 5, Sum of primes **Patterns and Algebra** Order/Grouping Property, Square/Triangular number pattern **Geometry** Transformations, Tessellations, Polygons **Measurement** Area, Perimeter **Vocabulary** Data and Problem Solving terms	**Number Names** p. 116C **Today's Number: 0** Place value Compute with 0 Order Property Slide, turn, flip Perimeter *pattern*	**Number Names** p.122A **Today's Number: 2** Even numbers Divisibility by 2 Square number pattern Tessellations Area of parallelograms *sequence*
PRACTICE *Written Practice: 20–30 min* **Number and Operations** Place value and the digit 0, Even/Odd numbers, Compute with zero, Divisibility, Prime/Composite numbers **Patterns and Algebra** Order/Grouping Property, Number sequence **Geometry** Transformations **Measurement** Perimeter, Area **Review** Fractions, Simplest form, Transformations, Equivalent amounts **Problem Solving** Strategies and skills	**Practice** p. 117 Place value and the digit 0 Compute with zero Translation, rotation, and reflection Add like fractions, Simplest form Guess, Check, and Revise Make a Table Make an Organized List Ignore Unneeded Information	**Practice** p. 123 Identify even numbers Divisibility by 2 Analyze number sequence Transformations Make a Diagram Make a Table Make an Organized List Use Logical Reasoning
GAME *Active Practice: 20–30 min* Identify prime and composite numbers Add and subtract whole numbers Estimate sums and differences Calculate exact sums and differences	**Game** p. 119 **Prime Time** Prime/Composite numbers Add/Subtract whole numbers	**Game** p. 119 **Prime Time** Prime/Composite numbers Add/Subtract whole numbers
FOCUS *Additional Support: 20–30 min* Events, Outcomes, Combinations, Tree diagram, Probability Spatial relationships, Recognize shapes, Congruence, similarity, and symmetry Fraction concepts, Number types	**Data Study** p. 121 **Combinations and Probability** Events, outcomes, combinations Tree diagram, Probability	**Data Study** p. 121 **Combinations and Probability** Events, outcomes, combinations Tree diagram, Probability

© Great Source. Copying is prohibited.

PLANNER

WEDNESDAY	THURSDAY	FRIDAY
Game 0–9 Digits Cards with zeros removed, paper and pencil **Concept Builder** scissors, bags	**Game** 0–9 Digits Cards with zeros removed, paper and pencil **Concept Builder** materials prepared previously	**Game** see Tuesday and Thursday **Newsletter** SE p. 137 (Send home with the Concept Builder materials.)
Number Names p. 124A	**Number Names** p. 130A	**Number Names** p. 132A
Today's Number: 3 Odd numbers Divisibility by 3 Triangular number pattern Triangle tessellations Area of right triangles *frequency*	**Today's Number: 5** Prime and composite numbers Divisibility by 5 Grouping Property Tessellations Area *trend*	**Today's Number: Review** Number types Sum of primes Grouping Property Polygons Perimeter and area Vocabulary review
Practice p. 125	**Practice** p. 131	**Practice** p. 133
Identify odd numbers Divisibility by 3 Area of right triangles Equivalent fractions Guess, Check, and Revise Make a Table Write an Equation Take Notes	Identify prime and composite numbers Divisibility by 2, 3, 5 Grouping Property Equivalent amounts Act It Out Make a Model Make a Diagram Find Needed Information	Prime and composite numbers Divisibility Perimeter and area Transformations Act It Out Make a Diagram Make a Table Solve in More Than One Way
Game p. 127	**Game** p. 127	**Game** pp. 119 or 127
Inverse Estimations Estimate sums and differences Calculate exact sums and differences	**Inverse Estimations** Estimate sums and differences Calculate exact sums and differences	**Choice** **Prime Time** or variation **Inverse Estimations** or variation
Concept Builder p. 129	**Concept Builder** p. 129	**Read and Reason** p. 135
Make & Take: Tangrams To Go Examine spatial relationships Recognize shapes, Congruence, similarity, and symmetry	**Make & Take: Tangrams To Go** Examine spatial relationships Recognize shapes, Congruence, similarity, and symmetry	Parts of a whole Fractional pieces Prime, even, and square numbers

© Great Source. Copying is prohibited.

NUMBER NAMES TODAY'S NUMBER 0

NUMBER **Place value**

- Our number system is based on groups of 10s.
- *Can you tell what is alike about the digits in the numbers 10 and 1?* (the digit 1 is in both numbers) *Different?* (the digit 0 is in the number 10) *What does the digit 0 show?* (the digit 0 is a placeholder to show that there are no extra ones)
- ✎ *What's the place value of the digit 0 in 103?* (tens) *What does it represent?* (sample answers: there are no extra tens; 0 tens and 1 hundred; 10 tens) *What's the place value of the digit 0 in 3,075?* (hundreds) *70,824?* (thousands) *104,637?* (ten thousands)

Math at Hand 003–004

10 and 1
Place value of 0:

10**3** _____tens_____

3,**0**75 _____hundreds_____

70,**8**24 _____thousands_____

10**4**,637 _____ten thousands_____

OPERATIONS **Compute with 0**

- ✎ *When you add 0 to any number, what do you know about the sum?* (The sum is that same number.) Invite volunteers to write some examples. *Does the order of the addends matter?* (no)
- ✎ *What happens when you multiply any number by 0?* (The product is 0.) Invite volunteers to write some examples. *Does the order of the factors matter?* (no)

Math at Hand 118–119, 136

__33__ + 0 = __33__

0 + __65__ = __65__

Other examples:

__249__ × 0 = __0__

0 × __1,180__ = __0__

Other examples:

PATTERNS AND ALGEBRA **Order Property**

- ✎ The *Order Property of Addition* states that the order of the addends does not change the sum. *Can you write an example of the property?* (see recording pad) Invite students to write other examples.
- ✎ A similar property also works for multiplication. *Can you write an equation to show an example of the property?* (see recording pad) Invite volunteers to write other examples.
- The *Order Property* is also called the *Commutative Property*.

REACHING ALL LEARNERS Use counters and arrays to show the property is true for addition and multiplication.

Math at Hand 216–219

__25__ + __13__ = __38__

__13__ + __25__ = __38__

Other examples:
Answers will vary.

__3__ × __5__ = __15__

__5__ × __3__ = __15__

Other examples:
Answers will vary.

KEY ✎ = record on pad

© Great Source. Copying is prohibited.

GEOMETRY Slide, turn, flip

✎ *When a picture moves in one direction, it is called a* slide, *or* translation. *Can you write* translation *beneath the diagram that shows the change?*

✎ *When a picture turns around a point, it is called a* turn, *or* rotation. *Write* rotation *beneath the diagram that shows the change.*

✎ *When a picture flips over a line, it is called a* flip, *or* reflection. *Write* reflection *beneath the diagram that shows the change.*

Math at Hand 375–379

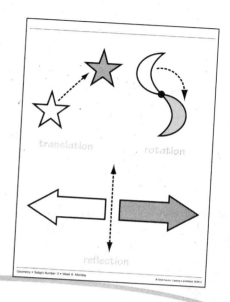

MEASUREMENT Perimeter

• *The distance around the outside of any polygon is called the* perimeter. *How many sides do you see in this shape?* (5) *Are they the same lengths?* (no) *How can you find the perimeter of this shape?* (add the lengths of the sides)

✎ *What is the perimeter?* (see recording pad)

✎ **Problem Solving** *I am a rectangle with a perimeter of 26 units. One side of me is 8 units long. What are the lengths of the other sides?* (8 units, 5 units and 5 units) *Draw a picture of the rectangle. Label its sides.*

REACHING ALL LEARNERS Draw and label a rectangle to help students visualize the problem solving.

Math at Hand 295

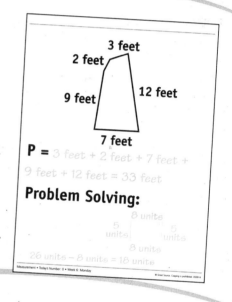

VOCABULARY *pattern*

• *Tell how patterns are used in every day life.* (sample answers: on quilts, parade marching order, tiles on the wall, weekly school schedule of classes)

• *How can you tell if something is a pattern?* (if certain groups repeat or change in a predictable way)

• *What is useful about a pattern?* (sample answers: patterns help us predict, help us identify trends, create a rhythm)

Math at Hand 401

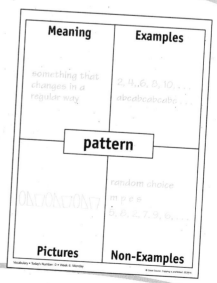

© Great Source. Copying is prohibited.

PRACTICE

Written Practice

CONCEPTS AND SKILLS

- Place value and the digit 0
- Compute with zero
- Translation, rotation, and reflection
- Review adding fractions with like denominators, writing fractions in simplest form
- Problem Solving Strategies and Skills: *Guess, Check, and Revise, Make a Table, Make an Organized List, Ignore Unneeded Information*

PREVIEW THE PRACTICE

- *What can you tell about adding 0 to any non-zero number?* (The sum is the non-zero number.)
- *What is special about multiplying any number by 0?* (The product equals 0.)

SUPPORT THE PRACTICE

- Problems 1–4 work with place value of the digit 0. Use a place value chart to illustrate.
- Problems 5–8 apply adding with and multiplying by 0. Remind students to pay attention to the numbers as they work.
- Problems 9–11 illustrate 3 transformations. Revisit today's Geometry recording pad, if needed.
- Problems 12–15 review adding fractions with like denominators. Some answers might need to be in simplest form.
- Problem 16 provides practice choosing a strategy to solve the problem. Making a list might help students get started.

PRACTICE TODAY'S NUMBER ⓪

Name _____

NUMBER AND OPERATIONS

Name the place value of the underlined digit. ◄1–4. MAH 003–004

1. 2<u>0</u>8 _____tens_____ place
2. 60<u>0</u> _____ones_____ place
3. 5,<u>0</u>54 _____hundreds_____ place
4. 3<u>0</u>2,571 _____ten thousands_____ place

Fill in the blank to complete the equation. ◄5–8. MAH 118–119, 136

5. 316 __+__ 0 = 316
6. 597 __×__ 0 = 0
7. 1,405 __×__ 0 = 0
8. 73,024 __+__ 0 = 73,024

GEOMETRY

Name the change. Write *translation*, *rotation*, or *reflection*. ◄9–11. MAH 375–379

9.

10.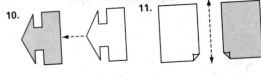

11.

_____rotation_____   _____translation_____   _____reflection_____

REVIEW

Add. Write in simplest form, if needed. ◄12–15. MAH 159

12. $\frac{3}{5} + \frac{2}{5} =$ _____ $\frac{5}{5} = 1$
13. $\frac{5}{8} + \frac{2}{8} =$ _____ $\frac{7}{8}$
14. $\frac{3}{7} + \frac{3}{7} =$ _____ $\frac{6}{7}$
15. $\frac{2}{9} + \frac{4}{9} =$ _____ $\frac{6}{9} = \frac{2}{3}$

© Great Source. Permission is granted to copy this page.

SUMMER SUCCESS: MATH **117** MAH: *Math at Hand*

REACHING ALL LEARNERS

Help students visualize the transformations in problems 9–11. Cut out a figure to demonstrate the changes.

Math at Hand

If students need help, encourage them to refer to the MAH items shown on the student page.

© Great Source. Copying is prohibited.

Complete each step. ◄MAH 16. MAH 396

16. Leon is selling boxed dried fruit to raise money for football camp in the fall. Each box costs $4.50. Leon plans to carry plenty of change because most people pay with a $5 bill. How many different ways can Leon make change for a $5 bill, if he does not use pennies?

a. Underline the question you need to answer.

b. Loop details about the change to be given.

c. Mark the strategy/strategies you will use.

d. Solve the problem. Explain your thinking.

2 quarters

1 quarter, 2 dimes, 1 nickel

1 quarter, 1 dime, 3 nickels

1 quarter, 5 nickels

5 dimes

4 dimes, 2 nickels

3 dimes, 4 nickels

2 dimes, 6 nickels

1 dime, 8 nickels

10 nickels

e. Answer the question.

There are 10 ways to make change for 50¢, without using pennies.

POSSIBLE STRATEGIES

- Guess, Check, and Revise
- Make a Table
- Make an Organized List

Sample strategy:
Make an Organized List

© Great Source. Permission is granted to copy this page.

REACHING ALL LEARNERS

If students have difficulty with the problem, provide play coins or counters to use as manipulatives.

© Great Source. Copying is prohibited.

PROBLEM SOLVING

Work in small groups of 3 or 4 students.

- Encourage students to find ways to identify needed information to solve the problem.
- *What information do you need to answer the question?* (how much change Leon needs to give for a $5 bill, the kind of change Leon can make)
- *How can you use the information?* (to make an organized list)

SCORING

a. Last sentence underlined: 1 pt

b. Details about the change circled: 1 pt

c. Choose and apply an appropriate strategy: 1 pt

d. Explanation of solution: 1 pt

e. Correct answer: 1 pt

GLOSSARY TO GO

Today's Vocabulary *pattern*

Have students complete an entry for today's vocabulary term in their Glossaries. Encourage students to use both words and drawings.

MATH JOURNAL

- *Write an example to show what happens when you add with zero.* (sample answer: add any number and 0, the sum is that number; for example: 8 + 0 = 8; 0 + 53 = 53)

GAME

Active Practice

CONCEPTS AND SKILLS

- Identify prime and composite numbers
- Add and subtract whole numbers

MATH TALK

Model the correct use of these words and encourage students to use them as they work.

- **composite number** a number that has more than 2 different factors
- **factor** a whole number that divides evenly into another
- **prime number** a number that has exactly 2 different factors, 1 and itself

MATERIALS

For each pair: 4 sets of 0–9 Digits Cards, paper and pencil

GAME

Prime Time

Object: Be the first to reach 200 points by creating prime numbers.

MATERIALS

4 sets of 0–9 Digits Cards, paper and pencil

DIRECTIONS

1. Each player makes a recording sheet and keeps track of the other player's score. Each player gets 100 points to start the game.

2. Shuffle the Digit Cards and place them facedown in a draw pile.

3. Players take turns drawing one card at a time until both players have a pair of cards. Then players reveal their cards at the same time.

4. Each player tries to create a prime number using the two digits drawn. Suppose you draw a 5 and a 3. You can make 53 or 35. Since 35 is composite and 53 is prime, you declare 53 as your prime number. To get 53 points get added to your score, you must also name the next prime number.

   If instead you draw a 2 and a 1, the numbers that you can make are the composites 12 and 21. You cannot make a prime number. You declare 12, the lower of the numbers, as your composite number. 12 points get subtracted from your score. **(With my 5 and 3 cards, I can make the prime number 53. The next prime number is 59. I score 53 points!)**

5. Play continues for 3 rounds. The first player to reach 200 points wins. The first player whose score drops to 0 or below, loses. If after 3 rounds no player reaches 200 or 0, the player with the higher score wins.

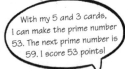

With my 5 and 3 cards, I can make the prime number 53. The next prime number is 59. I score 53 points!

© Great Source. Permission is granted to copy this page.

REACHING ALL LEARNERS

Simplify Provide a hundreds chart with prime numbers shaded.

Variation Change the rules of the game so that composite numbers are added, while prime numbers are subtracted.

Math at Hand

- Factors, 051
- Prime Numbers, 053
- Composite Numbers, 055
- Even and Odd Numbers, 063
- Adding with Whole Numbers, 119–122
- Subtracting with Whole Numbers, 129–133

© Great Source. Copying is prohibited.

Day 1

- Review the concepts of prime and composite numbers using manipulatives to construct arrays. Write the number 7 on the chalkboard. Draw an array to show 1 row of 7.

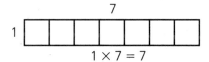

Explain that 7 is a prime number because 1 and 7 are the only factors of 7. A prime number has the factors of 1 and itself.

- Write the number 8 on the chalkboard. Draw an array to show 1 row of 8. Draw another array to show 2 rows of 4. Explain that 8 is a composite number because 1, 2, 4, and 8 are factors of 8. A composite number has additional factor pairs other than 1 and itself.

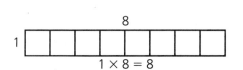 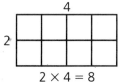

- Demonstrate how to play the game. Have volunteers play a demonstration game.
- Show students how to keep score, starting with 100 points.

Day 2

- Review the rules and procedures discussed yesterday.
- Assign partners to play the game.

Encourage students to ask themselves.

- *How do I know this number is prime?*
- *Does this number have any other factors besides 1 and itself?*
- *Did I use the greater of two possible prime numbers?* (For example, with the cards 3 and 7, both 37 and 73 are prime numbers. Other examples for two prime numbers: 17 and 71; 13 and 31.)

Teacher: I have a 1 and a 7. I can make 17 or 71. Both are prime, which one do I want to keep?

Student: 71, you want the bigger number. It will increase your score.

T: What is the next prime after 71?

S: 73.

T: So, what is my score?

S: You started with 100. So, 100 plus 71 gives you 171.

T: My next two numbers are 8 and 6. What numbers can I make?

S: 68 or 86.

T: Are either of these prime?

S: Nope, both are composites because they are even numbers.

T: What does that mean if the number is even?

S: It is composite. It has 2 and other numbers as factors.

T: Are all even numbers composite?

S: No, 2 is even but it is prime.

T: Because I can't make a prime number, I must subtract the composite number from my score. Which number should I subtract? What's my new score?

S: Subtract 68, because it's smaller. Your new score is 103.

If students need more help, use the hints below, or refer to the *Math at Hand* items shown to the left.

- **Can students identify prime and composite numbers?** Provide practice using divisibility rules to determine factors of numbers. Give students a list of divisibility rules.

- **Do students use the correct vocabulary?** Model how to use the targeted vocabulary.

© Great Source. Copying is prohibited.

DATA STUDY

Additional Support

CONCEPTS AND SKILLS

- Events and outcomes
- Possible combinations
- Tree diagram
- Probability of an event

MATH TALK

Model the correct use of these terms and encourage students to use them as they work.

- **combinations** a way of arranging items in a group; placing them in a different order does not create a new combination

- **probability of an event** a ratio expressed as a fraction to show the number of favorable outcomes to the number of all possible outcomes

- **sample space** a list of all possible outcomes of an event; a tree diagram may be used find all possible outcomes

MATERIALS

Colored paper*

*Optional materials

GET STARTED

- Read and discuss the directions on page 121 of the student book.
- Assign partner pairs of mixed abilities to work together.

DATA STUDY

Name _____

Combinations and Probability

What is the probability of picking a sandwich of your choice?

MAKE A PREDICTION

A deli makes one each of every possible combination of sandwiches using 2 kinds of bread (wheat, rye), 3 kinds of meat (ham, turkey, beef), and 2 kinds of cheeses (cheddar, Swiss). Each sandwich is wrapped in wax paper, but is not labeled.

- What is the probability of picking a ham sandwich? Explain your answer.
  1 chance in 3, because there are 3 types of meat

MAKE A TREE DIAGRAM

- Use the information to make a tree diagram.
- Make an organized list of all possible combinations.

ANALYZE THE DATA

1. Look at the tree diagram. How many different combinations of sandwiches are there in all? _____12_____ Write a fraction to show the probability of picking a turkey and cheddar cheese sandwich on wheat bread. $\frac{1}{12}$

2. How many different combinations of sandwiches are possible with ham? _____4_____
   What is the probability of picking a sandwich with ham? Explain your answer.
   There are 4 out of 12 possible ways to make a sandwich with ham; $\frac{4}{12} = \frac{1}{3}$.

3. What is the probability of picking a sandwich made with tuna? Explain.
   0. Tuna is not a choice.

4. Do you have a 50–50 chance of picking a sandwich made with rye bread? Explain.
   Yes, since 6 of the 12 possible combinations are made with rye bread, that's $\frac{1}{2}$ of the sandwiches.

© Great Source. Permission is granted to copy this page.

SUMMER SUCCESS: MATH   **121**   *Math at Hand 291*

REACHING ALL LEARNERS

Demonstrate the possible outcomes. Use color paper to model the breads, meat, and cheeses. For example, on 6 sheets of white paper write *rye*, on 6 other sheets write *wheat*. Repeat with different colors for the meat and cheese selections. Then proceed to assemble the combinations.

Math at Hand

- Events and Outcomes, 286
- Notation and Calculating Probability, 287
- Sample Space, 290
- Tree Diagrams, 291

© Great Source. Copying is prohibited.

Day 1

Ask students to read the problem at the top of student page 121. *What kind of bread-meat-cheese sandwich would you like using the choices given?* (Answers will vary. Have students share the different ways they could make a sandwich.)

Ask students to look at the tree diagram on student page 122. *What are the 3 ingredients?* (bread, meat, cheese) *Which ingredient has 3 options?* (meat) *How many possible outcomes are there in all?* (12) *How do you know?* (sample answer: count the lines in the cheese column)

Day 2

Review with students the work they have done so far. *What was the question for this project?* Work together to complete the tree diagram.

Write the bread, meat, and cheese sandwich options on the board in three columns. Tell students to complete the tree diagram on student page 122. Ask them how a tree diagram can help them find all possible combinations for making a sandwich with three ingredients.

Discuss with the class their answers to the questions at the bottom of student page 121. Then ask them to consider the following:

- *Do you think there is a way to find the total number of combinations of sandwiches without making a tree diagram?* (Since there are 2 breads, 3 meats, and 2 cheeses, multiply $2 \times 3 \times 2$ to get a total of 12 different combinations.)

- *What does it mean to have a "50–50 chance" of something happening?* (It means half of the time something will happen and half of the time it won't.)

- **What If?** *Suppose customers wanted more choices for their sandwiches, such as adding chicken. How many different kinds of sandwiches would be possible?* (If chicken were used to make the bread-meat-cheese sandwiches, there would be $2 \times 4 \times 2$, or 16 different combinations.)

Teacher: Can you name all the different combinations of turkey and Swiss cheese sandwiches that are possible?

Student: There's turkey and Swiss on rye.

S: And turkey and Swiss on wheat bread.

T: How many turkey and Swiss combinations are there? Look at the tree diagram.

S: I see 2.

T: What is the total number of combinations possible?

S: I can count 12 in all.

T: Can you think of a fraction to show the probability of a turkey and Swiss sandwich?

S: That would be 2 out of 12.

S: Or, $\frac{2}{12}$.

S: Or, the probability of picking a turkey and Swiss sandwich is $\frac{1}{6}$.

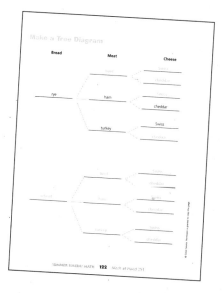

© Great Source. Copying is prohibited.

NUMBER NAMES TODAY'S NUMBER 2

1	2	3	4
6	8	10	12
25	34	46	58
60	73	77	88
92	107	235	480

NUMBER Even numbers

✎ *An even number of things can be divided into 2 equal-size groups. Loop the even numbers on the recording pad.* (see recording pad)

- *What pattern do you notice about the digits in the ones place?* (sample answer: all the ones have 0, 2, 4, 6, or 8)
- *Tell two ways you can describe an even number.* (sample answer: An even number can be divided evenly into 2 groups, and it has the digits 0, 2, 4, 6, or 8 in the ones place.)

Math at Hand 063

34	yes	no
50	yes	no
126	yes	no
6,709	yes	no
35,901	yes	no

Other examples:

sample answers:

1,000   312   504   456   88

OPERATIONS Divisibility by 2

✎ *A number is divisible by another number when the remainder is 0. How can you show that 34 is divisible by 2?* (sample answer: I can split 34 into 2 equal groups with 17 in each.) *How about 50?* (sample answer: I can split it into 2 groups, with 25 each.)

✎ *Look at the numbers. Do you see a pattern or a "rule" that lets you know a number is divisible by 2?* (sample answer: see if the digit in the ones place is an even number.) Invite volunteers to write examples of large numbers divisible by 2. (see recording pad)

Math at Hand 062

Shape	# of Squares
□	1 × 1 = 1
⊞	2 × 2 = 4
(3×3 grid)	3 × 3 = 9
4th shape?	4 × 4 = 16
6th shape?	6 × 6 = 36

PATTERNS AND ALGEBRA Square number pattern

✎ *Continue the pattern. What will the 4th shape look like?* (4 by 4 squares) *Draw the shape.*

✎ *If the pattern continues, how many squares will make up the 6th shape?* (6 × 6 = 36) *Draw the shape.*

- *What patterns do you see?* (sample answers: the shapes are squares; the sides increase by 1 each time; the number of squares increase by 3, by 5, by 7, and so on)

REACHING ALL LEARNERS Use graph paper to help students visualize the shapes and to complete the 4th and 6th shapes.

Math at Hand 495

© Great Source. Copying is prohibited.

KEY ✎ = record on pad

GEOMETRY Tessellations

- *We call a pattern of shapes that totally covers a flat surface a tessellation. Figures that tessellate must fit together without any overlap.*

- ✎ *Which figure do you think tessellates? Draw a picture to show how you know.* (see recording pad)

- ✎ **Problem Solving** *Draw a figure that does not tessellate.* (sample drawing: the oval and heart do not tessellate)

REACHING ALL LEARNERS Use cut outs to show the tessellations.

Math at Hand 381

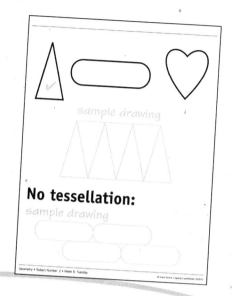

MEASUREMENT Area of parallelograms

- *Describe what you see in the top diagram.* (sample answer: a parallelogram is changed into a rectangle)

- *How can the top diagram help you find the area of the parallelogram?* (sample answer: change the parallelogram into a rectangle)

- ✎ *Use what you know about areas of rectangles to find the area of the parallelogram. What is the area of the parallelogram?* (Area = 6 mi × 4 mi = 24 mi²)

REACHING ALL LEARNERS Use cut outs to show the changes in the top diagram.

Math at Hand 302

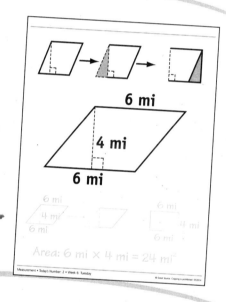

VOCABULARY *sequence*

- *How are these lists of numbers alike: 8, 9, 10, 11, 12, . . . and 199, 198, 197, 196, . . .?* (They are in order, and change by 1.) *How are they different?* (One series in increasing, the other is decreasing.)

- *What are some other examples of a sequence of numbers?* (Answers will vary.)

- *Are these numbers in a sequence: 4, 7, 1, 5, 9?* (no) *Can you tell why?* (sample answer: There is no order or pattern.)

Math at Hand 493, 534

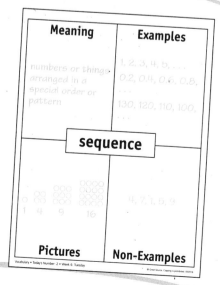

© Great Source. Copying is prohibited.

PRACTICE

Written Practice

CONCEPTS AND SKILLS

- Identify even numbers
- Divisibility by 2
- Analyze number sequence
- Review transformations
- Problem Solving Strategies and Skills: *Make a Diagram, Make a Table, Make an Organized List, Use Logical Reasoning*

PREVIEW THE PRACTICE

- *Is 2 an even number?* (yes) *How do you know?* (sample answer: 2 of any thing can be split equally between 2 people with nothing left over)

SUPPORT THE PRACTICE

- Problems 1–5 list random numbers for students to identify the even number. Remind students to look at the digit in the ones place.
- Problems 6–10 let students play the role of the teacher. Help students verbalize a comment for problem 10.
- Problems 11–13 analyze a sequence of square numbers. Help students recognize the connection between the drawing and the multiplication equation.
- Problems 14–16 review the 3 transformations. Revisit yesterday's Geometry recording pad, if needed.

Name _____

NUMBER AND OPERATIONS

Loop the even number or numbers. ◄1–5. MAH 063

1. 17　(22)　(18)　(30)

2. (46)　51　99　(14)

3. (804)　911　(532)　(200)

4. (1,470)　(3,020)　(8,888)　8,589

5. How can you describe an even number?

　　Sample answers: It has a 2, 4, 6, 8, or 0 in the ones place; it can be divided into 2
　　equal-size groups; it is divisible by 2.

Help the teacher correct this paper. Write a note to the student.

Write the number in standard form only if it is divisible by 2. ◄6–10. MAH 062

6. ninety-five _____ ✓

7. two thousand, twelve ___2,012___ ✓

8. seven hundred forty ___740___ ✓

9. sixty-three ___63___ ✗

10. Comment: ___In #9, 63 has a 3 in the ones column, so it is not an even___
　　___number.___

PATTERNS AND ALGEBRA

Fill in the blank and draw the missing picture. ◄11–13. MAH 495

11.

$1 \times 1 = 1$　　$2 \times 2 = 4$　　$3 \times 3 = 9$　　$4 \times 4 = 16$　　$5 \times 5 = 25$

12. What do you notice about the multiplication facts?

　　Sample answer: The factors are the same.

13. What do you notice about the pictures?

　　Sample answer: Except for 1×1, each picture forms a square figure.

SUMMER SUCCESS: MATH **123** MAH: *Math at Hand*

© Great Source. Permission is granted to copy this page.

REACHING ALL LEARNERS

Some students might need counters or other types of manipulatives to help with the problems.

Math at Hand

If students need help, encourage them to refer to the MAH items shown on the student page.

© Great Source. Copying is prohibited.

Name the change. Write *translation, rotation,* or *reflection.* ◄14–16. MAH 375–379

14.

reflection

15.

rotation

16.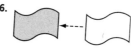

translation

PROBLEM SOLVING · **UNDERSTAND · PLAN · TRY · LOOK BACK**

Complete each step. ◄MAH 17. MAH 396

17. Mrs. Klein goes to the market every 4th day and goes to the library every 6th day. If she does both on January 1, what is the next date she will go to the market *and* the library on the same day?

a. Underline the question you need to answer.

b. Loop the details about the days.

c. Mark the strategy/strategies you will use.

d. Solve the problem. Explain your thinking.

POSSIBLE STRATEGIES

- Make a Diagram
- Make a Table
- Make an Organized List

Sample strategy: Make a Table

1 M, L	2	3	4	5 M	6	7 L
8	9 M	10	11	12	13 M, L	14
15	16	17	18	19	20	21
22	23	24	25	26	27	28
29	30	31				

e. Answer the question.

On January 13, Mrs. Klein will go to the market and the library.

© Great Source. Permission is granted to copy this page.

REACHING ALL LEARNERS

If students have difficulty with the problem, help them make a calendar by drawing a 7 by 5 grid. Or, use a calendar for the current month.

© Great Source. Copying is prohibited.

PROBLEM SOLVING

Work in small groups of 3 or 4 students.

- Encourage students to find ways to identify needed information to solve the problem.
- *What information do you need to answer the question?* (the pattern of days Mrs. Klein goes to the market and the library)
- *How can you use the information?* (to map out the events on a calendar that starts with January 1)

SCORING

a. Last sentence underlined: 1 pt

b. Details about the pattern of events circled: 1 pt

c. Choose and apply an appropriate strategy: 1 pt

d. Explanation of solution: 1 pt

e. Correct answer: 1 pt

GLOSSARY TO GO

Today's Vocabulary *sequence*

Have students complete an entry for today's vocabulary term in their Glossaries. Encourage students to use both words and drawings.

MATH JOURNAL

- *What are square numbers?* (sample answer: numbers you get by multiplying a number times itself. For example, $2 \times 2 = 4$ and $3 \times 3 = 9$. You can use dots, in a square array, to represent the numbers.)

NUMBER NAMES TODAY'S NUMBER 3

(1)	2	(3)	(5)
6	(7)	(9)	12
(17)	(25)	(29)	(33)
46	(51)	62	88
(93)	100	(249)	(315)

NUMBER Odd numbers

✎ *An odd number of things cannot be divided into 2 equal-size groups. Loop the odd numbers.* (see recording pad)

- *What pattern do you notice about the digits in the ones place?* (sample answer: all the ones have 1, 3, 5, 7, or 9)

- *How are odd numbers different from even numbers?* (sample answer: odd numbers do not divide evenly into 2 groups, they always have 1 extra)

REACHING ALL LEARNERS Use counters to demonstrate the difference between odd and even numbers.

Math at Hand 063

33	(yes)	no
18	(yes)	no
27	(yes)	no
608	yes	(no)
301	yes	(no)

Other examples:

sample answers:

1,587   312   504   456   888

OPERATIONS Divisibility by 3

✎ *How can you show that 33 is divisible by 3?* (sample answer: I can split 33 into 3 equal groups with 11 in each) *How about 18?* (sample answer: I can split it into 3 groups, with 6 each)

- *Here is a rule of thumb to remember: Add up the digits in any number, until you get a 1-digit sum. If the sum is divisible by 3, then the number is divisible by 3. Try out the rule with the numbers on the recording pad.*

✎ *Write some examples of large numbers divisible by 3.* (see recording pad)

Math at Hand 062

Shape	# of Dots	# Added
o	1	
oo	3	2
ooo	6	3
oooo	10	4
ooooo	15	5
oooooo	21	6

PATTERNS AND ALGEBRA Triangular number pattern

✎ *Look at the pattern. How many dots are in the 5th group?* (15) *How many more is that compared with the 4th group* (5 more)

✎ *How many dots do you think the 6th group will have?* (21) *Why?* (sample answer: it is the 6th group, so it has 6 more dots than the previous one) *Draw the 6th group and fill in the chart.*

- *Why do you think* triangular number *might be a good name to call the numbers 1, 3, 6, 10, 15, 21?* (sample answer: because I can make them fit into a triangular group of shapes)

Math at Hand 494

© Great Source. Copying is prohibited.

KEY ✎ = record on pad

GEOMETRY Triangle tessellation

- *How do you know this is a tessellation?* (There are no gaps or overlaps.)

✎ *All triangles tessellate. Use the grid to draw an example.* (Drawings will vary.)

✎ *Not all shapes tessellate. Draw one that does not tessellate.* (Example: circle, oval, star, regular pentagon)

REACHING ALL LEARNERS Cut out triangles for students to trace, if needed.

Math at Hand 381

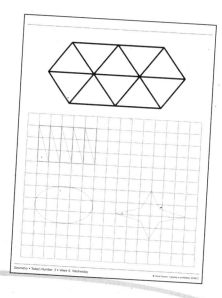

MEASUREMENT Area of right triangles

- *What do you know about this shape?* (sample answers: it is a triangle with 3 sides and 3 vertices) *What is special about one corner?* (sample answers: it is a square corner, a 90° angle) *What do we call this shape?* (a right triangle)

✎ *How can 2 of these right triangles make a rectangle? Use the grid to draw it. Label the sides.*

✎ **Problem Solving** *How can you find the area of the rectangle?* (count the units; use length × width) *How would you find the area of the triangle?* (take half of the area of the rectangle)

Math at Hand 303

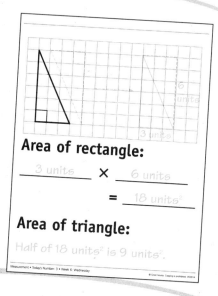

VOCABULARY *frequency*

- *When we say the frequency of an event is high, what do we mean?* (sample answer: something is happening a lot)

- *What can we learn from the frequency of an event?* (sample answer: we can spot a trend)

- *Name some examples of when knowing the frequency is useful.* (sample answer: knowing how often it rains helps you decide what to pack for a camping trip)

Math at Hand 268, 524

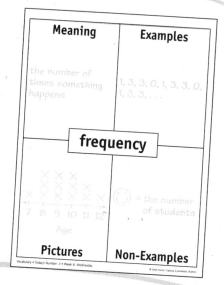

© Great Source. Copying is prohibited.

PRACTICE

Written Practice

CONCEPTS AND SKILLS

- Identify odd numbers
- Divisibility by 3
- Area of right triangles
- Review equivalent fractions
- Problem Solving Strategies and Skills: *Guess, Check, and Revise, Make a Table, Write an Equation, Take Notes*

PREVIEW THE PRACTICE

- *What is the rule of thumb for divisibility by 3?* (Add up the digits in any number, until you get a 1-digit sum. If the sum is divisible by 3, then the number is divisible by 3) *Give an example.* (sample answer: 732 → 7 + 3 + 2 = 12, 1 + 2 = 3, 3 ÷ 3 = 1)

SUPPORT THE PRACTICE

- Problems 1–4 ask students to select the odd numbers from a given set. Remind them to focus on the digit in the ones place.

- Problems 6–11 require students to decide whether a number is divisible by 2, 3, or both. Revisit yesterday and today's Operations recording pads, if needed.

- Problems 12–13 have students work with area of right triangles. Help students recognize the relationship between the area of rectangles and right triangles.

- Problems 14–18 review equivalent fractions using points on a number line. Help students see that Point C is midway between 0 and 1.

- Problem 19 is a problem for students to select from 3 strategies to solve the problem.

PRACTICE TODAY'S NUMBER **3**

Name _____

NUMBER AND OPERATIONS

Loop the odd number or numbers. ◄ 1–5. MAH 063

1. (17) (21) 8 (39)

2. (85) (51) (99) (13)

3. (803) 914 536 208

4. (1,473) 3,022 (8,881) (8,589)

5. How can you describe an odd number?

Sample answers: It has a 1, 3, 5, 7, or 9 in the ones place; it cannot be divided into 2 equal-size groups; it has 1 leftover when divided by 2.

What is the number divisible by? Loop 2 or 3, or both. ◄ 6–11. MAH 062

6. 351 divisible by: 2 (3) both

7. 9,600 divisible by: (2) 3 (both)

8. 46 divisible by: (2) 3 both

9. 704 divisible by: (2) 3 both

10. 2,982 divisible by: (2) (3) (both)

11. 405 divisible by: 2 (3) both

MEASUREMENT

What is the area of the triangle? Show your work. ◄ 12–13. MAH 303

12.

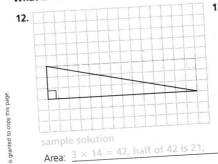

sample solution
Area: 3 × 14 = 42, half of 42 is 21;
21 units²

13.

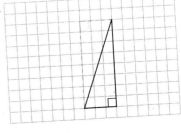

Area: 3 × 8 = 24, half of 24 is 12;
12 units²

© Great Source. Permission is granted to copy this page.

REACHING ALL LEARNERS

Use counters to illustrate a number. Help students see that those that line up are even numbers. Those that have 1 more are odd numbers.

Math at Hand

If students need help, encourage them to refer to the MAH items shown on the student page.

© Great Source. Copying is prohibited.

Write two equivalent fractions to name the point on the number line. ◄14–18. MAH 031

14. Point A = _____ $\frac{1}{8}$ _____ $\frac{2}{16}$

15. Point B = _____ $\frac{1}{4}$ _____ $\frac{2}{8}$

16. Point C = _____ $\frac{1}{2}$ _____ $\frac{2}{4}$

17. Point D = _____ $\frac{5}{8}$ _____ $\frac{10}{16}$

18. Point E = _____ $\frac{3}{4}$ _____ $\frac{6}{8}$

PROBLEM SOLVING • **UNDERSTAND** • **PLAN** • **TRY** • **LOOK BACK**

Complete each step. ◄19. MAH 396

19. Mr. Davidson is (three times older than his son.) Together, (their ages equal 52.) How old is Mr. Davidson?

   a. Underline the question you need to answer.

   b. Loop the details about the ages.

   c. Mark the strategy/strategies you will use.

   d. Solve the problem. Explain your thinking.

   _____

   _____

   _____

   _____

   e. Answer the question.

   Mr. Davidson is 39 years old.

   _____

POSSIBLE STRATEGIES

- Guess, Check, and Revise
- Make a Table
- Write an Equation

Sample strategy: Guess, Check, and Revise

Son (Guess)	5	16	11	13
Mr. Davidson	5 × 3 = 15	16 × 3 = 48	11 × 3 = 33	13 × 3 = 39
Check	5 + 15 = 20	16 + 48 = 64	11 + 33 = 44	13 + 39 = 52
Revise	too low (increase son's age)	too high (lower son's age)	too low, but getting closer (increase son's age)	just right

© Great Source. Permission is granted to copy this page.

REACHING ALL LEARNERS

If students have difficulty with the problem, begin the process of guessing and checking. Model the analysis of whether the combined age is too high or too low.

© Great Source. Copying is prohibited.

PROBLEM SOLVING

Work in small groups of 3 or 4 students.

- Encourage students to find ways to identify needed information to solve the problem.

- *What information do you need to answer the question?* (the combined age of the father and son, the relationship between their ages)

- *How can you use the information?* (to guess, check, and revise)

SCORING

   a. Last sentence underlined: 1 pt

   b. Details about the ages circled: 1 pt

   c. Choose and apply an appropriate strategy: 1 pt

   d. Explanation of solution: 1 pt

   e. Correct answer: 1 pt

GLOSSARY TO GO

Today's Vocabulary *frequency*

Have students complete an entry for today's vocabulary term in their Glossaries. Encourage students to use both words and drawings.

MATH JOURNAL

- *What is one strategy you learned that will help you tell the difference between an odd or an even number?* (sample answer: an even number of things can be divided into 2 equal groups; an odd number has 1 left over.)

GAME

Active Practice

CONCEPTS AND SKILLS

- Estimate sums and differences
- Calculate exact sums and differences

MATH TALK

Model the correct use of these words and encourage students to use them as they work.

- **addend** any number being added
- **difference** the amount that remains after one quantity is subtracted from another
- **sum** the result of addition

MATERIALS

For each pair: 4 sets of 0–9 Digits Cards with the zeros removed, paper and pencil

GAME

Inverse Estimations

Object: To create an addition or subtraction equation with an answer as close as possible to the target number.

MATERIALS

4 sets of 0–9 Digits Cards with the zeros removed, paper and pencil

DIRECTIONS

1. Use the recording sheet on p. 128.
2. Shuffle the Digit Cards and place them facedown to form a draw pile.
3. Players begin with Target A. Each player draws 6 cards and arranges them to make two 3-digit addends with a sum as close to the target as possible. The sum should be calculated on scrap paper and then written on the recording sheet. The player with the sum closer to the target wins the round and circles the winning sum on the recording sheet. **(My cards have a sum of 475. You got 450. Mine's closer to 500!)**
4. Collect all the cards and shuffle them to make a new draw pile before beginning each target.
5. Continue with the remaining targets, circling each winning sum or difference.
6. At the end of 4 rounds, the player with more circled answers wins. In case of a tie, play an extra round.

My cards have a sum of 475. You got 450. Mine's closer to 500!

Inverse Estimation

Target Numbers	Player 1	Player 2
A. Sum = 500; use 6 cards	475	450

© Great Source. Permission is granted to copy this page.

REACHING ALL LEARNERS

Simplify Use smaller target numbers. Allow students to work with 2-digit sums and differences until they are more familiar with the game.

Variation Allow the students to alternate the responsibility of setting the targeted sum or difference before each round.

Math at Hand

- Estimating Sums and Differences, 100–101
- Adding with Whole Numbers, 119–122
- Subtracting with Whole Numbers, 129–133

© Great Source. Copying is prohibited.

Day 1

- Review the vocabulary associated with addition and subtraction.
- Demonstrate regrouping within the context of addition and subtraction if students have displayed a lack of understanding with either operation.
- Demonstrate by writing on the chalkboard and by verbalizing the thinking process used to estimate sums and differences.

- Demonstrate how to play the game and how to keep score. Have volunteers play a demonstration game.

Day 2

- Review the rules and procedures discussed yesterday.
- Assign pairs of students to play the game.

Encourage students to ask themselves:

- *Did I estimate correctly?*
- *Should I round or use another method to estimate?*
- *What would happen if I switch the digits in the tens place?*

Teacher: I have drawn a 4, 2, 8, 3, 5, and 1. What two digits would be good to put in the hundreds place?

Student: Use 2 and 3 to make something in the 200s and 300s.

T: Are there other choices?

S: You could use 4 and 1, or 3 and 1.

T: The estimation of 200 plus 300 is great. What about the other digits?

S: One number can be 248. Putting the 8 in the tens place will make the number way too large.

T: What about the other number?

S: Make the other number 315. We need a small number in the tens place. We are already over 500.

T: What is the sum of 248 and 315?

S: 563

T: Is this the closest we can get to 500?

S: Using 3 and 1 in the hundreds place may be closer since the estimation of 300 and 100 is 400.

T: Let's see, the sum of 385 and 124 is 509. Is this good?

S: Yes, but you can also try 352 and 148.

S: That sum is even better. It's exactly 500. Bingo!

If students need more help, use the hints below, or refer to the *Math at Hand* items shown to the left.

- **Do students estimate correctly and use the estimates as a strategy?** Use a number line to practice rounding.

- **Can students add and subtract?** Check to be sure students align the digits correctly before they compute.

© Great Source. Copying is prohibited.

CONCEPT BUILDER
MAKE & TAKE

Additional Support

CONCEPTS AND SKILLS

- Examine spatial relationships
- Recognize squares, triangles, trapezoids, and parallelograms
- Explore congruence, similarity, and symmetry

MATH TALK

Model the correct use of these terms and encourage students to use them as they work.

- **congruent** having exactly the same size and shape
- **parallelogram** a 4-sided figure with 2 pairs of parallel and congruent sides
- **similar** having the same shape, but not necessarily the same size
- **trapezoid** a 4-sided figure with exactly 2 parallel sides

MATERIALS FOR DAY 1

For each student: Tangrams (SE page 129), scissors, bags

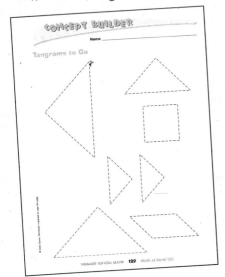

Tangrams to Go **Day 1**

GET READY

Follow the instruction below to prepare tangrams to use for demonstration.

BUILD THE TANGRAMS

1. Have students look at the tangrams found on page 129 of their books. Have students name and describe each shape as accurately as they can. Draw their attention to the triangles. Have students identify congruent and similar triangles.

2. Have the students cut out the shapes. Remind them to cut carefully.

3. Students should write their names or initials on each shape and on the storage bag. Store the shapes in the bags until tomorrow.

FOCUS ON THE MATH

- *How many triangles are needed to form a square?* (2) *Do the triangles have to be congruent right triangles?* (yes) *Why?* (If the triangles are not congruent right triangles, the sides of the square will not be equal.)

- *How many triangles are needed to form the parallelogram?* (2) *Do the triangles have to be congruent?* (yes) *Why?* (If the triangles are not congruent, the sides of the parallelograms might not be parallel.)

© Great Source. Copying is prohibited.

Tangrams to Go **Day 2**

1. Ask students make a square using two congruent triangles. Since there are 2 pairs of congruent triangles, 2 different size squares are possible.

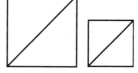

2. Students can experiment with the shapes to make rectangles using 2 or more of the shapes.

3. Have students explore combining the shapes to make several different trapezoids.

4. Have students use all 7 shapes to make one large square.

5. Have students create their own designs. Encourage them to use their imagination. Working in pairs, students can trace the outlines of these designs on a separate sheet of paper.

MODEL THE ACTIVITY

Be sure students can name and describe the tangram pieces. Accept informal names for the shapes. Reinforce geometric terms, when possible.

Ask students to name the similarities and differences between a square and a parallelogram. For example, help students see that a square is a rectangle. This is because a rectangle has 2 pairs of equal and parallel opposite sides. So does a square. Since rectangles are parallelograms, then squares are also parallelograms. But, a parallelogram is not necessarily a square, since some parallelograms do not have right angles.

REFLECT ON THE MATH

Encourage students to ask themselves:
- *Do I know which shape is a trapezoid?*
- *If the shape doesn't fit, can I change its direction?*
- *Maybe I should make a sketch of the bigger shape?*

REACHING ALL LEARNERS

Remind students to rotate the tangram pieces to find the best fit.

Math at Hand
- Plane Figures, 356

© Great Source. Copying is prohibited.

Tangram shapes prepared yesterday

Note: Send these materials home with the Newsletter at the end of the week.

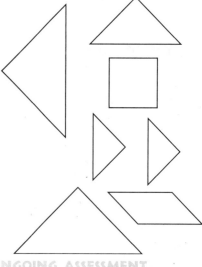

ONGOING ASSESSMENT

If students need more help, use the hints below, or refer to the *Math at Hand* items shown to the left.

- **Are students able to use geometric terms to name and describe the tangram pieces?** Remembering the term "parallelogram" may be challenging, students will be familiar with the other shapes. Relate the parallelogram to a rectangle. Discuss the difference between the shape and appearance of the angles in the parallelogram and the rectangle.

- **Are students able to demonstrate congruence, similarity, and symmetry by manipulating the tangram pieces?** Demonstrate the folding of a shape to check for symmetry. Emphasize the overlaying of one shape on top of another to check for congruence. Model the process of aligning the angles of two shapes to check for similarity.

NUMBER NAMES TODAY'S NUMBER 5

© Great Source Copying is prohibited.

Prime numbers:

2, 3, 7, 11, 13, 17, 19, 23, and so on

Composite numbers:

4, 6, 8, 9, 12, 25, 30, and so on

NUMBER Prime and composite numbers

✎ *Prime numbers have exactly 2 different factors, 1 and itself. So, is 5 a prime number?* (yes) *Can you name some other prime numbers?* (sample numbers: 2, 3, 7, 11, 13, 17, 19, 23, and so on)

✎ *Composite numbers have more than 2 different factors. **Can you name some composite numbers?*** (4, 6, 8, 9, 12, 25, 30, and so on)

✎ **Problem Solving** *Does the number 1 have exactly 2 different factors?* (no) *Does it have more than 2 factors?* (no) *So, is the number 1 a prime or composite number?* (neither)

Math at Hand 053–055

5, 10, 15, 20, 25, 30 · · ·

600	(yes)	no
415	(yes)	no
52	yes	(no)
35,795	(yes)	no

Examples:

1,005 70 905 2,000 1,050

OPERATIONS Divisibility by 5

• *When you look at the multiples of 5, what pattern do you see in the ones place?* (5, 10, 15, 20, 25, 30 . . .)

• *So, to tell whether a number is divisible by 5, what rule or pattern can you use?* (sample answer: if the digit in the ones place is 0 or 5, then the number is divisible by 5)

✎ *Is 600 divisible by 5?* (yes) *Is 415?* (yes) *Is 52?* (no) *Is 35,795?* (yes)

✎ *What are some other examples of number that are divisible by 5?* (see recording pad)

Math at Hand 062

(5 + 3) + 2 = __10__

5 + (3 + 2) = __10__

Other examples:

Answers will vary.

(5 × 4) × 3 = __60__

5 × (4 × 3) = __60__

Other examples:

Answers will vary.

PATTERNS AND ALGEBRA Grouping Property

✎ The *Grouping Property of Addition* states that the grouping of 3 or more addends does not change the sum. *Can you write an example of the property?* (see recording pad) Invite students to write different examples.

• *A similar property also works for multiplication. Can you write an equation to show an example of the property?* (see recording pad) Invite volunteers to write different examples.

• The *Grouping Property* is also called the *Associative Property.*

REACHING ALL LEARNERS Use counters and arrays to show the property is true for addition and multiplication.

Math at Hand 220–222

KEY ✎ = record on pad

GEOMETRY Tessellations

- *Look at the pentagons. Do they tessellate?* (no) *How come?* (sample answers: there are gaps; they don't cover the entire surface.)
- *Name some shapes that can tessellate.* (sample answers: square, triangle, rectangle, and so on)
- *Name some shapes that do not tessellate.* (sample answers: circles, ovals)
- ✎ *Sometimes, you can combine 2 shapes to create a tessellation. Use the grid to draw an example.* (Drawings will vary.)

Math at Hand 381

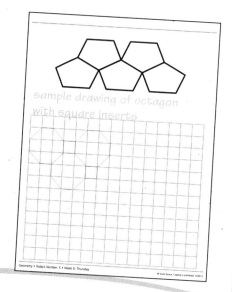

MEASUREMENT Area

- *What is the area of a shape?* (the space inside the shape)
- ✎ **Problem Solving** *What are some different ways you could find the area of the pentagon?* (sample answer: count the squares and half squares; separate the shape into smaller ones, find the area of each, then add them)
- Invite a volunteer to show how s/he would find the area. (Methods will vary. Be sure to ask the volunteer to explain his/her method.)

Math at Hand 299

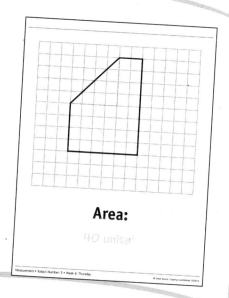

VOCABULARY *trend*

- *How can you identify trends?* (sample answer: look for patterns in things that have increased or decreased)
- *What could you learn from a trend?* (sample answer: you could find out whether something is popular with certain groups)
- *Could you name a trend that is based on something that is happening a lot?* (Answers will vary.)

Math at Hand 264, 277

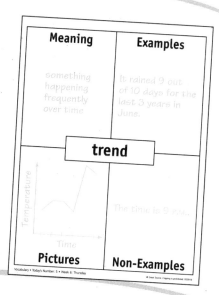

© Great Source. Copying is prohibited.

PRACTICE

Written Practice

CONCEPTS AND SKILLS

- Identify prime and composite numbers
- Divisibility by 2, 3, 5
- Grouping Property
- Review equivalent amounts
- Problem Solving Strategies and Skills: *Act It Out, Make a Model, Make a Diagram, Find Needed Information*

PREVIEW THE PRACTICE

- *Is the number 1 a prime or a composite number?* (neither) *Explain.* (a prime number has two different factors, one and itself; a composite number has more than 2 factors)

SUPPORT THE PRACTICE

- Problems 1–3 ask students to identify prime numbers from a given set. Revisit what is a prime number.
- Problems 4–6 ask students to identify composite numbers from a given set. Revisit what is a composite number.
- Problems 7–10 focus on divisibility by 2, 3, 5. Revisit earlier Operations recording pads, if needed.
- Problems 11–14 apply grouping symbols. See today's Patterns and Algebra recording pad.
- Problems 15–18 review equivalent fractions, decimals, and percents. Use a number line to help students visualize the equal amounts.

PRACTICE TODAY'S NUMBER 5

Name _____

© Great Source. Permission is granted to copy this page.

NUMBER AND OPERATIONS

Loop the prime number or numbers. ◄1–3. MAH 053

1. ⟨17⟩ 21 8 10 ⟨43⟩   2. 85 ⟨53⟩ 99 ⟨13⟩ ⟨79⟩

3. How can you define a prime number? _____
   Any number with exactly two different factors, one and itself.

Loop the composite number or numbers. ◄4–6. MAH 055

4. ⟨27⟩ ⟨21⟩ 7 ⟨39⟩ 1   5. ⟨85⟩ 71 ⟨99⟩ ⟨120⟩

6. How can you define a composite number? _____
   Any number with more than 2 factors.

What is the number divisible by? Loop 2, 3, 5 or all. ◄7–10. MAH 062

7. 453   divisible by: 2 ⟨3⟩ 5 all   8. 9,600   divisible by: 2 3 5 ⟨all⟩

9. 770   divisible by: ⟨2⟩ 3 ⟨5⟩ all   10. 248   divisible by: ⟨2⟩ 3 5 all

PATTERNS AND ALGEBRA

Use what you know about the Associative Properties to write the missing number. ◄11–14. MAH 216–219

11. $(29 + 71) + \underline{}83 = 29 + (71 + 83)$

12. $(\underline{}75 \times 21) \times 3 = 75 \times (21 \times 3)$

13. $\underline{}835 + (177 + 409) = (835 + 177) + 409$

14. $6 \times (8 \times 2) = (6 \times \underline{}8) \times 2$

REACHING ALL LEARNERS

Use the Hundred Chart to identify all the prime numbers from 1 to 100.

Math at Hand

If students need help, encourage them to refer to the MAH items shown on the student page.

© Great Source. Copying is prohibited.

Write an equivalent decimal and percent for the fraction. ◀15–18. MAH 020, 035, 044

15. $\frac{1}{4}$ _____ 0.25; 25%

16. $\frac{5}{10}$ _____ 0.5; 50%

17. $\frac{1}{10}$ _____ 0.1; 10%

18. $\frac{1}{5}$ _____ 0.2; 20%

PROBLEM SOLVING · UNDERSTAND · PLAN · TRY · LOOK BACK

Complete each step. ◀19. MAH 396

19. A group of friends are eating lunch at a picnic table. Mary is sitting across from Cory and next to Penny. Penny is to the left of Bob. And, Bob is across from Tom. If Alanna joins the group, between which two friends can she sit?

   a. Underline the question you need to answer.

   b. Loop the positions of the friends.

   c. Mark the strategy/strategies you will use.

   d. Solve the problem. Explain your thinking.

POSSIBLE STRATEGIES

- Act It Out
- Make a Model
- Make a Diagram

Sample strategy:
Make a Diagram

Cory	Alanna	Tom
	picnic table	
Mary	Penny	Bob

   e. Answer the question.

   Alanna can sit between Cory and Tom.

© Great Source. Permission is granted to copy this page.

SUMMER SUCCESS: MATH **132** MAH: *Math at Hand*

© Great Source. Copying is prohibited.

REACHING ALL LEARNERS

If students have difficulty with the problem, assemble groups of students to act out the problem.

PROBLEM SOLVING

Work in small groups of 3 or 4 students.

- Encourage students to find ways to identify needed information to solve the problem.
- *What information do you need to answer the question?* (the sitting positions of the friends around the picnic table)
- *How can you use the information?* (to make a diagram)

SCORING

   a. Last sentence underlined: 1 pt

   b. Sitting positions circled: 1 pt

   c. Choose and apply an appropriate strategy: 1 pt

   d. Explanation of solution: 1 pt

   e. Correct answer: 1 pt

GLOSSARY TO GO

Today's Vocabulary *trend*

Have students complete an entry for today's vocabulary term in their Glossaries. Encourage students to use both words and drawings.

MATH JOURNAL

- *How can an algebraic property help you work with numbers?* (sample answer: A property tells what is always true about how numbers behave.)

NUMBER NAMES TODAY'S NUMBER Review

Even numbers:
sample answers: 12, 14, 36, 58, 90, and so on

Odd numbers:
sample answers: 11, 23, 35, 47, 59, and so on

Prime numbers:
sample answers: 2, 5, 7, 11, 13, 17, and so on

Composite numbers:
sample answers: 12, 15, 27, 30, 55, 96, and so on

Number • Today's Number: Review • Week 6: Friday   © Great Source Copying is prohibited. 053011

NUMBER Number types

- *What do you know about even numbers?* (sample answer: they have in 0, 2, 4, 6, 8 in ones place) *Odd numbers?* (sample answer: they have 1, 3, 5, 7, 9 in ones place)
- ✎ *Write some even and odd numbers.* (see recording pad)
- *What is different about prime and composite numbers?* (prime numbers have exactly 2 different factors, 1 and itself; composite numbers have more than 2 factors.)
- ✎ *Write some prime and composite numbers.* (see recording pad)

Math at Hand 053–055, 063

Goldbach's conjecture:

20 = 13 + __7__

20 = 17 + __3__

sample answers:

__52__ = __5__ + __47__

__36.__ = __5__ + __31__

__90__ = __7__ + __83__

Operations • Today's Number: Review • Week 6: Friday   © Great Source Copying is prohibited. 053013

OPERATIONS Sum of primes

- A mathematician named Christian Goldbach said that every even number greater than 2 can be written as the sum of two prime numbers.
- ✎ *Test out Goldbach's idea.* Complete the equations.
- ✎ *Can you provide three more?* (see recording pad)
- *Does Goldbach's idea work?* (yes)

REACHING ALL LEARNERS Students may want to make a list of prime numbers to use as they find the sums.

Math at Hand 053

---

23 + (15 + 5) =

sample answers   = __23__ + __20__

= __43__

Reason: 15 + 5 is 20, I can add 23 + 20 mentally

(25 × 4) × 37 =

= __100__ × __37__

= __3700__

Reason: 25 × 4 is 100, the product of 37 × 100 is easy to do mentally

Patterns and Algebra • Today's Number: Review • Week 6: Friday   © Great Source Copying is prohibited. 053013

PATTERNS AND ALGEBRA Grouping Property

- ✎ *Show how the grouping of addends can make it easier to find the sum.* (see recording pad) *Explain your thinking.* (sample answer: 15 + 5 is 20, I can add 23 + 20 mentally)
- ✎ *Show how the grouping can make it easier to find the product.* (see recording pad) *Explain your thinking.* (sample answer: 25 × 4 is 100, the product of 37 × 100 is easy to do mentally)
- *What is another name for the* Grouping Property? (Associative Property)

REACHING ALL LEARNERS Use single-digit numbers to illustrate the property.

Math at Hand 220–222

© Great Source Copying is prohibited.

GEOMETRY Polygons

- Regular polygons have all sides the same length and all angles the same measure.

✎ *Look at the polygons on the recording pad. Which ones appear to be regular?* (see recording pad)

✎ *How will you know if one of these shapes will tessellate?* (the shape completely cover a space with no gaps or overlaps) *Draw a regular polygon that will tessellate.* (Drawings will vary.)

REACHING ALL LEARNERS Students may need to cut-out shapes for the tessellation.

Math at Hand 357, 381

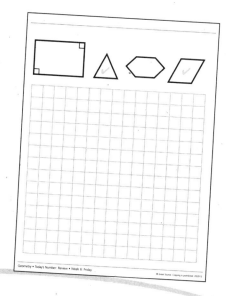

MEASUREMENT Perimeter and area

- **Problem Solving** *You have 10 square tiles. You are testing different patterns to position them.*

✎ *What is the perimeter of each pattern?* (see recording pad)

✎ *Which pattern has the greater area?* (neither) *Why is that?* (the amount of space covered by each square remains the same)

REACHING ALL LEARNERS Use cut-outs to help students recognize the different perimeters.

Math at Hand 295, 299

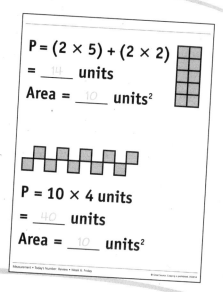

$P = (2 \times 5) + (2 \times 2)$

$= \underline{14}$ units

Area = $\underline{10}$ units²

$P = 10 \times 4$ units

$= \underline{40}$ units

Area = $\underline{10}$ units²

VOCABULARY Review

Let's work together to do today's matching exercise. Draw a line to match each word with an example that describes it.

- *Which example is most different?* (the pattern of shapes)
- *What is it called when events happen in a particular order?* (a sequence of events)
- *What does it mean when you say, "there is a trend?"* (something is happening again and again)
- *What is another way to say something is happening often?* (high frequency)

Math at Hand 264, 268, 277, 401, 493

Match

_C_ pattern	A. 3 out of 4 times
_D_ sequence	B. happens a lot
_B_ trend	C. ΔΔOΔΔOΔΔO
_A_ frequency	D. special order

© Great Source. Copying is prohibited.

PRACTICE

Written Practice

CONCEPTS AND SKILLS

- Prime and composite numbers
- Divisibility
- Perimeter and area
- Review transformations
- Problem Solving Strategies and Skills: *Act It Out, Make a Diagram, Make a Table, Solve in More Than One Way*

PREVIEW THE PRACTICE

- *How can you write 10 as a sum of two prime numbers?* (7 + 3) *Is there more than one pair of prime numbers that add up to 10?* (yes, the other pair is 5 + 5)

SUPPORT THE PRACTICE

- Problems 1–8 apply prime and composite number concepts. Revisit today's Number and Operations recording pads, if needed.

- Problems 9–14 review the divisibility of given numbers. Remind students to look at the digits in the ones place for divisibility by 2 and 5. Or, find the sum of the digits in the number for divisibility by 3.

- Problems 15–16 examine perimeter and area. Revisit today's Measurement recording pad, if needed.

- Problems 17–19 review transformations. Help students see that the shaded image is the result of the change.

PRACTICE TODAY's NUMBER **Review**

Name _____

NUMBER AND OPERATIONS

Write the number as the sum of two prime-number addends. ◄1–8. MAH 053–055

1. 8 = __5__ + __3__   **2.** 16 = __11__ + __5__   **3.** 20 = __3__ + __17__
1, 7   3, 13   7, 13
4. 26 = __19__ + __7__   **5.** 32 = __29__ + ____   **6.** 50 = __31__ + __19__
3, 23; 7, 19; 13, 13   13, 19   3, 47; 7, 43; 13, 37

7. What do all the sums have in common? _____
They are all even, composite numbers.

8. What do all the addends have in common? _____
They are all odd, prime numbers.

What is the number divisible by? Circle 2, 3, 5 or all. ◄9–14. MAH 062

9. 228 ②③ 5 all   **10.** 5,200 ② 3 ⑤ all

11. 75 2 ③⑤ all   **12.** 300 2 3 5 (all)

13. 6,030 2 3 5 (all)   **14.** 904 ② 3 5 all

GEOMETRY AND MEASUREMENT

Make a shape with 6 squares. Find the area and perimeter of your shapes. ◄15–16. MAH 295, 299

Drawings will vary. Check student's work. Sample answers provided.

15.

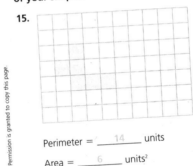

Perimeter = __14__ units

Area = __6__ units²

16.

Perimeter = __12__ units

Area = __6__ units²

SUMMER SUCCESS: MATH **133** MAH: *Math at Hand*

REACHING ALL LEARNERS

Help students recall the prime numbers. Use a copy of the Hundred Chart with prime numbers highlighted.

Math at Hand

If students need help, encourage them to refer to the MAH items shown on the student page.

© Great Source. Permission is granted to copy this page.

© Great Source. Copying is prohibited.

Name the transformation. Write *translation, rotation,* or *reflection.* ◀17–19. MAH 295, 299

17.

18.

19.

_____ reflection

_____ rotation

_____ translation

PROBLEM SOLVING · **UNDERSTAND** · **PLAN** · **TRY** · **LOOK BACK**

Complete each step. ◀20. MAH 396

20. The Furst family has 5 children. Frank is younger than Floyd, but older than Fredda. Felix is 18 months older than Floyd. Felicia is the baby. How would you line up the children from oldest to youngest?

   a. Underline the question you need to answer.

   b. Loop the details about the children.

   c. Mark the strategy/strategies you will use.

   d. Solve the problem. Explain your thinking.

_____

_____

_____

_____

_____

_____

   e. Answer the question.

   Felix, Floyd, Frank, Fredda, and Felicia.

_____

_____

POSSIBLE STRATEGIES

• Act It Out
• Make a Diagram
• Make a Table

Sample strategy: Make a Diagram

Clue 2 { Felix (oldest)

Clue 1 { Floyd / Frank / Fredda

Clue 3 { Felicia (youngest)

© Great Source. Permission is granted to copy this page.

REACHING ALL LEARNERS

For students having difficulty aligning the children in the problem, role play to act out the parts. Invite volunteers to be one of the 5 children, and then position them as described in the problem.

© Great Source. Copying is prohibited.

PROBLEM SOLVING

Work in small groups of 3 or 4 students.

• Encourage students to find ways to identify needed information to solve the problem.

• *What information do you need to answer the question?* (the names and clues about each child's age or position in the family)

• *How can you use the information?* (to make a diagram)

SCORING

   a. Last sentence underlined: 1 pt

   b. The information about the children circled: 1 pt

   c. Choose and apply an appropriate strategy: 1 pt

   d. Explanation of solution: 1 pt

   e. Correct answer: 1 pt

GLOSSARY TO GO

Today's Vocabulary Review

Have students review and share the entries made for this week's vocabulary words, *pattern, sequence, frequency,* and *trend.* Ask students to add more words and/or drawings to the maps if they can.

MATH JOURNAL

• *Write about your favorite Summer Success game. What math skill did you learn from playing the game?* (Answers will vary. Check that students use math terms to describe what they learned from playing a specific game.)

Additional Support

CONCEPTS AND SKILLS

- Parts of a whole
- Fractional pieces

MATH TALK

Model the correct use of these terms and encourage students to use them as they work.

- **fraction** a way to show part of a whole or part of a group
- **whole** all of something

SUPPORT PROBLEM 1

Read the story aloud, then have a volunteer read the problem again.

- *What is the story about?* (a pizza and its parts)
- *What is the math about?* (making sense of fractional parts)
- *Are there any answer choices you can rule out?* (24) *Why?* (It is too big a number for slices of pizza.)

READ AND REASON

Name _____

Fill in each blank with the choice that makes the *most* sense.
Do not use any choice more than once.

1. Brittany ordered a pizza. It was cut into _____ 8 _____ pieces. She put away half, or _____ 4 pieces _____, for the family. She ate _____ 2 slices _____, or one fourth, and her two friends each ate _____ one-eighth _____ of the pizza.

ANSWER CHOICES

- 24
- 4 pieces
- 8
- one-eighth
- 2 slices

Explain your thinking.

a. How did you begin?
   Sample answer: I drew a picture of a pizza.

b. Which answer did you rule out? Explain why.
   24. It is too big a number.

c. How are you sure that your answers make sense in the story?
   Sample answer: I reread it to make sure my answers all made sense.

SUMMER SUCCESS: MATH **135**

© Great Source. Permission is granted to copy this page.

REACHING ALL LEARNERS

Help students visualize the problem by drawing an 8-piece pizza.

Math at Hand

- Fraction of a Whole, 030
- Equivalent Fractions, 035

© Great Source. Copying is prohibited.

Fill in each blank with the choice that makes the *most* sense. Do not use any choice more than once.

2. Tori says that ___prime___ numbers are the numbers that have one and itself as factors. She says that ___2___ is the smallest prime. She also says that ___7___ is prime, but ___9___ is not because it is a square number.

ANSWER CHOICES

- 2
- prime
- 7
- 9
- 15

PRIME   NOT PRIME

a. How did you begin?

Sample answer: I thought about prime numbers, even numbers, and square numbers.

b. Which choices did you rule out? Explain why.

15. It is not a square number.

c. How do you know your answers make sense in the story?

Sample answer: I picked out the primes and looked for a square number.

© Great Source. Permission is granted to copy this page

CONCEPTS AND SKILLS

- Prime numbers
- Even numbers
- Square numbers

MATH TALK

Model the correct use of these terms and encourage students to use them as they work.

- **even number** a whole number that is divisible by 2
- **prime number** a number that has exactly two different positive factors, itself and 1
- **square number** the number of items in a square array. The first two square numbers are 4 and 9

SUPPORT PROBLEM 2

Read the story aloud, then have a volunteer read the problem again.

- *What is the story about?* (describing different types of numbers)
- *What is the math about?* (prime, even, and square numbers)
- *Are there any answer choices you can rule out?* (15) *Why?* (It is not a square number.)

REACHING ALL LEARNERS

Discuss the meaning of prime, even, and square numbers.

Math at Hand

- Prime Numbers, 053
- Even and Odd Numbers, 063
- Square Numbers, 495

© Great Source. Copying is prohibited.

NEWSLETTER

This Newsletter is sent home with students at the end of the week, along with the completed *Tangrams To Go* Concept Builder materials.

The first page suggests a simple way for students to share with their parent or guardian basic math skills they have been practicing in summer school.

NEWSLETTER

Summer Success: Math

What a fantastic week we've had in summer school. Your child learned a lot about different types of numbers, algebraic properties, and all sorts of geometry and measurement topics.

Transformations is a big word that means to move from one position to another. Ask your child to share with you what s/he learned about translation, rotation, and reflection.

- Describe the movement. (a slide) Is this a translation, rotation, or reflection? (translation)

- Describe the movement. (a flip) Is this a translation, rotation, or reflection? (reflection)

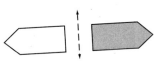

- Describe the movement. (a turn) Is this a translation, rotation, or reflection? (rotation)

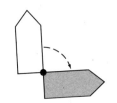

On the backside of this page are directions for using the project called *Tangrams To Go*. Invite your child to share this activity with you.

 Thank you for helping to strengthen the tie between home and school. Enjoy the time you spend with your child!

© Great Source. Permission is granted to copy this page.

© Great Source. Copying is prohibited.

NEWSLETTER

Family Math with Tangrams to Go

This week in summer school your child made a set of tangram shapes. Your child used the shapes to explore concepts in geometry.

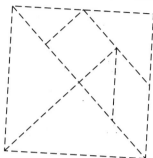

1. Have your child describe each shape as accurately as possible. He or she should be able to show you congruent and similar triangles. Encourage your child to describe similarities and differences among squares, rectangles, and parallelograms.

2. Work with your child to combine the shapes to make as many different squares, rectangles, and trapezoids as possible.

 Enjoy using the *Tangrams to Go* with your child. Remember, using math in the real world helps your child understand that math is important in and out of school.

138

© Great Source. Permission is granted to copy this page.

The back side of this week's Newsletter includes instructions for the parent or guardian to help their student demonstrate the *Tangrams To Go* Concept Builder activity at home.

© Great Source. Copying is prohibited.

GLOSSARY TO GO

Week 1 Terms

USING GLOSSARY TO GO

The purpose of creating personal glossaries is to help students acquire and use the language of math so that it makes sense to them. Use the terms and pictures shown here as guidelines to help students formulate their own pictures and definitions.

GLOSSARY TO GO

operations

work with numbers using addition, subtraction, multiplication, and/or division

$$20 + 3 = 23$$
$$10 - 6 = 4$$

decimal number

a number with a dot separating the ones and tenths places

3.7
$1.00

compare

to tell whether quantities are equal to, or less than, or greater than each other

$$0.25 = \tfrac{1}{4}$$
$$1 < 7$$
$$0.50 > 0.25$$

fraction

a number that tells how many equal parts a whole has been divided into, and how many parts you are looking at

$\tfrac{1}{2}$

$\tfrac{1}{4}$

$\tfrac{3}{4}$

© Great Source. Permission is granted to copy this page.

© Great Source. Copying is prohibited.

algebra

a mathematical description of how things are related

3 oranges = 2 bananas

equation

a number sentence that shows 2 equal values

$$3 + 3 = 6$$
$$2 \times 0.30 = 0.60$$

expression

a mathematical relationship that names a number

$$6 + n$$
$$(2 + 3) - 1$$

variable

a quantity that can change

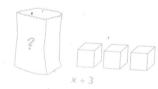

$$x + 3$$

© Great Source. Permission is granted to copy this page.

Week 2 Terms

LEARNING FROM GLOSSARY TO GO

When looking over students' work in their glossaries, check to make sure their definitions are mathematically accurate. Help them use their own words even as they correct errors.

© Great Source. Copying is prohibited.

GLOSSARY TO GO

Week 3 Terms

USING GLOSSARY TO GO

The purpose of creating personal glossaries is to help students acquire and use the language of math so that it makes sense to them. Use the terms and pictures shown here as guidelines to help students formulate their own pictures and definitions.

© Great Source. Permission is granted to copy this page.

geometry

the study of shapes, solids, position, and direction

plane figure

solid figure

solid figure

geometric figures with 3 dimensions

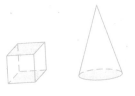

prism

a solid with 2 identical bases and faces that are parallelograms

triangular prism

rectangular prism

pentagonal prism

net

flat shape that can be folded into a solid figure is a net of that figure

Net for a cylinder:

Net for a triangular pyramid:

VOCABULARY GROUP 3

© Great Source. Copying is prohibited.

measure

the dimensions, quantity, length, or capacity of something

8 feet — 2 feet

area

the space covered by a shape

5 ft — 2 ft

area = 10 square feet

$5 \times 2 = 10$

volume

the amount of space inside a container

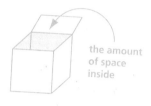

the amount of space inside

capacity

the maximum amount that can be held by a container

one liter

1 cup

Week 4 Terms

LEARNING FROM GLOSSARY TO GO

Students' drawings help them place the words used to describe a mathematical term in their visual memory. Check to make sure that students are illustrating the mathematical term shown, and are doing so accurately.

© Great Source. Permission is granted to copy this page.

© Great Source. Copying is prohibited.

GLOSSARY TO GO

Week 5 Terms

USING GLOSSARY TO GO

The purpose of creating personal glossaries is to help students acquire and use the language of math so that it makes sense to them. Use the terms and pictures shown here as guidelines to help students formulate their own pictures and definitions.

© Great Source. Permission is granted to copy this page.

data
information

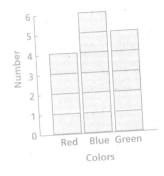

graph
a drawing that shows data

Age of students

 11 years old

 12 years old

survey
the process of collecting information by asking a question for people to answer

Favorite sport

Soccer ||

Swimming ||||

Basketball |||

Baseball ||||

strategy
a plan for getting to an answer when solving a math problem

Make a Diagram

Sun   Earth
About 93 million miles

© Great Source. Copying is prohibited.

pattern

something that changes in a regular way

sequence

numbers or things arranged in a special order or pattern

frequency

the number of times something happens

trend

something happening frequently over time

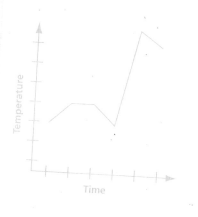

Encourage students to exchange and compare their glossaries with each other. Invite them to discuss definitions with each other and try to find ways to understand and remember their new math language.

© Great Source. Permission is granted to copy this page.

© Great Source. Copying is prohibited.

REVIEW FOR THE POST TEST IN NUMBER

Revisiting the summer's experiences will help students recall what they have learned. Remind students of all the discussion with Number Names and the numbers that were discussed. Ask what numbers they remember best and why.

Name _____

NUMBER

Choose the best answer or write a response for each question.

1. Which diagram shows $\frac{1}{3}$ of the figure shaded?

   (A) ▲▲▲

   (B) ●●●○

   (C) ▦

   (D) ◁▷

2. Which group of numbers is listed from least to greatest?

   (A) 0, 0.35, 0.40, 1

   (B) 0, 0.35, 0.40, 1

   (C) 1, 0.40, 0.35, 0

   (D) 0, 1, 0.35, 0.40

3. How many thousands are in the number 21,920?

   (A) 20 thousands

   (B) 21 thousands

   (C) 9 thousands

   (D) 1 thousands

4. Which is the odd number?

   (A) 12

   (B) 40

   (C) 33

   (D) 26

5. Which fraction describes the shaded area on the Hundred Chart?

   (A) $\frac{10}{100}$

   (B) $\frac{20}{100}$

   (C) $\frac{30}{100}$

   (D) $\frac{40}{100}$

6. Which symbol best compares the numbers?

   0.75 ____ 0

   (A) <

   (B) >

   (C) =

   (D) not given

© Great Source. Permission is granted to copy this page.

Use the Post Test to measure student achievement during the summer. Like the Pretest, the Post Test has six sections and assesses identical concepts and skills. If you used only certain sections of the Pretest, use the same in the Post Test, or use the sections that you focused on during the summer.

Be sure to praise students for their progress over the summer!

© Great Source. Copying is prohibited.

Name _____

7. Which model shows $\frac{1}{5}$?

(A)

(B)

(C)

(D)

8. Which is the factored form of the number 1,000,000?

(A) 10 × 10,000

(B) 10 × 10

(C) 10 × 10 × 10

(D) 10 × 10 × 10 × 10 × 10 × 10

9. What is the sum?

$5.25 + $0.75 = ___

(A) $6.00

(B) $7.00

(C) $6.25

(D) $1.75

10. What is the product?

100 × 0.30 = ___

(A) 0.30

(B) 3.0

(C) 30

(D) 300

11. What is the difference?

$1 - \frac{1}{5} =$ ___

(A) $\frac{2}{5}$

(B) $\frac{4}{5}$

(C) $1\frac{1}{5}$

(D) $\frac{1}{5}$

12. Which operation best completes the equation?

1 ___ 597 = 597

(A) ×

(B) +

(C) −

(D) ÷

© Great Source. Permission is granted to copy this page.

REVIEW FOR THE POST TEST IN OPERATIONS

Review the different operations, what their signs are and what they each mean. Remind students of mental math strategies they have used to find, estimate, or check for reasonableness of answers.

© Great Source. Copying is prohibited.

POST TEST

Reinforce for students the power that comes from looking for patterns to solve a problem. Revisit some patterns they discovered and predictions the patterns allowed them to make.

Name _____

PATTERNS AND ALGEBRA

Use the fractions to answer problems 13–14.

$$\frac{1}{15}, \frac{2}{15}, \frac{3}{15}, \frac{4}{15}, \text{_____}$$

13. What is the missing fraction?

 (A) 5

 (B) $\frac{5}{5}$

 (C) $\frac{5}{15}$

 (D) $\frac{5}{10}$

14. Which rule best describes the pattern?

 (A) count backwards by $\frac{1}{15}$

 (B) subtract by $\frac{1}{15}$

 (C) count on by $\frac{1}{15}$

 (D) multiply by $\frac{1}{15}$

15. Look at the equations.

 $\frac{1}{2} \times 0 = 0$

 $100 \times 0 = 0$

 $0.75 \times 0 = 0$

 $648 \times 0 = 0$

 Now, complete the sentence.

 Any number times 0…

 _____ equals 0.

16. Which number pattern follows the rule shown?

 Add 0.2 to the term before.

 (A) 0.2, 0.3, 0.4, 0.5

 (B) 0.3, 0.5, 0.7, 0.9

 (C) 0.8, 0.6, 0.4, 0.2

 (D) 0.2, 0.2, 0.2, 0.2

Use the table to answer problems 17–18.

In	Out
3.5 →	3
10.5 →	10
7.5 →	7
____ →	4
6.5 →	6

17. What is the missing term?

 (A) 4.5

 (B) 5.5

 (C) 6.5

 (D) 7.5

18. Which equation best describes the terms in the table?

 (A) In − 0.5 = Out

 (B) In × 0.5 = Out

 (C) In ÷ 0.5 = Out

 (D) In + 0.5 = Out

© Great Source. Permission is granted to copy this page.

SUMMER SUCCESS: MATH **147** Post Test

© Great Source. Copying is prohibited.

GEOMETRY AND MEASUREMENT

19. Which ordered pair names the location of Point *D*?

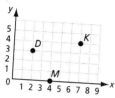

- (A) (4, 7)
- (B) (7, 4)
- (C) (2, 3)
- (D) (0, 4)

Use the diagram to answer problems 20–21.

30 m
45 m

20. What is the perimeter of the rectangle?

- (A) 180 meters
- (B) 150 meters
- (C) 75 meters
- (D) 45 meters

21. What is the area of the rectangle?

- (A) 1,350 square meters
- (B) 150 square meters
- (C) 75 square meters
- (D) 38 square meters

Use the diagram to answer problems 22–23.

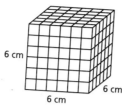

6 cm
6 cm
6 cm

22. What is the total area of the 6 faces of the cube?

- (A) 12 square centimeters
- (B) 18 square centimeters
- (C) 36 square centimeters
- (D) 216 square centimeters

23. What is the volume of the cube?

- (A) 18 cubic centimeters
- (B) 39 cubic centimeters
- (C) 216 cubic centimeters
- (D) 1,296 cubic centimeters

24. Which diagram shows a translation?

- (A)
- (B)
- (C)
- (D)

© Great Source. Permission is granted to copy this page.

REVIEW FOR THE POST TEST IN GEOMETRY AND MEASUREMENT

Review the new geometry vocabulary and visualization of shapes students have encountered. Invite students to look around the room and name the tool and the unit they would use to measure various attributes of classroom objects.

© Great Source. Copying is prohibited.

POST TEST

REVIEW FOR THE POST TEST IN DATA

Discuss what graphs students made and studied during the summer, and discuss the information learned from the data. This will draw on their real world connection with what they have learned.

DATA

Use the table to answer problems 25–26.

5-Subject Binder

Store 1	Store 2	Store 3	Store 4
$3.99	$4.59	$4.60	$4.89

25. Which equation would you use to find the range of prices for the binder?

- (A) $4.89 ÷ $3.99 = $1.23
- (B) $4.89 − $3.99 = $0.90
- (C) $4.89 × $3.99 = $19.51
- (D) $4.89 + $3.99 = $8.88

26. Which two operations would you use to find the average price?

- (A) subtraction and division
- (B) multiplication and division
- (C) addition and division
- (D) subtraction and multiplication

27. Which number is the median for the data?

11, 18, 21, 21, 35, 35, 47

- (A) 11
- (B) 21
- (C) 35
- (D) 47

Use the diagram to answer problems 28–30.

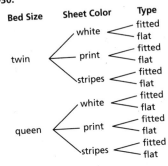

28. What type of diagram is this?

- (A) line plot
- (B) tree diagram
- (C) line graph
- (D) stem-and-leaf plot

29. What does the diagram tell you?

- (A) survey results
- (B) mean, median, mode
- (C) possible outcomes
- (D) probability

30. How many possible outcomes are there?

- (A) 2
- (B) 3
- (C) 12
- (D) 21

© Great Source. Permission is granted to copy this page.

© Great Source. Copying is prohibited.

Name _____

Solve each problem. Show your work.

31. Andy needs to set up 18 chairs in the gym. He has to put them in equal rows. How many different arrangements are possible?

Answer: _____ There are 6 arrangements.

Sample work:

□□□□□□□□□□□□□□□□□□

18 chairs, 1 row (or 1 chair, 18 rows)

□□□□□□□□□
□□□□□□□□□

9 chairs, 2 rows (or 2 chairs, 9 rows)

□□□□□□
□□□□□□
□□□□□□

6 chairs, 3 rows (or 3 chairs, 6 rows)

32. I am a hundredth decimal with one digit that is not zero. I am less than $\frac{5}{10}$, but greater than 0.30. I am between 0.50 and 0 on the number line. What decimal number am I?

Sample work:

0   0.30   0.40   0.50   1
           $\frac{3}{10}$ $\frac{5}{10}$

Answer: _____ 0.40

Refresh students' memories of all the problem solving strategies they have practiced using. Ask which they consider to be the most useful strategies, and why.

© Great Source. Permission is granted to copy this page.

© Great Source. Copying is prohibited.

CLASS RECORD

Teacher Name _____   **Class** _____

DIRECTIONS: Record each student's pre- and post-test scores.

Student Name	Pretest Score	Post-test Score

© Great Source. Copying is prohibited.

© Great Source. Permission is granted to copy this page.

WEEKLY PLANNER

WEEK NUMBER _____

MONDAY	TUESDAY	WEDNESDAY	THURSDAY	FRIDAY
Today's Number _____	Today's Number _____	Today's Number _____	Today's Number _____	Today's Number _____
Number Names & Practice	Number Names & Practice	Number Names & Practice	Number Names & Practice	Number Names & Practice
Game	Game	Game	Game	Game
Focus	Focus	Focus	Focus	Focus

INDEX

© Great Source. Copying is prohibited.

© Great Source. Copying is prohibited.

of geometric nets, 64B, 65–66, 66B, 78B

lines of symmetry, 12B, 22B

parallelograms, 58B, 102B, 122B, 129–130

pentagons, 130B

perimeter, 6E, 20B, 21–24, 22B, 78B, 116D, 132B, 133–134

plane figures vs. geometric solids, 50D, 56B

quadrilaterals, 6E, 22B, 44B, 95C

rectangles, 23–24, 50D, 51–52, 59–60, 100B, 122B, 124B

regular, 95C, 95–96, 132B

shape recognition, 23–24, 129–130

similarity in, 129–130

spatial relationships, 129–130

squares, 6E, 26, 78B, 95C, 129–130

symmetry in, 129–130

Tangrams To Go, 129–130, 137–138

tesselations, 124B, 130B, 132B

transformations

on coordinate grids, 88B

reflection, 78B, 116D, 117–118

rotation, 80B, 81–82, 116D, 117–118

translations, 72D, 116D, 117–118

types of, 123–124, 133–134

trapezoids, 95C, 129–130

triangles, 20B, 21–22, 22B, 34B, 50D, 51–52, 59–60, 114, 124B, 125–126, 129–130

with four sides, 6E

Pounds and ounces, 80B

Predictions

using data, 11–12, 121–122

using patterns, 12A, 56A, 110A, 111–112

Prime numbers, 119–120, 130A, 131–134, 132A, 136

Prisms, 48, 58B, 72D, 73–74, 102B, 103–104

Problem solving, 8, 14, 16, 22, 24, 30, 36, 38, 44, 46, 52, 58, 60, 66, 68, 74, 80, 82, 88, 90, 96, 102, 104, 110, 112, 118, 124, 126, 132, 134

Problem solving strategies and skills

act it out, 13–14, 29–30, 37–38, 89–90, 109–110, 131–132, 133–134

check for reasonableness, 57

check solution, 22A

draw a diagram, 101–102, 103–104, 109–110

find a pattern, 7

find needed information, 7, 13–14, 15–16, 35–36, 37–38, 101–102, 103–104, 131–132

guess, check and revise, 23–24, 81–82, 95–96, 103–104, 117–118, 125–126

ignore unneeded information, 43–44, 117–118

look for a pattern, 67–68, 79–80, 111–112

make a diagram, 15–16, 29–30, 35–36, 37–38, 43–44, 65–66, 67–68, 73–74, 87–88, 89–90, 111–112, 123–124, 131–132, 133–134

make a model, 37–38, 43–44, 65–66, 87–88, 101–102, 109–110, 131–132

make an organized list, 7, 15–16, 21–22, 23–24, 29–30, 57, 59–60, 73–74, 79–80, 81–82, 89–90, 95–96, 117–118, 123–124

make a table, 7, 15–16, 21–22, 23–24, 35–36, 57, 59–60, 73–74, 79–80, 81–82, 87–88, 95–96, 117–118, 123–124, 125–126, 133–134

solve in more than one way, 21–22, 23–24, 29–30, 59–60, 79–80, 111–112, 133–134

strategy, defined, 108B

take notes, 67–68, 81–82, 125–126

types of, 108B, 110B

use logical reasoning, 65–66, 73–74, 87–88, 89–90, 95–96, 109–110, 123–124

work backward, 13–14

write an equation, 13–14, 21–22, 35–36, 43–44, 57, 59–60, 65–66, 67–68, 101–102, 103–104, 111–112, 125–126

Product, 61–62, 105–106. *See also* Multiplication

Pyramids, 56B, 58B

Quadrilaterals, 6E, 22B, 44B, 95C

Reasoning. *See* Logical reasoning problems

Rectangles, 23–24, 50D, 51–52, 59–60, 100B, 122B, 124B

Rectangular prisms, 48, 58B, 80B, 102B

Reflection, 78B, 116D, 117–118

Rotation, 80B, 81–82, 116D, 117–118

Rounding, 36A, 37–38, 99–100, 109–110

Rulers, 63–64, 107–108, 115–116

Sequences, 122B, 123–124, 132B

Similarity, 129–130

Spatial relationships, 129–130

Square number patterns, 122A

Square numbers, 6E, 136

Squares, 6E, 26, 78B, 95C, 129–130

Subtraction. *See also* Computation

decimals, 12A, 13–14, 14A, 20A, 21–22, 31–32, 34A, 35–36, 36A, 42A, 43–44, 45–46

differences, estimate and calculate, 125–126

fractions, 12A, 13–14, 14A, 20A, 21–22, 56A, 57, 58A, 59–60, 64A, 65–66, 66A

order of operations, 66A

3- and 4-digit numbers, 39–40

whole numbers, 119–120

Sum of primes, 132A

© Great Source. Copying is prohibited.